THE RISE OF THE KOREAN ECONOMY

THE RISE OF THE
KOREAN ECONOMY

Byung-Nak Song

HONG KONG
OXFORD UNIVERSITY PRESS
OXFORD NEW YORK
1990

Oxford University Press

Oxford   New York   Toronto
Petaling Jaya   Singapore   Hong Kong   Tokyo
Delhi   Bombay   Calcutta   Madras   Karachi
Nairobi   Dar es Salaam   Cape Town
Melbourne   Auckland

and associated companies in
Berlin   Ibadan

First published 1990
Published in the United States
by Oxford University Press, Inc., New York

British Library Cataloguing in Publication Data
Song, Byung-Nak, 1939–
The rise of the Korean economy.
1. Korea. Economic conditions, history
I. Title
330.9519
ISBN 0-19-583979-X

Library of Congress Cataloging-in-Publication Data
Song, Pyŏng-nak, 1939–
The rise of the Korean economy / Byung-Nak Song.
p.   cm.
Includes bibliographical references.
ISBN 0-19-583979-X: $37.00 (U.S.: est.)
1. Korea (South)—Economic policy—1960–   2. Korea (South)—
Economic conditions—1960–   3. Korea (South)—Foreign economic
relations.   I. Title.
HC467.S6365   1990
338.95195'009'045—dc20   90-30241
CIP

Printed in Hong Kong by Calay Printing Co., Ltd.
Published by Oxford University Press, Warwick House, Hong Kong

Preface

THE image of a country usually changes only slowly. However, over the course of a generation or so the popular image of Korea has changed from that of a bleak, poverty-stricken, and war-torn country to that of a promising, newly industrializing country at the threshold of the final stage of development. Westerners have come to view Korea as the 'second Japan'—or as one of the four Asian dragons (alongside Hong Kong, Singapore, and Taiwan). The rapid economic growth and transformation of Korea since the early 1960s has almost completely transformed the image and status of Korea in the world community, as well as the standard of well-being and the lifestyle of the Korean people.

Korea became more or less self-sufficient in savings, managerial talent, business infrastructure, and in other areas from about 1986. Korea's international balance of payments shifted from a chronic deficit to a global surplus at around the same time. Also, the recipient-donor relationship with the United States changed as Korea realized a surplus with its chief economic partner. As a result Korea no longer needs to worry about foreign debt or to depend on foreign aid from advanced countries. Korea now exports an increasing amount of capital or technology-intensive goods including colour television sets, automobiles, and personal computers—industries in which Korea has emerged as one of the leading contenders in the world market. All these changes resulted from the success of Korea's export-oriented growth strategy under which exports expanded enormously from 55 million US dollars to 55 billion US dollars between 1962 and 1988.

Korea is well positioned to become a key centre, not only geographic but also economic, in the emerging 'era' of East Asia, and a focal point in a new world economic alignment in which Seoul will be an integral part of a system of pivotal Asian cities such as Beijing and Shanghai to the west, Tokyo and Osaka to the east, Pyongyang and Vladivostok to the north, and Hong Kong and Taibei to the south. The Korean economy is becoming increasingly integrated with the East Asian and global economies as it moves towards a new era of economic progress and prosperity.

The Korean economic 'miracle' has attracted much attention

among economists, policy makers, and interested citizens in both developing and developed countries. It is of vital importance to know how Korea has managed such rapid growth in the past, and whether she can successfully manage the transition to becoming, like Japan, an advanced non-Western country. In spite of the increasing demand from foreigners for books on the Korean economy, there are very few such books written in English by Koreans. Although a vast and detailed body of studies on the Korean economy exists, it is largely in Korean and inaccessible to foreign readers. This book is intended to meet the need for an English language text which draws extensively on Korean as well as foreign-language research materials. It describes and explains various aspects of Korea's economic growth during the postwar period, with particular emphasis on the period of rapid growth since the early 1960s. It also assesses Korea's present and future economic prospects, and attempts to summarize the major debates on policy issues among Korean as well as foreign experts. Although this book draws on the materials in my book on the Korean economy written in 1980 and revised in 1984, it is not a translation but an entirely new book in its concept, structure, and coverage.

Because Korea is often compared to Japan, the only country outside the West to achieve an advanced economy, and the country perhaps most similar to Korea, I have attempted as far as possible to compare and contrast the similarities and differences between the two economies. Reference is also made in some cases to the economy of Taiwan, Korea's major competitor among the other 'Asian dragons'. As Korean economic growth and management have been profoundly influenced by Korean culture and history, including the experiences of colonial rule and national division, this book includes separate chapters on historical and cultural influences on development. The cultural aspects of the Korean management system are also examined in relation to those of Japan and the United States.

The book also seeks to examine the failures or less successful episodes that have accompanied success in the growth of exports and the economy. These include the problem of dealing with increasing protectionism against Korean imports in foreign countries and, at home, the rapidly increasing expectations of the Korean people for better housing, greater economic equality, and a higher quality of life.

In writing this book and formulating my ideas, I have bene-fited greatly from exchanges with a vast number of Korean and foreign experts. Because they literally number in the hundreds, it is impossible to acknowledge them all individually. However, I am particularly indebted to Professor Dwight H. Perkins of Harvard and James Tobin of Yale for kindly reading the entire manuscript and offering me pages of helpful advice and valuable corrections. Special thanks are also due to Professor Edwin S. Mills of Princeton for many valuable suggestions as to the overall contents and direction of the book. Another friend, John Sloboda, read the entire manuscript and provided suggestions that helped make the manuscript more readable. I would also like to express my sincere gratitude to Irma Adelman, Anthony Downs, John F. Kain, Kyu Sik Lee, Fu-chen Lo, John R. Meyer, Jeffrey B. Nugent, Wilfred Owen, Yung Chul Park, Il Sakong, Miyohei Shinohara, Raymond J. Struyk, and Jeffrey Williamson for helpful discussions, suggestions, and comments on my earlier studies. Finally I would like to acknowledge the assistance in researching this book provided by Joosung Jun, Inpyo Lee, Tack Yoon, James Forrester, Byung-Yeon Kim, Duane Vorhees, Hun-Koo Ha, Ki-Ho Yoon, and Yong Sung Jeong. I hope that the book lives up to the expectations of all these people, and I thank them for helping me.

BYUNG-NAK SONG

Contents

Tables

Figures

Chronology, 1945 to 1988

1945	August	Independence begins with Japanese surrender.
	September	Partition and occupation of Korea by the USA and USSR begins; two zones divided at the 38th parallel.
		US Military Government established in South Korea.
1948	August	South Korean government established. Syngman Rhee becomes first president; authority transferred from US Military Government to newly established Republic of Korea (August 15).
1950	April	Land Reform Law promulgated.
	June	Bank of Korea established. North Korea invades South Korea; United States leads 16-country United Nations force.
1953	July	Korean War Armistice agreement signed at Panmunjom.
	December	National income data compiled for the first time in Korea.
1954	April	Korea Development Bank established.
1955	September	First population census conducted.
1958	January	Illiteracy eradication campaign begins.
1959	March	Stock market opens.
1960	April	President Syngman Rhee toppled by April 19 Student Revolution. Parliamentary government established. Chang Myon becomes Prime Minister.
1961	May	May 16 Military Coup led by General Park Chung Hee, who takes over from government of Prime Minister Chang Myon.
	July	Economic Planning Board established.
1962	January	First Five-Year Economic Development Plan (1962–1966) begins.
	February	Construction of the Ulsan industrial complex begins.

	May	Korea Trade Promotion Corporation (KOTRA) established.
	December	President's Monthly Export Promotion Conference begins.
1963	January	Export-import linkage scheme initiated.
	October	General Park elected President; the Third Republic begins.
	December	Manpower exports begin (132 miners to West Germany).
1964	May	Comprehensive economic policies announced. Korean won devalued.
1965	February	Korean soldiers join US forces in Vietnam War.
	March	Unitary exchange-rate system introduced.
	June	Treaty normalizing relations with Japan signed.
	September	Interest rates reformed.
1966	February	Korea Institute for Science and Technology established.
	July	The law for the promotion of foreign investment enacted.
	August	Foreign capital inducement law enacted.
1967	January	Korea Foreign-Exchange Bank established.
	March	Korea joins GATT.
	April	Kuro export industrial complex established in Seoul.
		Ministry of Science and Technology established.
	June	First foreign bank (Chase Manhattan) opens branch office.
1968	January	USS Pueblo captured by North Koreans.
	April	Construction of Pohang iron and steel mill began.
1969	January	Ten-Year Plan for modernization of rural areas formulated.
	March	Dual farm-price policy began.
	April	World Bank voices uncertainty about Korea's ability to repay foreign debt.
	May	Satellite-relay receiving station established at Kumsan.

	July	Seoul-Inchon expressway opens.
	October	Constitutional Amendment passed to allow President Park to run for more than two terms.
	December	Law for the promotion of local industries enacted.
1970	June	Seoul–Pusan expressway opens.
	December	Taejon–Chonju expressway opens.
1971	March	Construction of first nuclear power plant begins.
	August	*Saemaul Undong* (New Village Movement) begins.
	September	First National Land Development Plan (1972–1981) formulated.
	October	North and South Korea hold first talk.
	December	Opening of the Seoul-Kangnung expressway.
1972	April	Korean Air opens trans-Pacific route.
	July	Korea Development Institute established.
	August	August 3 Emergency Measure freezes informal debts of private companies.
	October	Martial law declared and National Assembly dissolved.
		Yushin (Revitalization) Constitution introduced, President Park re-elected, and the Fourth Republic begins.
1973	January	Long-term economic goals of achieving per capital GNP of $1,000 and exports of $10 billion by 1981 announced.
		US grant aid ceases.
	May	Government policy for developing heavy and chemical industries announced.
	June	Family rituals standards announced. Central railway line (155.2Km) electrified. Greenbelts around major cities formed.
	July	Completion of Pohang iron and steel mill. First oil crisis.
1974	January	National Emergency Measures No. 1, No. 2, and No. 3 announced.
	March	Designation of 6 industrial bases nationwide.
	August	Seoul subway (9.5km) opened and railway lines in the Seoul region (98.6km) electrified.

1975	April	US economic assistance programme phased out. Pusan port development plan implemented. First general trading companies (GTCs) established.
	October	Yongdong–Tonghae expressway opened.
1976	January	Asset formation savings scheme for wage earners enacted.
	February	Antitrust and Fair Trade Law enacted.
	April	Export-Import Bank established.
	September	National health insurance scheme introduced.
1977	November	VAT (value added tax) system introduced.
	December	Export target of US$10 billion achieved four years ahead of schedule.
1978	July	Completion of the first nuclear power plant.
	October	Middle East construction boom reaches its peak. Measures for curbing real-estate speculation enacted. First Korean guided missile produced.
1979	October	President Park assassinated by the head of the Korean Central Intelligence Agency and Prime Minister Choi Kyu-ha becomes acting President. Second oil crisis begins.
1980	January	New economic policy shifts emphasis away from economic growth alone to a concern about economic stability and equity.
	April	Riot in Sabuk coal mine.
	May	General Chun Doo Hwan seizes power under martial law. Kwangju riots begin, last nine days. Special Committee for National Security Measures formed.
	July	4,992 government officials purged for corruption.
	October	World-wide poor harvest and food shortage hit the Korean economy.
	December	Colour television broadcasting begins.
1981	January	Democratic Justice Party formed.
	March	President Chun Doo Hwan inaugurated and the Fifth Republic begins.
	May	Fair Trade Commission formed.
	August	Liberalization of foreign trade begins.
	September	Seoul named host of 1986 Asian Games and 1988 Summer Olympics.

1982	January	37-year-old nightly curfew lifted.
	April	Production of supersonic jet aircraft.
	October	Second National Land Development Plan (1982–1991) begins.
1983	July	Korean population reaches 40 million.
	September	Korean airliner shot down by USSR after straying off course.
	October	North Korean terrorist bombing in Rangoon, Burma, kills 17 senior South Korean Cabinet officials; President Chun narrowly escapes.
1984	June	Completion of Taegu–Kwangju Olympic Expressway.
	September	President Chun's state visit to Japan. Establishment of Korea Fund investment in Korean stock market.
1985	January	Three 'lows'—low oil price, low interest rates, and low US dollar value—spur export boom.
1986	September	Asian Games held in Seoul.
	November	Exports exceed imports for the first time since development began.
	December	Savings exceed investment for the first time since the First Five-Year Plan began.
1987	January	Import liberalization and trade negotiations become national and international issues.
	March	Student riots spread nationwide.
	June	June 29 democratization declaration by ruling party Presidential candidate Roh Tae-Woo.
	July	Massive damage by typhoon Selma, death toll exceeds 700.
	August	Labour disputes break out nation-wide.
	October	New constitution becomes effective.
	December	Roh Tae-Woo elected as President.
1988	February	President Roh Tae-Woo inaugurated as President and the Sixth Republic begins.
	July	Iran-Iraq War ends. Policy of limiting real-estate transactions announced.
	October	Policy of opening-up trade with North Korea announced.
	September	1988 Summer Olympics.

1 Introduction

KOREA was among the very poorest countries in the world following the devastation of the Korean War (1950–3). Until the end of the 1950s per capita income was much lower than for most of Korea's neighbours. The Philippines at one time was considered by poverty-stricken Koreans as an all but unreachable role model for their own war-torn country. The period from 1953 to 1961 was one of very slow recovery from the war with massive assistance from the United States. The trend curve changed abruptly, however, with the beginning of the First Five-Year Plan in 1962. Thereafter, Korea's climb up the ladder of development accelerated. Normalization of relations with Japan in 1965, fiscal and financial reforms in the mid-1960s, supplying *matériel* for the Vietnam War, the Middle East construction boom in the 1970s, and low oil prices, cheap dollars, and low interest rates in the late 1980s all facilitated this rise. By 1970 Korea had achieved NIC (newly-industrializing country) status, and had surpassed North Korea and the Philippines in terms of per capita income. Korea continued its rapid growth in the 1970s despite the two oil crises, and by the late 1970s had overtaken Malaysia—then the second most advanced ASEAN nation—as well as Cuba. In the mid-1980s Korea overtook countries such as Mexico, Argentina, Brazil, Portugal, Poland, Yugoslavia, and Hungary. By the time of the 1988 Summer Olympics—Korea had become known as one of the highest income developing countries—a group including Israel and the three so-called 'little Asian dragons', namely: Hong Kong, Singapore, and Taiwan.

What was behind Korea's rapid growth—'the miracle of the Han River'? How did Korea rise from rags to riches so quickly? How has the economic and social structure of the country been transformed in the process of growth? What have been the consequences of this rapid growth? Will Korea become another advanced country, like Japan, with a non-Western cultural background? These questions have attracted increasing attention among economists and observers from all over the world. The purpose of this book is to examine these causes, processes, and consequences of the rapid expansion and transformation of the Korean economy.

There already exists a large body of studies on these issues by both Korean and foreign scholars. Some studies focus solely on macroeconomic trends and policies. But economic development is a multidimensional and complex process involving changes in many non-economic factors. It is intertwined with cultural, social, and institutional changes and is affected by historical background, natural resources, geopolitical location, population characteristics, and other factors. We do not believe that developing countries that want fast growth can succeed simply by adopting macroeconomic policies similar to those in Korea.

This study chiefly covers the post-Korean War period with special reference to the high-growth period after 1963. Because Korea's experience has paralleled Japan's in many respects, discussion of the rise and transformation of the Korean economy is often cast in relation to the Japanese case.

Korea is a small country in terms of area—about the size of Portugal or Hungary, and a quarter of that of California or Japan. It is a large country by population, however. With 42 million people in 1989, Korea is comparable in population with the major Western industrial countries during their rise from developing to developed country status.

Its small territory and large population make Korea one of the most densely populated and confined countries in the world. Congestion is everywhere. Korea's land-use policy has been such that at present over 30 million Koreans, or about three-quarters of the total population, live in 245 urban areas, the total area of which is only about 3 per cent of the total land. In addition, the whole country is so mountainous that only a little more than a fifth of it is arable. The problems of growth without adequate natural resources, a common denominator with Japan and other East Asian countries, are examined in more detail in Chapter 2.

Chapter 3 examines historical factors in Korea's growth. Korea's cultural and geographical proximity to China and Japan has inevitably linked Korea's fate and fortunes to the 'rise and fall of empires' in China and Japan. For instance, Korea was colonized by Japan when Chinese power and influence waned around the turn of the nineteenth century. Until then, China's influence had predominated in Korea, and Korea's tradition of centralized and bureaucratic government are often cited as a prime example of this influence. At the same time, domestic innovation and invention was conducive to the development of a socio-cultural environment favourable for modern economic growth. Chapter 3 examines the enduring impact of historical factors, as well as the subsequent impact of Japanese occupation on Korea's general economic and social famework, organization and management, infrastructure, and institutions.

The fall of Japan in 1945 and the cold war tensions that followed resulted in the division of the country into North and South and the tragic Korean War. The Korean War left over one million people dead and destroyed about half of all the infrastructure of the country. It also destroyed traditional authority and class barriers and hastened the rejection of old-fashioned ways of thinking and habits. In destroying the old order, the War also destroyed many barriers to the development of a modern economy.

Because of the division of the country and a constant military menace from the North, Korea spends about 6 per cent of its GNP on defence every year and maintains the fifth largest military force in the world. Chapter 3 also looks at the impact of the North-South division on Korea's development choices and patterns.

The continuing influence of traditional values and their integration with modern attitudes to form a new synthesis of development-oriented modes of thought and organization is a frequently overlooked aspect of the modernization process. Chapter 4 therefore looks at the amalgam of traditional Confucian ethics and adapted Christian ethics in Korea that form what Tu Wei-Ming of Harvard calls the 'new Confucian ethic'. This new Confucian ethic has provided the functional equivalent of Max Weber's 'Protestant ethic' in the West as the basis for Koreans' attitude towards work, self-discipline, desire for education, strong family ties, loyalty to the country and organizations, and flexible adaptability to change.

Chapter 5 examines basic patterns in Korea's economic growth, the primary macroeconomic sources of growth, and related issues. The chapter traces the shift from a subsistence economy after the Korean War through the take-off process in the 1960s to Korea's emergence as a newly industrializing country in the 1970s and 1980s. Because of the similarity between the two countries, Japan's experience is often used to provide a comparative perspective on Korea's development.

The central role which exports and export-promotion strategies have played in Korea's development clearly justifies the separate treatment of trade issues in Chapter 6. The chapter discusses the characteristics of Korea's trade promotion efforts in relation to those of neighbouring countries. The philosophy behind Korea's export-oriented growth strategy and the major policy instruments used to implement this strategy are also examined.

Chapter 7 examines the impact of trade on the industrial structure and focuses on industrial policy as a factor in expanding Korean exports. Although industrial policy is rather a vague concept in the United States and other advanced countries, it is at the core of national growth policies in Korea and Japan. The relationship of industrial policy to the hyperactive growth of large business conglomerates (*jaebol*) and to Korea's high level of industrial concentration is also considered, as is the role played by Korea's relatively large public enterprise sector.

Economic planning has also played a crucial role in the process of growth. In Chapter 8 we review Korea's experience with formal five-year plans and discuss the Korean style of economic planning and policy formation, partly in comparison with the Japanese case. Korea is noted for its strong leadership commitment to development and successful implementation of development plans. Korea has been, in Gunnar Myrdal's terms, the 'hardest state' as far as plan implementation is concerned. Korean growth was promoted extensively by the government through various incentive systems, and appears to have generally been efficient. A case study of the planning procedures involved in the process of the formulation of the Sixth Five-Year Plan (1987–91) is presented, and an attempt is made to derive some implications from the Korean experience with economic planning that may be relevant to other developing countries.

Chapter 9 moves the focus to an examination of consumption and savings behaviour. Alternative hypotheses concerning savings behaviour in Japan are evaluated in the context of the Korean experience. Korea is often cited as an example of how growth can be combined with maintaining a relatively balanced income distribution. How was this achieved? Is this a permanent or transitional pattern? How has equity changed in the process of economic growth? These issues are dealt with in Chapter 10, as are ongoing changes in the sense of class consciousness and sensitivity to social and economic disparities. The chapter also looks, through the prism of social indicators, at objective measures of change in the quality of life of Koreans.

To give the reader a better understanding of the inner workings of Korean enterprises, and the decision-making processes and organizational aspects of the Korean economy generally, Chapter 11 explores the major characteristics of the Korean management system in comparison to that of Japan and the United States.

Chapter 12 looks at the broader dynamics of Korea's external economic relations. As one of the most trade-oriented countries in the world, Korea is heavily dependent upon foreign countries for resources, technology, and markets. During the early stages of development Korea depended heavily upon other countries, especially the United States for aid and capital. Korea was in the past the third highest aid-receiving country in the world after Vietnam and Israel, and the fourth largest debtor nation in the world after Brazil, Mexico, and Argentina. How well Korea manages her relationships with other countries, including its nascent contacts with China and the USSR, is crucial for Korea's continued growth in a future characterized by an increasingly interdependent global economy.

The final chapter attempts a summing up of the essential aspects of Korea's economic development, using a framework suggested by scholars of the Japanese economy. Looking forward, the chapter assesses the prospects for the Korean economy towards the year 2000. Projections for the Korean economy by the Korea Development Institute and distinguished experts such as Walt W. Rostow, Lawrence Klein, and Miyohei Shinohara are reviewed and analysed.

Finally that chapter attempts to derive some implications of the Korean experience for other countries as they attempt to clear, as Korea has, the constantly changing hurdles that mark the path of economic progress.

Part I
The General Background of the Economy

2   The Korean People and Their Land

THE Korean economy has been shaped by the Korean people and the land in which they live. The geopolitical location, climate, and natural resources of the Korean peninsula are unchangeable facts that affect the basic course of the Korean economy. The pattern and direction of Korea's economic development are also determined by the Korean people themselves. Therefore, this study of the Korean economy begins with an introduction to the Korean people and their land.

Ethnic Origins of the Korean people

When I visited Tibetan villages in Nepal and travelled through northern China, I found that many of the people looked like Koreans. Korean diplomats have told me that the Mongolian people also closely resemble Koreans. Ethnically, Koreans belong to the same family of races as the Japanese and Chinese. However, the typical Japanese is closer in physical build to the South Chinese, whereas Koreans are more like the North Chinese—taller and sturdier than the Japanese or most Southeast Asians.

Experts on the origins of the Koreans people assert that the ancient Koreans were a horse-riding people. Perhaps for this reason Koreans traditionally appear to have been highly mobile. According to the residence registration statistics of the National Bureau of Statistics, over 20 per cent of all Koreans changed their address every year in the 1980s.[1] Of course, such an ethnic heritage is altered by changes in socio-economic conditions, and the mentality and culture of modern Koreans clearly differ greatly from those of traditional Koreans.

Development without Natural Resources

Akio Morita's remark about Japan's resource poverty—that the land provides almost no raw materials except water, and that less than a quarter of the land is usable—almost exactly describes Korea's situation as well.[2] Korea, like Japan, has to rely on foreign countries for most mineral resources such as oil, iron ore, copper, gold, silver, and só on, which are crucial for industrialization. If anything, Japan seems to be relatively better off than Korea in terms of resource endowment. For instance, Japan has more land per capita than Korea. Japan is roughly the same size as California, while South Korea is little more than one-fourth the size of Japan. Being an island, Japan also has better oceanic resources than Korea. Due to its milder climate, moreover, Japan's energy requirements also are relatively lower than Korea's. Japan also has better forestry and agricultural resources.

In a few areas, however, Korea has a comparative advantage over Japan. For instance, Korea has larger rivers and greater potential for developing hydroelectric power. Korea also has a relatively higher proportion of arable land—21.5 per cent of the total land area versus 14.1 per cent in Japan (see Table 2.1). Korea also is better endowed with such mineral resources as limestone, tungsten, and lead. In particular, Korea has almost infinite amounts of limestone for cement. This has enabled Korea to expand its domestic construction industry, which served as the springboard for the expansion by Korean construction companies into the Middle East in the 1970s. Overseas construction earnings in the Middle East enabled the Korean economy to recover from the first oil price 'shock' as well as pay back a large proportion of the foreign debt Korea had incurred in the early 1970s.

The relationship between the Korean people and their land is closest in agriculture. Agriculture is still the main source of income for some eight million Koreans. There are important differences between agriculture in Korea and Japan, however (see Table 2.1). For example, the share of agriculture in the GNP of Japan was only 2.6 per cent in 1985, much lower than the Korean figure of 10.8 per cent. Dependence on agriculture is, accordingly, much higher in Korea. Moreover, the proportion of non-agricultural income in farm household income was 83.2 per cent in Japan, much higher than the Korean figure of 39.6 per cent in 1988.

Both Korean and Japanese farm households cultivate extremely small plots of land. The average acreage cultivated by farm households was 2.9 acres in Korea and 3.1 acres in Japan in 1985, much smaller than the several hundred acres typically cultivated by the American farm family. With the exception of such city states as Singapore and Hong Kong, Korea has the world's smallest average cultivated area per farm household.

The limited amount of arable land forces Korean farmers to cultivate their land intensively and enhance field productivity as much as possible. In fact, agricultural productivity is known to have been relatively high throughout Korea's history. In 1977, for instance, Korea's rice productivity per acreage was the highest in the world, due in part to the introduction of a new variety of rice especially developed for Korean conditions.

None the less, because of the scarcity of land, Korea must import large amounts of food from foreign countries. Korea's self-sufficiency in food grains—except for rice—has steadily decreased since the early 1960s. Korea grew 93.9 per cent of its own grain needs in 1965, but this decreased to 38.4 per cent by 1988. Overall, Korea imports more than 60 per cent of the grain it consumes—including 97.5 per cent of the corn and 84.3 per cent of the soybeans in 1988. At the same time, Korea has become nearly self-sufficient in rice in recent years. This was due to the rise in rice productivity as well as the shift of many urban Koreans away from rice and toward greater consumption of wheat and other grains. Because Koreans have been dependent upon rice for thir survival throughout their long history, self-sufficiency in rice has a special meaning, and, as such, self-sufficiency in rice has been the central element in Korea's agricultural policy.

Korea's limited natural resources have circumscribed her policy choices for agricultural development, with the result that Korea's dependence on imported foods probably will continue to rise. Korea's relative disadvantage in agriculture will also accelerate with the rise in wages. This will be especially true in the production of grains and other foodstuffs that require relatively large amounts of land.

For a land-poor country like Korea, it is extremely important to use land efficiently. There appears to be great room for improvement in this respect. However, Korea's past policy of maximizing agricultural production by preventing the transfer of arable land into non-agricultural uses has contributed to a serious land shortage in urban areas. For example, the administrative area of Seoul (627 square kilometers) has not increased since 1973, in spite of the rapid increase in population and the level of development. Since then the population of Seoul has

Table 2.1 Major Agricultural Indicators for Korea and Japan

	1955	1960	1965	1970	1975	1980	1988
1. Agricultural population							
a) In millions							
Korea	13.3	14.6	15.8	14.4	13.2	10.8	7.3
Japan	36.6	34.4	30.1	26.6	23.2	21.4	19.3
b) Share of total							
population (%)							
Korea	61.9	58.3	55.8	45.8	38.2	28.9	17.3
Japan	41.0	36.8	30.6	25.4	20.7	18.3	15.7
2. Share of agriculture							
in GNP (%)							
Korea	43.9	36.5	37.6	26.4	24.7	14.4	10.8
Japan		10.1	7.0	5.9	5.3	3.8	2.6
3. Cultivated area per							
household (acres)							
Korea	2.22	2.13	2.22	2.11	2.33	2.52	2.89
Japan		2.48	2.62	2.65	2.78	2.90	3.08
4. Ratio of arable land to							
total land (%)							
Korea	20.3	20.6	22.9	23.3	22.7	22.2	21.5
Japan		16.4	16.2	15.4	14.8	14.5	14.1

5. Share of agriculture in total employment (%)						
Korea	36.2	55.7	50.4	45.9	34.0	20.7
Japan	30.0	22.8	17.9	12.6	9.8	7.2
6. Percentage of non-farm income						
Korea	29.5	20.8	24.2	18.1	34.8	39.6
Japan	45.0	52.0	63.5	66.4	78.9	83.2[a]
7. Family size (persons)						
Korea	6.0	6.3	5.8	5.6	5.0	4.2
Japan	6.2	5.3	4.8	4.5	4.4	4.3[a]
8. Farm households ('000)						
Korea	2,349	2,507	2,483	2,379	2,162	1,826
Japan	6,057	5,665	5,402	4,953	4,661	4,240
9. Korea's arable land						
(1,000 acres)	5,024	5,575	5,678	5,535	5,453	5,284
(1,000 hectares)	2,033	2,256	2,298	2,240	2,196	2,138

Note: a: 1987.

Sources: Data for the years 1955–80 are from Byung-Nak Song, *The Korean Economy*, second edition, Seoul, Bakyoungsa, 1984. Data for the year 1988 are from The Bank of Korea, *Economic Statistics Yearbook*, 1989; Economic Planning Board, *Major Statistics for the Korean Economy*, 1989; Ministry of Agriculture and Fisheries, *Major Statistics of Agriculture and Fisheries*, Seoul, MAF, 1989. Japanese Statistics are from Japanese General Affairs (Somucho) Agency/Bureau of Statistics, *Statistics of Japan*, 1988; The Prime Minister's Office/Statistical Bureau; *International Statistics*, 1983; Ministry of Agriculture and Fisheries, *Major Statistics of Agriculture and Fisheries in Japan*, 1988, 1989; and Economic Planning Agency, *Handbook of the Japanese Economy 1989*, Tokyo, EPA, 1989.

almost doubled, and the per capita income of 'Seoulites' has increased more than threefold. Because of such a policy, the price of land and housing has increased tremendously, as has population density and congestion. As land resources are very scarce in Korea, the government has devised various measures to use land efficiently. But the result has turned out to be contrary to government expectations. For instance, it is extremely difficult for firms to obtain a piece of land for industrial use. Soo Il Kwack[3] indicated that firms need to go through a great deal of red tape. There are 60 different procedures involving 199 government offices to deal with. The number of documents involved in these procedures can be as many as 374. Many Koreans become highly emotional about the transfer of arable land, especially rice paddies, to urban use. According to Kenichi Omae, a Japanese economic columnist, a similar policy has been the major cause for the tremendous rise in land prices in Tokyo and other Japanese cities.[4] For the future, Korea will need a land-use policy that can smoothly transfer agricultural land into industrial and urban use.

Because of Korea's comparative disadvantages in agriculture, the industry-oriented growth strategy will continue to be the most appropriate as long as there are still many people in rural areas to be absorbed into urban ones. In the case of Japan and other countries, it was the farms that supplied the surplus capital needed for industrialization in the early stages of development. However, in the case of Korea they supplied mainly the surplus labour needed for industrial growth. Their supply of capital was extremely limited. Although Korea does not have good land resources, Korean agriculture did not slow down but actually developed faster due to industrial expansion.

Land Use

The fact that Korea is the third most densely populated country in the world means that Korea's per capita land area is the third smallest. Moreover, Korea's terrain is very hilly, and only one-fifth of the land is arable. Korea's per capita GNL (gross national land) and per capita arable land were only 0.58 acres and 0.13 acres, respectively, in 1987 (see Table 2.2). Increases in population will push these figures lower, making efficient utilization of land extremely important.

Table 2.2 Land Use in Korea, 1970 and 1987

	1970		1987	
	Sq. Km.	%	Sq. Km.	%
Entire Country (km^2)	98,480	100.0	99,170	100.0
Arable	22,980	23.3	21,430	21.6
Rice paddies	12,730	12.9	13,520	13.6
Dry field	10,250	10.4	7,920	8.0
Forest	66,114	67.1	65,160	65.7
Other	9,386	9.6	12,580	12.7
Urban Areas	8,412	100.0	19,851	100.0
Residential	601	7.1	969	4.9
Roads	193	2.3	625	3.1
Industry	—		154	0.8
Educational	—		109	0.5
Park	16	0.2	16	0.1
(Subtotal)	(810)	(9.6)	(1,873)	(9.4)
Arable	2,511	29.9	4,805	24.2
Forest	4,307	51.2	11,092	55.9
River, etc.	370	4.4	928	4.7
Other	414	4.9	1,153	5.8
Rural Areas	90,068		79,319	
Urban Population ('000)	15,810		33,294	
Per Capita Area (acre)				
Entire land	0.75		0.58	
Arable land	0.18		0.13	
Urban area	0.13		0.15	

Sources: Economic Planning Board, *Major Statistics of the Korean Economy,* 1988; Ministry of Agriculture and Fisheries, *Major Statistics of Agriculture and Fisheries*, 1988; and Ministry of Home Affairs, *Municipal Yearbook of Korea*, 1971, 1988.

The extreme scarcity of space in Korea, especially in Seoul and other metropolitan areas, has caused a rapid rise in land and housing prices. Pieces of land in urban areas become increasingly important forms of wealth and key determinants of income distribution. The present scarcity of land in large cities appears to be the result of overall nation-wide land scarcity and the low priority that has been given to housing and the environment by policymakers and ordinary Koreans alike. A third factor may be Korea's incorrent land-use policy.

Since the early 1960s the core of the Korean agricultural policy has been to expand rice production and achieve self-sufficiency. For this purpose the government has expanded rice paddies through reclamation, land clearing, and conversion of dry fields into rice paddies. The government also tried to prohibit the shift of arable land into non-agricultural or urban use through the designation of 'absolute arable land' and 'relative arable land'. Rice paddies legally classified as absolute arable land can never be transferred into non-agriculture use. In the case of relative arable land, the transfer to other use is possible but involves heavy sanctions involving many government offices. As a consequence of this land-use policy the area of rice paddies increased between 1970 and 1987 in spite of the rapid expansion of urban areas.

There still remains a great deal of arable land in urban areas. As seen in Table 2.2, 24.2 per cent of all urban land is arable. Also, because of the mountainous nature of the Korean landscape, 55.9 per cent of the entire urban area is hilly or forested. The net amount of land available for various urban uses is only a little over 9 per cent of all the urban areas. The shortage has been aggravated by the green-belt system which was introduced by the government in 1973 to prevent the spatial expansion of large cities, but has resulted in 79 per cent of urban Koreans living on only 2 per cent of the national land.[5]

Regions and Population Distribution

Korea is divided administratively into nine provinces, one special city (Seoul), and five directly-administered cities. The six major cities have administrative status equal to the provinces, and these fifteen administrative areas together constitute the basic regional units in Korea. Most statistical data are compiled on the basis of these regions. The main economic regions also are based on these admininstrative areas, as shown in Table 2.3.

Planning regions for Korea were devised for the first time for the National Land Development Plan (1972–81) in 1971.[6] This first plan divided the whole country into the four 'large development or river basin regions' based on the major river basins. These four regions were further divided into eight major regions.

The eight regions presented in Table 2.3 and Figure 2.1 are about the same as those suggested in the original national land plan, but more realistic than those in the plan in that they are based on the present regional transportation and communication networks linking Korea's special city, Seoul, the five directly administered cities, 28 major cities (see Figure 2.1), and 179 *eup* or townships in 137 counties throughout the country (as of 1989). The smallest administrative unit in Korea is a *dong*. There are 2,059 *dong* in urban areas and 34,553 *dong* in rural areas.

From a development standpoint, Korea's two most important regions have been the Seoul region and the Pusan-Kyongnam or Pusan region. Together, the two regions contained 58.3 per cent of the total population in 1988: 40.9 per cent in the Seoul region and 17.4 per cent around Pusan (See Table 2.3).

The Seoul region consists of Seoul Special City and surrounding Kyonggi Province. The Pusan region consists of the special city of Pusan and the surrounding province of Kyongsang Nam Province. It encompasses the south-eastern coastal zone including such major industrial cities as Pohang (iron and steel), Ulsan (automobiles, shipbuilding, and petrochemicals), and Changwon (heavy manufacturing industries), in addition to Pusan itself (general export manufacturing, commerce, and port facilities).

Seoul had grown very rapidly since Korea's economic takeoff in the 1960s, but the Pusan region only began its rise with the promotion of heavy industries after 1972. Now, however, the Pusan area is Korea's second most rapidly growing region.

In response to the rapid growth of population and industries in the city of Seoul since the early 1960s, the government has employed various policies to discourage what was viewed as the undesirable overconcentration of population and industries in the Capital region. The government also adopted various policies designed to disperse population and manufacturing industries away from Seoul. Most of these dispersal plans, such as the industrial relocation plan, the new capital city plan, the plan for relocating head offices of major public enterprises, and the rural resettlement plan, have ignored the forces of the market, however, and have not been particularly effective.[7] Instead, they have often harmed those same private firms that were pressured by the government to relocate.

Korea's lagging regions are the Kwangju and Chonju regions, whch lie in the chiefly agricultural zone in the south-western part

Table 2.3 The Population of the Eight Main Regions, 1966–1988 (thousands)

	1966	1970	1975	1980	1985	1988
Total population	29,193	31,466	34,707	37,436	40,448	41,975
1. Seoul (Capital) Region						
Seoul Special City	3,803	5,536	6,890	8,364	9,639	10,310
Inchon City*					1,387	1,552
Kyonggi Province	3,108	3,358	4,039	4,934	4,794	5,306
Total	6,911	8,894	10,929	13,298	15,820	17,168
Share in total						
population (%)	23.7	28.3	31.5	35.5	39.1	40.9
2. Pusan-Kyongnam Region						
Pusan City*	1,430	1,880	2,453	3,160	3,515	3,701
Kyongsangnam Province	3,176	3,120	3,280	3,322	3,517	3,613
Total	4,606	5,000	5,733	6,482	7,032	7,314
Share in total						
population (%)	15.8	15.9	16.5	17.3	17.4	17.4

3. Taegu-Kyongpuk Region	4,477	4,559	4,859	4,955	5,040	5,060
Taegu City*					2,031	2,166
Kyongsangbuk Province					3,010	2,894
4. Kwangju Region	4,050	4,006	3,984	3,780		3,725
Kwangju City*					(906)	1,131
Cholla Nam Province					3,748	2,594
5. Chonju Region						
Cholla Puk Province	2,523	2,434	2,456	2,288	2,202	2,143
6. Chungchong Region	4,455	4,341	4,471	4,380	4,393	4,381
Chungchong Puk Province	1,550	1,481	1,522	1,424	1,391	1,368
Chungchong Nam Province	2,905	2,860	2,949	2,956	3,002	3,013
7. Taebaek Region						
Kangwon Province	1,833	1,866	1,862	1,791	1,725	1,683
8. Cheju Region						
Cheju Province	337	365	412	463	489	501

Note: * Directly administered city. Kwangju was designated a DAC after the 1985 population census.

Sources: Computed from Economic Planning Board. *Major Statistics of Korean Economy, 1987* and the *Population and Housing Census,* various years. Figures for 1988 are from Economic Planning Board. *Future Population of Korea by Region.* Seoul, EPB, 1989. Population figures for 1988 are based on resident registration statistics.

Fig 2.1 Main Regions and Cities

Key: ■ Regional centres

⊙ 28 major cities with population over 100,000 (as of 1988)

of the country. The people of this area have long considered themselves discriminated against, as well as neglected in development and investment plans by the successive governments that to a large degree have been dominated by persons from the Taegu and Pusan regions. The Kwangju and Chonju regions have lost population since 1966, and are long-standing centres of anti-government sentiment. Unfortunately, these regions are not well positioned for the development of large-scale manufacturing industries. Especially limiting is the absence of good natural harbours that could be developed as international trading ports.

Urban Population and Urban Areas

There was a saying a few years ago that Koreans were living in the 'age of 70 per cent'. That is, that over 70 per cent of Koreans were living in rural areas, over 70 per cent of the total land area was mountainous, and that over 70 per cent of the country's GNP originated in rural-agricultural activites. That situation has changed drastically. At present, about 90 per cent of Korea's GNP is generated by urban, non agricultural activities, over 70 per cent of the population live in Korea's 160 cities and urbanized towns, and over two-thirds live in urban areas with over 50,000 in population (See Table 2.4).

According to Mills and Song the proportion of Koreans living in urban areas in the 1950s was similar to the average level observed in other typical developing countries. Since then, however, Korea's urbanization has been much faster than the pattern typically observed in such countries.[8] Korea's urbanization level of 68.7 per cent in 1987 (see Table 2.4) is much higher than registered in most middle-income countries.[9] Mills and Song indicate that this is largely due to the rapid growth of the manufacturing sector in Korea.

Since the early 1960s the number of urban areas as well as the urban population has increased substantially. Koreans living in settlements with over 20,000 inhabitants increased more than threefold and the number of urban areas grew by about 50 per cent. During this process of urbanization cities of different sizes grew at different rates. Cities with populations of over one million grew the most rapidly, increasing their share of the urban population from 40.0 per cent to 55.9 per cent between 1960 and 1987. Conversely, small urban areas with 20,000–50,000 inhabi-

Table 2.4 The Distribution of Urban Population by City Size Class, 1960–1987

Population of Cities ('000)	1960		1966		1970		1975		1980		1987	
	%	No. of Cities	%	No. of Cities	%	No. of Cities	%	No. of Cities	%	No. of Cities	%	No. of Cities
Over 1,000	40.0	2	42.5	2	54.1	3	52.8	3	57.0	4	55.9	4
500–1,000	6.6	1	11.2	2	7.3	2	9.5	3	5.5	2	8.3	5
200–500	9.9	3	7.7	3	4.3	2	7.1	5	12.9	11	12.6	12
100–200	7.4	5	9.8	10	10.4	12	11.1	17	9.8	18	7.5	15
50–100	14.4	20	10.2	18	10.1	22	7.0	22	5.1	21	7.8	36
20–50	21.7	74	18.6	77	13.8	74	12.5	90	9.7	115	7.9	88
Total	100.0	105	100.0	112	100.0	115	100.0	140	100.0	171	100.0	160
Urban Population ('000)												
Cities over 50,000 (A)	7,121		10,010		13,550		17,658		22,470		28,573	
Cities over 20,000 (B)	8,950		12,301		15,683		20,269		24,940		31,020	
Total Population (C)	24,954		29,160		31,435		34,679		37,407		41,575	
Share of urban population												
(A/C)	28.5		34.3		43.1		50.9		60.1		68.7	
(B/C)	35.9		42.2		49.9		58.4		66.7		74.6	

Sources: Computed from Ministry of Home Affairs, *Municipal Yearbook of Korea, 1972, 1974, 1982, and 1988,* and Economic Planning Board, *Population and Housing Census,* various years.

tants have accommodated an increasingly smaller share of the total population since 1960.

Seoul has shown the most remarkable growth, its population increasing from 3.8 million in 1966 to over 10 million at the end of 1988. The rapid concentration of population and industry in Seoul has long been regarded by political leaders as a critical national issue and the basic cause for various internal problems. And because Seoul is located within the range of North Korean artillery, the security of the capital city is considered highly vulnerable. The government has tried in various ways to deconcentrate and decentralize population and industries away from Seoul, but to little avail. Such measures include the green-belt system intending to limit the spatial expansion of Seoul, the new capital-city plan designed to relocate central government offices to a new administrative centre near Taejon City, plans to move the central offices of public enterprises away from Seoul, and so on. None of these measures has been successful in forestalling the continuing concentration of population in Seoul, and the government appears to have wasted enormous resources, both public and private, in pursuing what appear to be futile policies. The attention President Park Chung Hee gave to stemming the growth of Seoul was as intense as his efforts to promote trade. Working in the Blue House as a member of a special task force dealing with the issue of growth in Seoul and the capital region, I had the impression that to President Park it was one of the most important domestic issues.

The concentration of population and economic infrastructure in the capital region is a common problem in less developed countries. On the basis of Korea's experience, there appears to be no easy solution to this problem for most developing countries. They can try to relocate some residents and industries away from the capital city, but the social cost of doing so is likely to greatly exceed the social benefit. Instead, less developed countries should concentrate their efforts on solving whatever problems are created by population concentration, rather than on preventing the concentration itself.

Another important urban policy concerns small urban areas with populations of 20,000–50,000. In Korea these smaller centres play a crucial role for rural dwellers. Early in the development process, these cities provide rural villagers with access to urban services. These cities are where villagers obtain modern medical treatment, send their children to school, purchase farm supplies, and sell their produce. In this sense small cities and towns determine the quality of rural life. However, these cities generally have been neglected by the central government because of the preoccupation with the capital city's problems.

The growth of urban areas of different size appears to have shifted over the course of development. Large cities appear to have grown fastest in the early stages of development, middle-sized cities in the middle stages, and small cities in the late stages.

The middle stage of development may be said to start at an income level of US$2,000 (1980 dollars), according to Nobel laureate economist Arthur Lewis.[10] The late stage of development, for its part, begins after per capita income reaches about US$5,500 (1982 dollars), to borrow the framework of Chenery and Syrquin.[11] According to this classification scheme, Korea recently entered into the stage when middle-sized cities grow at a relatively high rate. This trend is observed in the relative decrease in share of population held by large cities since 1980 and the corresponding growth of middle-sized cities (see Table 2.4). This suggests that the proper way of allocating public investment in cities should parallel this pattern of city growth. That is, the government should plan on allocating a relatively large proportion of its investment resources to large, middle, and small cities in the early, middle, and late stages of development, respectively.

Korea's Population Problem

The overall population density in Korea is the third highest in the world after Bangladesh and Taiwan, if the city states are excluded. Total land per capita was only 0.58 acres in Korea in 1987. With two-thirds of this area hilly and not suitable for either agricultural or urban use, the pressure of population growth has always been seen as one of the most serious socio-economic problems facing Korea.

This was especially so after the Korean War (1950–3), when a postwar baby boom (1955–60) occurred despite the sluggish recovery of the economy.[12] At the start of the First Five-Year Economic Development Plan (1962–66), the yearly population growth rate was a high 2.6 per cent, as shown in Table 2.5— significantly above the economic growth rate of 2.2 per cent. As a result, the per capita GNP growth rate was negative at the time.

Fig. 2.2 Population Structure, 1970, 1980, and 1985

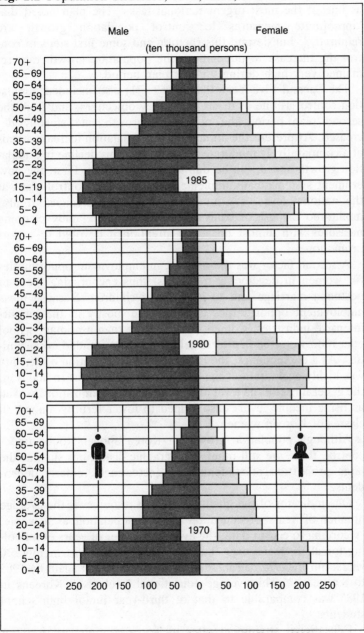

Source: Economic Planning Board, *Social Indicators in Korea*, 1988.

The First Five-Year Plan, however, identified population control as one of the most urgent national tasks. The plan noted that 'appropriate measures to control population growth are required,'[13] but despite this rhetoric and some first steps to control the increase in population, the population growth rate remained very high during the first plan period.

The Second Five-Year Plan (1967–71) also included population control as one of its six key policy objectives, and from the second plan period the population growth rate steadily decreased. At present the annual rate of population increase stands at a comparatively moderate 1.3 per cent. This decline in population growth appears to be due to several factors. First, the government systematically implemented population-control plans at the national level very much like military campaigns. It also monitored the use of contraceptives and other family planning measures with almost the same attention it devoted to export promotion.

A second factor was the increase in employment opportunities for women in developing industries, thus encouraging them to postpone marriage and to have fewer children. Because these employment opportunities initially were mostly in the labour-intensive industries, women with no more than a primary school education were the first to benefit from the expanded opportunities. As a consequence, the impact of industrialization on fertility was highly egalitarian in the early period of growth. In addition, the general rise in the level of education and urbanization, as well as rising income levels, also helped to lower fertility among all classes of Korean women.

Although population growth in Korea appears to be under control, there are still other demographic distortions such as the large proportion of students and, increasingly, elderly dependents.

One indicator of the quality of human resources is the average number of years of education for the population as a whole. According to census data, the average number of years of schooling for all Koreans over the age of six in 1966 was merely 5.0 years, but by 1975 had increased to 6.6 years, and again by 1985 to 8.6 years.[14] The average educational level of all Koreans in 1985 was comparable to that of third-year junior high school students.

Educational attainment rates in Korea continue to rise. For

Table 2.5 The Population of North and South Korea

| | North Korea | | South Korea | | | |
| | Population | | Population | | Population Density (persons per km²) | Urban Population (%) |
	Millions	Average Annual Growth Rate (%)	Millions	Average Annual Growth Rate (%)		
1920			17.3		79	3.3
1930			20.4	1.7	93	4.5
1935			22.2	1.7	101	7.4
1940			23.5	1.2	107	11.6
1944			25.1	1.6	114	13.9
1949	9.7		20.2	−4.4	205	17.5
1955	9.0	−1.3	21.5	1.1	218	24.4
1960	10.0	2.1	25.0	3.0	254	28.3
1966	12.4	3.6	29.2	2.6	296	35.6
1970	13.9	2.8	31.4	1.9	319	43.1
1975	15.9	2.6	34.7	2.0	351	50.9
1980	18.0	2.4	37.4	1.5	378	57.3
1985	20.4	2.5	40.4	1.5	414	64.0
1988	21.8	2.2	42.0	1.3	429	68.7

Note: Foreigners are excluded. Figures before 1945 include North Korea. North Korean population figures are at mid-year as estimated by the United Nations.

Sources: Byung-Nak Song, *The Korean Economy*, second edition, Seoul, Backyoungsa Co. 1984. Figures were computed from Economic Planning Board, *Population and Housing Census*, various years, and *Major Statistics of the Korean Economy*, various years.

instance, students enrolled in secondary school made up 94 per cent of their age group, the highest among developing countries. The rate is even higher than the average figure of 93 per cent for 19 advanced countries.[15] In addition, the proportion of Korean high school graduates going on to colleges or universities was a high 46.1 per cent in 1987—much higher than Japan's rate of 30 per cent and virtually identical to the rate in the United States in 1983.

3 The Historical Roots of Modern Growth

THE way the Korean economy has grown, and the way the Korean people have shared the fruits of economic growth, have been greatly influenced by Korea's history and culture. In this chapter we explore the historical roots of the contemporary Korean economy, returning to examine the cultural aspects of the Korean economy in Chapters 4 and 11.

Korea's successful economic growth in modern times has deep roots. In particular, the Confucian emphasis on education and discipline, the tradition of an industrious agricultural labour force, and the traditional innovative potential of the Korean people appear to form the foundation of Korea's recent advance. No less importantly, however, the period of Japanese colonial rule (1910–45) and the North-South division of the country also have profoundly shaped the structure and distortions of Korea's modern economic growth.

In this chapter we begin with a very brief review of those historical events or factors that appear to be most useful in helping our understanding of the roots of Korea's culture, ethics and values, economic base, social structure, and innovative potential. Following this we examine the long-term trend of Korea's economic development.

Korea's long-term development may be divided into the following three periods. The first is the period of very slow development of the traditional agrarian economy during the Chosun dynasty (1392–1910). The second is the period of colonial development and destruction during the Korean War which covers the period from the beginning of Japanese colonization in 1910 to the end of the Korean War (1950–3). The third is the period of post-war recovery and rapid growth since 1954. Korea's development during the first and second periods will be discussed in this chapter, and the third period in the following chapters. As economic and social development during the traditional period (prior to 1910) formed more or less the basis of development of the economy in later years, we will examine development during the traditional period in more detail. As Korea is one of the oldest countries in the world, it has also accumulated a number of inventions and innovative achievements during its long history. Prior to the examination of her long-term development we will review Korea's brief history in relation to innovative achievements.[1]

The Second Oldest Independent Nation in the World

The history of Korea as an independent country goes as far back as AD 668, when the Silla Kingdom (57 BC – AD 935) completed the conquest of two other early Korean kingdoms—Koguryo and Paekche. With the unification of the country under the Silla, the Korean people came under the rule of a single monarch— marking the beginnings of a unified culture and history that was to persist, with only occasional interruptions, until this century.

From the unification of the country by Silla until the colonization of the country by Japan in 1910, Korea remained an independent nation—a period spanning more than twelve centuries. Edwin Reischauer says that Korea and Japan have, after China, the longest histories as independent nations in the world.[2] Since AD 668 Korea has been a country consisting of a single race, language, and culture. The strong sense of unity—racial, cultural, and linguistic—is a fundamental quality of Koreans that dates back to the seventh century.

Korea's Unique Heritage

Korea's noteworthy innovative spirit began after the unification of the country by Silla. The most important innovative spirit during the unified Silla period is associated with Chang Pogo, known as the 'merchant prince' or the 'master of the Yellow Sea.'[3] Chang Pogo developed and maintained an extensive maritime trade network connecting regions in Korea, China, and Japan in the ninth century—a time when international maritime trade was still in its infancy even in Europe, which was then emerging from the Dark Ages. Chang Pogo is known to have built many vessels and established trading posts and warehouses in China's Shandong peninsula.

Chang's headquarters were located on Wando Island, situated in the south-western part of Korea. The stones of this maritime enterpreneur's hilltop fortress can still be seen. In recent years, several ancient vessels filled with celadon and Chinese wares were discovered in coastal waters not far from Wando Island. Large quantities of ancient celadon and other chinaware recovered from these sunken trade vessels are preserved at the national museum in Kwangju.

As the unified Silla weakened, one of the rebel leaders, Wang Kon, established the Koryo Kingdom (918–1392), which he did with the support of landords and merchants, and by accepting the voluntary surrender of the last Silla king. The West's name for 'Korea' originates in the name 'Koryo'.

The key invention during the Koryo period was the world's first documented use of movable metal printing type. This Korean development, dated at 1234, preceded Gutenberg's use of moveable metal type in Germany by about two hundred years. Although the exact date of the first use of moveable metal type in Korea is still under debate, it is generally considered to have evolved from the long history of wood-block printing, especially of Buddhist scriptures.

The Koryo dynasty produced the world's most comprehensive and oldest collection of Buddhist scriptures, known as the 'Tripitaka Koreana'. It consists of 81,258 large wooden printing blocks and took sixteen years to complete, being finished in 1251. The Koryo leaders undertook the massive project to reproduce the scriptures in order to secure Buddha's protection from incessant invasions by the Mongols. This helped accelerate printing technology, both wood-block and metal type, during the Koryo period.

Koryo is also famous for its developments in astronomy and ceramics. Even Chinese experts have praised Koryo blue celadon —famous for its refined shape and 'kingfisher blue' glaze—as 'the best under heaven'. Japanese historians acknowledge that the Japanese later learned celadon technology from Korean potters. During the Japanese Invasion of Korea (1592–7), whole villages of Korean potters were taken as captives to Japan so that their skills could be utilized.

Koreans even constructed a suspension bridge over the Imjin River during the Koryo period.[4] The bridge stood in the present Demilitarized Zone, north of Seoul. It was a hundred years before similar bridges were built in the West. Other notable inventions during the Koryo period include a spinning wheel and a water clock.

In spite of the completion of the Buddhist Tripitaka and the continuous performance of religious rites throughout the country, the incursions by the Mongols continued. It is worth nothing that the Koryo dynasty resisted the invasion of the brutal Mongols for about 30 years—no other people, except the people of China's Southern Sung dynasty, succeeded in holding back the Mongols for such a long period.

As the Mongols' power gradually faded in the fourteenth century, Japanese pirates started to plunder coastal villages on a large and systematic scale. This caused the people to lose faith in Buddhism, which did not appear to protect them, and rivalry and conflict intensified between Buddhist and Confucian scholars. Friction between scholarly officials and the warrior classes also grew, due largely to the fact that at the time the Tripitaka project was being promoted, the warrior classes were ignored and discriminated against. Towards the end, the Koryo dynasty badly needed generals who could organize a defense against the Japanese pirates and against Chinese incursions from the north. General Yi Songgye was one of the most capable and respected of the country's military leaders. After enlisting the support of key senior officials, General Yi overthrew the declining Koryo monarchy and established a new dynasty called Choson.

The Choson Kingdom (1392–1910) established by General Yi —also known as the Yi dynasty after the ruling family—adopted Confucianism as the state religion. Buddhism was officially suppressed, although not eradicated, and as a consequence Buddhist monks retreated deep into the mountains. The oppression of Buddhism continued throughout the Choson dynasty. This is the main reason why there are no large scale Buddhist temples or monasteries in Seoul, such as there are in Kyoto or Tokyo.

The reign of King Sejong, the fourth Yi king (1419–50), was marked by a flowering of inventiveness. The world's first scientific rain guage—or 'pluviometer'—was invented under King Sejong's sponsorship in 1442. It preceded Gastell's rain gauge (1639) by nearly two centuries. As a result of the system of government-maintained rain gauges, Korea has the oldest continuous record of rainfall measurements in the world. Korea's tradition of rice culture is among the oldest, and the rain gauge contributed greatly to increasing rice yields. According to Dwight Perkins of Harvard University, rice productivity in Korea was one of the highest in the world even before the annexation of the country by Japan in 1910.[5]

The creation in 1443 of *hangŭl*, Korea's phonetic alphabet, by King Sejong and a hand-picked group of scholars is considered one of the Yi dynasty's crowning intellectual achievements. Edward B. Adams, an educator born and raised in Korea, describes the *hangŭl* alphabet as follows: 'It is a combination of twenty-four extremely simple symbols, which in combination can represent almost any conceivable sound. Even the sigh of the wind, the chirp of birds, and the barking of dogs can be exactly described by the "hangŭl" phonetic system.'[6] Koreans during the Choson dynasty, according to Dwight H. Perkins, 'surpassed in the field of education their stronger Japanese and Chinese neighbours, at least in the field of mass education.'[7] This was due to the invention of *hangŭl*. Being phonetic, *hangŭl* is much easier to learn than Chinese characters. The invention of *hangŭl* no doubt contributed greatly to a higher educational level for almost all classes in Korea during the Choson dyansty.

Another famous invention of the Choson period was the world's first ironclad warship. In 1592 Korea's most famous admiral, Yi Sun-shin, built his first 'turtle ship' (*kŏbukson*)—so-called because of its shape and iron-plate covering. Admiral Yi used his heavily armed turtleships to rout the Japanese armada during the Japanese invasions of 1592–8. In victory, Admiral Yi was slandered and criticized at the court by jealous and corrupt political rivals. But, vindicated by history, Admiral Yi is regarded in East Asia as one of the world's best naval strategists. Admiral Togo, along with all the Japanese soldiers and sailors under his command, visited Yi Sun-shin's hometown on his way to the battle with the Russians and performed religious rituals there to invoke the 'spiritual help' of Admiral Yi. Togo was to say that Admiral Yi was by far the best naval commander in the world, much better than himself or Admiral Nelson.

Unfortunately, Korean history in the West has often been seen through the distorting mirror of nationalistic Japanese writers and others whose basic knowledge is about Japan, not Korea. In his book *Korea's Colorful Heritage*, Jon C. Covell takes note of the many inventions and cultural achievements of traditional Korea.[8]

The historical spurts of innovation during the Silla, Koryo, and Yi dynasties are the distant roots of Korea's modern economic development. The spirit of the Koryo suspension bridge is echoed in world-class bridges built at Penang, Malaysia, and between

Namhae Island and the mainland along Korea's southern coast. And Admiral Yi's turtleship serves as the spiritual ancestor to Korea's modern shipbuilding industry—the world's largest in 1987. Another important achievement showing Korea's continuing inventive spirit is the seven consecutive championships held by Korean teams in the 'Olympics of Technology', formally known as the International Vocational Training Competition.

Development of the Traditional Agrarian Economy

In 1876, Korea was coerced by Japan to sign a commerce treaty and thereby forced to open its ports and land to Japan, the United States, and other countries. Prior to 1876, Korea's doors were tightly closed to all countries except China due to the isolationist policy of the Choson dynasty (1392–1910). This is one of the reasons why Korea was known in the past as the 'hermit kingdom'. At the time of its opening up to the West in the late nineteenth century, the Korean economy was a typical, traditional agricultural economy. Thereafter, however, it underwent a gradual structural change in terms of manufacturing, infrastructure, and banking and other service industries. This trend accelerated after the country's colonization by Japan in 1910.

Population, Land, and Society

The two major factors shaping the traditional, agricultural economy of the Choson dynasty appear to be the following. One is the steady growth of the population, which led to a corresponding fall in the amount of farming land per capita. The other is the strictly observed class system, which accorded agriculture priority over manufacturing and commerce. The actual ranking order in social status was *sa* (scholar), *nong* (farmer), *gong* (manufacturer or artisan), and *sang* (merchant). Artisans and merchants were thus considered the lowest occupations. The philosophy of *nongja chonha-ji taebon* ('the great foundation under heaven is agriculture') dominated the people's value system concerning occupations and economic activities. Thus, agriculture was bound to be the predominant economic activity throughout the Choson dynasty.

We can see from the figures given in Table 3.1 that the population of Korea increased from 5.5 million to 17.4 million during the Choson dynasty, (1392–1910). As a consequence farmland per capita declined continuously throughout the period. This was exacerbated by the fact that the size of the national territory remained unchanged from 1392 and that about two-thirds of the country was mountainous. When the first land survey of Korea was carried out by the Japanese in 1918, the amount of farmland per capita turned out to be only about 0.12 hectares, or less than one-third of an acre. The fact that such a small area of land supported such a large population implies that agricultural productivity has been relatively high throughout Korea's long history.

Korean society during the Choson dynasty consisted of three classes: the *yangban* or literati, *sangmin* or commoners, and *chonmin* or lowborn. *Chonmin* were slaves and this status was hereditary. Slaves could be bought and sold by their masters. Traditional slavery existed in many parts of the country, including my home town, until the end of World War II. Since the *yangban* class directed the economy, government, and culture of the period, Choson is often referred to as a '*yangban* society'. Its culture, way of thinking, and lifestyle were all dominated by Confucianism, and Choson was fittingly designated a Confucian state.

In such a Confucian state, only men belonging to the *yangban* class and having a deep knowledge of Confucianism were eligible for the prestigious government posts. The sole ambition of promising sons of *yangban* families in the Yi dynasty was to pass the *kwago*, or civil service examination, and reach the highest rank in the government.

Senior government officials were rewarded for their loyalty to the king with grants of land. Towards the end of the Choson society the *yangban* class owned most of the private land, which was freely traded.

With the rise in free transactions, land tended to become concentrated in the hands of a few rich landlords. As the population continued to rise, so did the number of landless people. An increasingly large number of people craved to cultivate any piece of land made available to them. As a consequence, the number of tenant farmers increased as time went by, and when the first land survey of Korea was conducted, about 40 per cent of farm families were found to rent the land they cultivated.

Table 3.1 Population, Growth Rate, and Per Capita Income, 1392–1988

	Population (000)	Growth Rate (%)	Per Capita Income (1985 US$)
1392	5,549		160
1592	13,737	0.45	
1776	18,003	0.15	
1876	16,884	−0.06	190
1910	17,427	0.09	235
1920	17,264	−0.09	228
1930	20,438	1.69	225
1940	24,326	1.74	230
1944	25,900	1.57	223
1950	20,389	−3.99	260
1955	21,502	1.06	267
1960	24,954	2.98	287
1970	31,435	2.31	667
1980	37,407	1.74	2,074
1985	40,420	1.55	2,150
1988	41,975	1.26	3,120

Note: The Choson (*Yi*) dynasty covers the period 1392–1910. The year 1592 saw the beginning of the seven-year Japanese invasion (the Imjin Wars); Korea was opened to the west around 1876. Figures for 1988 are based on resident registration statistics. Figures prior to 1950 include North Korea.

Sources: Population figures for the Choson period are from Tai Hwan Kwon and Yong Ha Shin, 'An Attempt to Estimate the Population of the Choson Dynasty', *Tong-a-Munhwa*, December 1977. This research was supported by a Harvard-Yenching research grant.
    The population figure for 1920 is based on the provisional household survey, which was the first population survey in Korea. Population figures from 1910 through 1985 are from the Economic Planning Board/National Bureau of Statistics, *Korea Statistical Yearbook*, various years. Traditional population figures are more reliable after 1639 because the *hoguchosa* (household and population survey) was conducted almost every three years from that time. Population figures after 1945 exclude North Korea. Income figures were estimated by the author on the basis of data given in Sang-Chul Suh, 1978, Lee Ki-baik, 1984, and Korea Overseas Information Service, 1987.

Commerce and Money

Commerce was less developed than agriculture during the Choson dynasty. According to Dwight Perkins, it was also less developed in Korea than in either Japan or China,[9] the two most important neighbouring countries. Thus the Korean economy during this period was more agrarian than the economies of

China and Japan. Being predominantly agrarian, the Korean economy during the Choson period did not develop much. Per capita income increased only slightly during the whole period as seen in Table 3.1.

Commercial activities during the Choson period were conducted largely on the *changnal* or 'market day' system. Because the majority of the population were villagers scattered throughout the countryside, merchants tended to be itinerant salesmen. There were, of course, 'settled merchants', but they were usually to be found only in the larger towns. A *changnal* was a regular market day on which villagers and itinerant merchants met each other to exchange agricultural products and handicrafts. As people generally travelled on foot or used primitive modes of transport such as ox-carts, the boundary of the trading district was set, in effect, by the distance villagers could travel by foot to and from the market in one day. This made it necessary for merchants to journey from place to place in order to bring their goods close to the villagers. The heavily-laden travelling merchants could themselves go only short distances, however, and it became the custom for them to circulate among just five neighbouring market towns, taking each one in turn. Thus markets occurred on a five-day cycle in any one place. Even when the seven-day week was introduced to Korea at the end of the nineteenth century, the market day continued to fall every fifth day regardless of the 'weekday'.

The *changnal* market system existed quite extensively right up to the 1950s, but with the rapid development of various transport and distribution systems it has virtually disappeared in urban areas, existing only in some remote rural areas, and in a somewhat limited form on the outskirts of the larger cities.

Private commerce expanded gradually from the seventeenth century, especially with the introduction of a money system early that century. But the poor monetary system greatly constrained further development of commercial activities.

Ho-jin Choe indicates that the use of coinage became widespread from around 1679.[10] Before then, there had been no real currency in Korea, with commodities such as cloth and grain serving as the medium of exchange. The money system remained relatively undeveloped until the end of Choson dynasty, however. One foreign traveller in Korea in the late nineteenth century, for example, reported needing six men or one pony to carry a money chest containing copper coins worth only US$50 at the time.[11]

Government Finance

Because of the inconvenient monetary system, the central government could not pay officials of various local government offices or finance government activities scattered throughout the country through cash payments. Instead the central government assigned them a certain amount of land, depending on the size of the local government. The output of this government land was used to cover local government expenses. However, the amount of land given to most of the local governments was usually insufficient, especially in times of drought or bad harvest. In these circumstances, local governments were forced to rely on donations coerced from the local population. This became a source of extensive corruption among local government officials during the Choson dynasty. The most notorious example of corruption involved *koulwons* (county chiefs), who wielded almost absolute power in procuring materials from the people under their jurisdictions. The tradition of providing government officials with necessary support from extraordinary levies is still powerful among many Koreans. This tradition greatly contributes to the close relationship between the government and business circles, but also, in the past, to corruption.

Foreign trade during the Choson dynasty was chiefly conducted by the government and within a court-to-court tribute format with China and Japan. It was thus carried out mainly for political rather than economic reasons. Some foreign trade was also carried out on a private basis, but the total volume of both public and private foreign trade was very small.

The Japanese Occupation—Change amid Trauma

Tu Wei-Ming, professor of Chinese history and philosophy at Harvard, states that Confucianism strongly encourages people to 'adapt' themselves to the existing social system, but does not encourage people to 'transform' society.[12] According to this view, the Confucian state of Choson might have continued to sustain its traditional social system if Western-style foreign powers had not come on the scene. Choson was led by kings and elite scholar-bureaucrats steeped in Confucianism, who were totally incapable of conducting the kind of socio-economic transformation the country needed for its survival in the face of the threat from foreign powers.

In addition, the leaders of the Choson dynasty were almost totally isolated from foreign ideas and almost completely lacked a world view. Whatever the kings and leaders of the Choson dynasty knew about the West was learned from Koreans who had visited China. The situation remained the same even during the Japanese colonial period—whatever Koreans learned about the West during that period was obtained via Japan and was usually filtered through Japanese eyes. This lack of a world view contributed directly to the loss of the country to Japan in 1910, to the division of the country into North and South after its liberation in 1945, and to the Korean War in 1950.

Korea lagged far behind her most powerful neighbours, namely, China, Japan, and Russia, which had already begun the economic and political transformation needed to survive in the modern world. As a consequence, Korea was easy prey for these strong imperialist powers. Japan eventually was able to formally colonize Korea in 1910, but even before then, Japan had introduced a series of measures into traditional Korea that initiated the transformation of the country, both economically and socially. Examples include the establishment of an electric power company in 1898; the construction of the Seoul-Pusan railroad in 1900; the creation of a *de facto* central bank for Korea through the branch office of the Daiichi Ginko Bank of Japan, and the reform of the Korean currency in 1905; the formation of the Oriental Development Corporation in 1912; and the expansion of mining and manufacturing activities by numerous Japanese companies.

Japan ruled Korea for 35 years, from 1910 to 1945. During this time the colonial Korean economy was run by the Japanese for the Japanese, and the beneficiary of Korea's economic expansion was chiefly Japan and Japanese settlers in Korea. Although the growth rate of the Korean economy during the whole colonial period was nearly 4 per cent per annum—probably higher than the growth rate of the Japanese economy itself[13]—the well-being of the ordinary Koreans worsened in absolute terms. In other words, gross *domestic* product per capita increased remarkably, but gross *national* product per capita for Koreans actually decreased.

For the years 1912–36, Ki-Baek Lee suggests an average increase in agricultural output of about 1.6 per cent per annum (see Table 3.2). This figure coincides with Ban Sung Hwan's estimate for roughly the same period. During this period, however, rice exports from Korea to Japan soared continuously, leading to an actual decline in per capita food consumption for Koreans. Indeed, by 1936, more than half of all agricultural output in Korea was being shipped to Japan. The great and cruel irony of the colonial period was that, as stated by Edward Mason, 'many Koreans experienced an absolute, not just a relative, decline in their standard of living.'[14]

Korea's per capita GNP when the Japanese left in 1945 was very low—comparable to that of the least developed countries today. Even with massive injections of American assistance in the 1950s, Korea's per capita GNP amounted to only US$260 (in 1985 prices) in 1960, even lower than that of India at present. Liberation from the Japanese left Koreans with little more than dire poverty.[15]

The following factors account for the deterioration of the Korean people's economic welfare during the colonial period.

Firstly, Korea was regarded by the Japanese mainly as a supplier of cheap rice. Infrastructure facilities such as irrigation and reservoirs that were built during the colonial period increased output largely for Japanese landlords, who shipped the rice to feed Japan's growing industrial workforce. The increased output of rice was sent mostly to Japan—according to one estimate, about half of Korea's total rice production during the 1912–31 period was sent to Japan.[16]

Secondly, Korea, as a colonial enclave economy, was a source of other resources as well. Japanese lumbering companies were given extensive logging rights. The excessive felling of trees stripped mountains of their cover, leading to erosion and flooding. Japanese fisherman were also given permission to exploit Korea's fishery resources. Mining of gold, tungsten, and other minerals was also extensive during the colonial period, especially in the North.

Thirdly, Korea was also regarded as a place to settle Japan's surplus population. According to Edward S. Mason and others

Table 3.2 The Production, Consumption, and Export of Rice, 1912–1936

Period	Average Production		Average Consumption in Korea		Average Exported	
	Million sok	Index	Million sok	Per Capita sok	Million sok	Index
1912–16	12.3	100	11.24	0.72	1.06	100
1922–26	14.5	118	10.16	0.59	4.34	409
1932–36	17.0	138	8.24	0.40	8.76	826
	Percentage Average Annual Growth Rate					
1912–16 1932–36	1.6		−1.6		10.6	

Note: One *sok* = 180.39 litres (= 5.01 bushels).
Source: Kee-baik Lee, 1984.

the number of Japanese in Korea increased from 170,000 to 770,000 between 1910 and 1945.[17] To this end, the Oriental Development Company was established by well-connected Japanese leaders in 1908, even before the formal annexation of Korea. In the first stage, Japan used the Oriental Development Company to assume control over Korea's state-owned land, lands managed by military troops, and properties of the royal family. In the next stage, the Japanese capitalists coerced Koreans into selling their land at low prices. The Japanese also introduced registration laws that worked to strip illiterate or uninformed Korean farmers of their land, forcing many to become either tenants or semi-tenants. By 1931, 12 million farmers—2.3 million farm households—had been reduced to such a status. Landless Korean farmers, many on the verge of starvation, migrated to Manchuria, Siberia and, as labourers, to Japan. By 1931 around 19 per cent of the total farm population had migrated under such circumstances.[18] The legacy of this exodus is that there are at present over two million Koreans resident in China, about half a million Koreans resident in the USSR, and over half a million Koreans resident in Japan.

Additionally the Japanese used cheap workers from Korea for the development of Japanese mining and manufacturing industries. And finally, Japan used Korea as a base for military training in preparation 'for the invasions of Manchuria and China. Young Koreans were also forcibly drafted as soldiers when Japan entered World War II.

Under Japan's colonial regime, Koreans were generally restricted to no more than a primary education. This reflected the belief that Koreans should have only the level of education required for the completion of the tasks they were expected to perform in the colonial system. Nonetheless, the level of formal modern education for Koreans rose during the period mainly due to the efforts of foreign Christian missionaries.

The Japanese used Koreans mainly in lower positions in organizations. As a result, Koreans had few opportunities to accumulate experience as leaders, managers, or negotiators. Forced into a 'sergeant's' role, they developed a disgruntled sergeant's mentality. This legacy persists, and modern Korea needs badly the mentality of committed 'officers' or 'generals', self-sacrificing leaders, and risk-taking entrepreneurs and innovators.

The severe lack of competent politicians, bureaucrats, scholars, businessmen, and technocrats is a common colonial heritage shared by most newly liberated nations, complicating the development of a stable national polity after independence. The retardation of the potential enterpreneurial class and the class of social leaders and philosophers may be one of the most harmful impacts of colonialism in Korea and elsewhere. Under Japanese rule, Koreans were largely isolated from experience in the international arena. When Japan tried to expand its imperial control through the so-called Greater East Asia Co-Prosperity Sphere, Korea's contacts outside the Japanese Empire were restricted even more. The social disintegration of the traditional social structure under Japanese rule, as well as the growth of distrust and suspicion between those who went along with the Japanese and those who actively participated in the resistance movement, left Koreans with a legacy of mistrust of government and of one another.

There were many other negative impacts as well, even though basic Korean cultural values changed little despite the massive Japanese effort to mold Koreans into second-class Japanese subjects. For example, neither Japanese Shintoism nor Japanese-style Zen Buddhism gained ground in Korea, despite Japan's efforts to implant its belief systems and discourage Korean beliefs—as well as Christianity. The Koreans remained Korean in spite of everything.

For all the undoubted negative features of Japanese colonialism there were some positive impacts as well. Education, infrastructure, and management experience in modern organizations are the most often quoted examples. Moreover, Koreans learned the Japanese ways of doing business and managing the economy, and Koreans probably are still the Asians who understand Japan best. Because of the colonial experience, Koreans are in a position to make selective use of various Japanese institutions.

The Impact of the North-South Division

Following the Korean War, the north-south division of the country by the truce of July 1953 split a relatively integrated economic whole into two incomplete parts. The best mines and most advanced heavy industries had been developed in the North during the colonial period. As a consequence, the North was in a better position than the South to rehabilitate its war-ravaged economy, although much of the physical industrial infrastructure in both North and South had been destroyed in the conflict. Destruction in Seoul was especially severe, as Seoul changed hands four times during the Korean War. Over 80 per cent of industrial and infrastructure facilities and more than half the dwellings were destroyed by the War.

The South, on the other hand, was developed by the Japanese as a supplier of cheap foodstuffs for Japan's industrial workforce, and little industrial infrastructure was left behind. As a result of partition and war, moreover, the mainly agricultural South was left with two thirds of the Korean population.

The creation of a Soviet-backed communist regime in the North produced a flood of refugees to the South, including many Christians, landlords, and businessmen. Overseas Koreans also returned in large numbers from China, Japan, and Soviet Manchuria, where they had fled, resettled, or been taken as draft labour during the colonial period. The South began its national reconstruction with too many people on too little land.

The presence of a continuing military threat from the North has profoundly influenced the direction and pattern of Korea's economic development. In particular, the military threat forces South Korea to spend about 6 per cent of its GNP on defense. It also forces the South to maintain the fifth largest standing army in the world. The impact of the armed forces on Korean society has been profound. Over 600,000 men are in the Armed Forces, with roughly one-fourth of these soldiers discharged back into society every year. The provision of re-entry employment opportunities for retiring military officers has been a special problem for the Korean economy. At the same time, the Korean military contributed greatly to the development of human skills especially in the early stages of development. Through the military, young Koreans, especially those from rural areas or with limited education, become acquainted with motor vehicles, electronic, and other equipment, and a variety of related skills. The military also exposed young Koreans to modern urban life and familiarized them with modern organizations and management techniques. Into the 1960s the military services were the major modern organizations in the country.

The threat from the North also helped unite South Koreans in their nation-building efforts. The sense of competition with the North also drove South Koreans to concentrate their energies on catching up and outperforming North Korea in economic and non-economic realms.

An Overview of Korea's Transition from Traditional to Modern Economy

The long-term process of Korea's economic development may be summarized as follows:

Firstly, before the opening-up of the country to the West in 1876; Korea was a traditional, almost wholly agrarian economy. Korea's manufacturing, commerce, and economic infrastructure were relatively less developed than in either China or Japan. During the pre-1876 period, Korea's economic development was mainly determined by changes in agriculture. The invention of the rain gauge, the gradual improvement in traditional farming techniques and development of an agricultural infrastructure allowed agricultural output to increase considerably during this period, although only slightly faster than the growth of the population, so that output per person increased only modestly (see Table 3.1).

Secondly, between the opening-up of the country in 1876 and subjugation to Japanese colonial rule in 1910, Korea experienced rapid economic growth and rise in per capita income. This was due chiefly to the expansion of infrastructure investment by Japanese investors, particularly the introduction of electricity and communication facilities, and the construction of railroads. Because harsh colonial exploitation had not yet begun, Koreans as well as Japanese benefited from the economic growth.

Thirdly, because the economy of colonial Korea was an appendage to the Japanese economy, its long-term trend of development during the colonial period (1910–45) resembled to a large extent that of the larger Japanese economy. Ohkawa and Rosovsky point out that the Japanese economy grew at one of the highest rates in the world after 1900 and reached a pre-war peak GNP in 1939.[19] Korea experienced a similar trend line but with the important difference that in its case it was gross domestic product (GDP) rather than gross national product (GNP) that grew rapidly. 'Domestic' production inside the Korean peninsula grew significantly but the income accruing to Koreans was low and most of the gains went to the Japanese.

The Korean economy during this period was characterized by a colonial type of dualism. Ohkawa and Rosovsky describe the Japanese economy during this period as characterized by a dualistic 'differential structure' wherein the gap in output per worker in the traditional (agriculture) and modern (industry) sectors grew increasingly large.[20] The dualism in the Korean economy was of a different and more divisive sort. The modern-industrial sector in the colonial Korean economy was owned and run mostly by the Japanese, whereas the traditional-agricultural sector was owned by both Koreans and Japanese, but ultimately redounded chiefly to the benefit of the Japanese. The gap in output per worker in the traditional and modern sectors of the Korean economy during this period also widened. Moreover, because a large fraction of Korea's agricultural output was shipped to Japan, real per capita consumption by Koreans actually fell during the last decade of the colonial period.

Fourthly, the period 1945–53 was one of interrupted development and social chaos. Economic development was greatly hindered after liberation by the division of the country into North and South in 1945, political turmoil during the American occupation (1945–8), and the Korean War (1950–3).

With the liberation of Korea and the departure of the Japanese population, the per capita income of Koreans increased rapidly between 1945–50 (see Table 3.1). The Korean War reduced to ashes many production facilities, houses, and infrastructure, and forced the Korean people to rebuild the economy from scratch.

Fifthly, the period between 1953 and 1961 was one of slow recovery of the war-ravaged economy, while economic policy focused on import substitution and massive investments in education. The emphasis on import substitution was clearly a mistake, but private and public investment in education turned out to pay off handsomely in terms of producing a well-educated labour force that would provide the backbone of the labour-intensive industries in the early 1960s.

Finally, the period from 1962 to 1989 has been one of rapid growth, beginning with the inauguration of systemic economic planning under the First Five-Year Plan (1962–6). Economic growth, beginning with the inauguration of systemic economic plans during this period is discussed in Chapter 8.

4 East Asian Culture and the New Confucian Ethic

The Most Homogeneous People in the World

Korean culture is, like Japanese culture, part of an East Asian culture, centred on China and characterized by extraordinary homogeneity. All Koreans speak one language, use a unique and indigenously developed alphabet—*hangŭl* invented by King Sejong the Great in 1443—and belong to the same racial stock— part of the Altaic family of races. Edwin O. Reischauer says in his widely read book *The Japanese* that 'education has been the chief tool in shaping the national uniformity of Japan.'[1] The same is true for Korea. All Koreans receive a virtually identical education in that they use the same textbooks and students graduating from senior high schools all take the same national college entrance qualification examination for entry to colleges or universities. As pointed out by Edward Mason and others, 'the most important part of modern Korea's East Asian heritage was the Confucian emphasis on education.'[2]

Another important factor shaping national homogeneity in Korea—different in this case from Japan—is the strong influence of the military. All young Korean males are expected to serve in the army or augment the police forces for a certain period of time. And after being discharged from the army they must continue to serve in reserve army units. Even middle-aged Korean males are required to receive civil defense training several times a year. In addition, Koreans throughout the nation respectfully mark the lowering of the national flag each evening around 6 p.m., while speakers in public areas play the national anthem. These types of activity make Korean society extremely uniform and homogeneous. Moreover, the relatively small size of the Republic of Korea means that the population is subject to nearly the same climate and natural environment. Nearly all parts of the country lie within the distance of a half-day or, at most, one-day round trip. Thus, the Korean people can maintain close relationships with their relatives very easily. Alvin Toffler indicates that this factor makes the Korean family system highly cohesive.[3]

These factors all help to integrate the Korean people into a tight, nation-wide cultural and social system, and Korea's extraordinarily homogeneous culture leads to the rapid spread of information and innovation among the population.

Religion in Korea and Japan

Korea's culture can be understood better if compared with her closest-neighbour, Japan. Regarding religion in Japan, Akio Morita, the co-founder of Sony Corporation, states:

We Japanese do not think of ourselves as a deeply religious people, although we are; we tend to believe that God resides in everything. We often joke that most Japanese are born Shinto, live a Confucian life, get married Christian-style, and have a Buddhist funeral. We have our rites and customs and festivals steeped in centuries of religious tradition, but we are not bound by taboos and feel free to try everything and seek the best and most practical ways of doing things.[4]

The majority of Japanese, although they belong to one or more religious bodies (see Table 4.1), do not regard themselves as serious believers in any religion. Indeed, because some Japanese claim to belong to more than one religious group, the number of believers as shown in Table 4.1 exceeds the total Japanese population. But in the case of Korea the number of believers is less than half of the total population: they totalled 42.6 per cent in 1985. Despite the influences of various religions, Edwin Reischauer says the ethics of the Japanese are derived mainly from Confucianism and Christianity.[5] And although the proportion of Christians in the Japanese population is less than one per cent, Christianity has had, according to Reischauer, a profound impact on Japanese ethics.

Christianity and Korean Culture

Christianity has played an extraodinary role in Korea's modernization, and Korea now has by far the highest proportion of Christians—nearly half of all professed religious believers— among the traditionally Confucian and Buddhist cultures of East Asia. According to the latest population and housing census, the proportion of Christians in the total population of Korea was 20.6 per cent (including 4.8 per cent Catholics) in 1985.[6] Spencer J.

Palmer indicates in his book *Korea and Christianity* that 'Korea is the only country of continental Asia today where the largest religious group is still Christian.'[7] The first resident Christian missionary, the American medical doctor Horace N. Allen, entered Korea in 1884. Yi Kwang-su, a famous and well-respected writer, believed that Christianity was a particularly important benefactor to Korea in that it presented Koreans with a new, that is, Western civilization. Yi divided the contribution of Christianity to Korea into the following eight categories:[8]

(a) Introduction of Western civilization
(b) Rearmament of a decaying morality
(c) Promotion and popularization of education
(d) Enhancement of the social status of women
(e) Rectification of the early marriage system
(f) Popularization of the Korean alphabet and vernacular literature
(g) Modernization of traditional values and philosophy
(h) Stimulation of individualism

The impact of Christianity on Korea's modernization is visible everywhere. Christian missions established modern schools, including the first medical school. The first hospital, the first tuberculosis sanatorium, and the first leprosy colonies were established and operated by medical missionaries. Korean women were first educated in mission schools.

Korean Christians also learned democratic processes of government through their participation in church activities. The use of vernacular Korean as a literary vehicle was popularized and given a major boost because the Bible and Christian hymns were translated in the native *hangŭl* alphabet, which had been considered inferior by traditional Confucian scholars. As a result, Christianity contributed greatly to the spread of literacy among Korean adults. Almost every large village now has a Christian church or a Christian prayer group, which plays a key role in introducing Koreans to Western values, attitudes, and civilization.

The New Confucian Ethic and Korea

Many Koreans have become concerned that acceptance of Christianity can lead to a loss of national identity unless combined with traditional ethical and cultural values. Many Koreans are worried

Table 4.1 Religious Statistics for Korea and Japan

	Korea (1985)		Japan (1984)	
	Thousands	Per Cent	Thousands	Per Cent
Religious believers				
Christianity	8,343	20.6	1,656	0.8
Buddhism	8,171	20.2	88,965	41.0
Confucianism	482	1.2		
Shinto and related religions			112,107	51.6
Others	207	0.5	14,378	6.6
Total (A)	17,203	42.6	217,106	100.0
Total population (B)	40,420	100.0	120,235	
Proportion of religious people (%), A/B	42.6		180.6*	

Note: *Reflects the large number of Japanese who purport to believe in more than one religion.

Sources: The Korean data are from Economic Planning Board, *Social Indicators in Korea*, 1987. The Japanese data are from Japan Institute for Social and Economic Affairs, *An International Comparison*, Tokyo, Keizai Koho Center, 1987.

that the values, morality, and ethics of modern-day Korea lag far behind the level of material progress.

Numerous scholars point out that the industrial progress of Korea and other East Asian nations is due to the Confucian ethic. Examples are Peter Berger, Herman Kahn, Roderick Macfarquhar, and others. Macfarquhar even coined a new term, 'the post-Confucian Challenge to the West', to emphasize the increasing importance of East Asian culture and industrial power.[9] These writers indicate that Confucian ethics have the following characteristics: an emphasis on education, the leadership of government and consensus formation, East Asian management style, and the East Asian entrepreneurial spirit or work ethic.[10]

Tu Wei-ming, Harvard professor of Chinese history and philosophy, notes in his book *Confucian Ethics Today*, however, that in East Asian countries the traditional Confucian ethics have been combined and modified by Western Christian ethics to form what Tu calls the 'new Confucian ethics'.[11]

Numerous experts on cross-cultural differences contrast East Asia and the West in terms of the traditional sense of obligations that bind people together in the former. Nathan Glazer of Harvard explains this point as follows: the difference between the East and the West is:

a difference exhibited in a net of obligations that bind individuals together and makes strong institutions of the family, principally, but by extension of the school and the work place—individual values and institutional needs are brought together in some kind of organic connection and with only moderate strains from individual psychological resistance.[12]

Two of the most famous experts on Japanese society, the American Ruth Benedict and the Japanese Chie Nakane, also agree on this point.[13] The observation appears to appropriately describe as well the basic difference between Korea and the West.

The differences between East Asian and Western cultures may be better understood if the Confucian ethic is examined in comparison with the Puritan ethic, which is often credited with being a foundation of the West's capitalist (or individualistic) economic philosophy.

Tu Wei-ming identifies the 'newly-emerging Confucian ethic as an amalgam of family or collectively-oriented values of the East and the pragmatic, economic-goal oriented values of the West'.[14] Tu notes that in the East Asian countries where the new Confucian ethic has penetrated, the national economies have prospered: Korea, Japan, Taiwan, Hong Kong, and Singapore are, of course, leading examples.

In contrast to the new Confucian ethic, the traditional value system in Korea lacked prosperity-promoting tenets. This can be observed in various traditional values of Koreans. For instance, the old Confucian view placed commerce and manufacturing at the bottom of the occupational and social hierarchy. In traditional Korean society the idealized social status order put, as previously mentioned, scholars or government officials at the top, followed by farmers (as the backbone of the agrarian society), artisans (as producers of useful goods) and, lastly, merchants (as unproductive profit-takers). It goes without saying that this growth-deterring value system had to be replaced by new values that emphasize business and entrepreneurial activities. ⇒

The old values have deep roots, however, and until very recently the most brilliant Korean students aspired to become government officials, lawyers, or professors. Being a professor is still regarded as the most respectable profession by Korean university students. And many Koreans still tend to disparage entrepreneurs and their devotion to business activities. Because such traditional values still carry force, balanced development among various occupations has not been possible.

In Korea, as elsewhere, if occupational choices are strongly biased toward or against particular kinds of activity, the economy suffers. Even the United States' economy is no exception: Lee Iacocca claims that one of the sources of its problems is that the United States graduates fifteen times as many lawyers—and only a fraction as many engineers and scientists—as Japan every year.[15] Korea's anti-business ethic is, however, being supplanted by adopted Western pro-business values via the new Confucian ethic. What are the distinctive characteristics of the new Confucian ethic with regard to economic growth?

For one thing, the new Confucian ethic places great emphasis on education and personal and familial relations. It also stresses personal cultivation, self-improvement, and spiritual and psychological discipline of the self. This is why education has become one of the most important socio-economic issues in Korea. It is very common in Korea for parents to sacrifice their lives solely for the education of their children. This is why both the Korean people and the government allocate an immense amount of resources to human capital formation. According to the estimates by Kim Myung Sook of the Korea Development Institute, total expenditures for education amounted to 13.3 per cent of GNP in 1984, including both private (6.9 per cent) and public (6.4 per cent) spending. This is much larger than the Japanese figure of 5.7 per cent in 1982, the American figure of 6.7 per cent in 1981, and the Singaporean figure of 4.4 per cent.[16] Korea's public spending on education alone is also very high by world standards.

In addition, the new Confucian ethic places unique emphasis on the family. The family is the basic unit of consumption, income distribution, and also social welfare in Korea. It is the nature of the Korean family system, especially the traditional extended-family system, that the needs of the family have priority over individual needs.

In terms of socio-cultural functions, the clan—a patrilineal group that defines itself in terms of a common distant ancestor—also plays an important role. Indeed, familial relations in Korea do not draw a sharp line between members of the extended family and members of the wider clan. The members of a clan are expected to help each other, and as a result many Korean firms are staffed by distant relatives of the owners and managed as a quasi-family unit. In this way, blood-ties and the system of reciprocal family obligations provides the organizational sinew of the enterprise, while also helping to reduce the potential for conflict between duty to family and duty to the organization that can occur among executives of a business firm who are not bound by kinship ties.

The new Confucian ethic also stresses a harmonious personal relationship among individuals and puts great importance on harmony, co-operation, concensus, and social solidarity among members of an organization. This contrasts with the Western emphasis on 'competition' among the members of an organization and may be the chief factor determining the distinctive characteristics of organization dynamics in Korea and other East Asian countries.

The Japanese anthropologist Chie Nakane points out in her paper 'Logic and the Smile: When Japanese Meet Indians', that Japanese tend not to confront disagreement directly, and smile to mask their discomfort in such situations.[17] Indians, on the other hand, have no qualms about confronting disagreement directly if they think their views are logically correct—notwithstanding the frictions this may cause in personal relations. The 'Japanese smile' and the 'Indian logic' form a striking contrast. Koreans are more outwardly emotional than the Japanese, but still much closer to them than to Indians in dealing with disagreements.

The harmonious integration of the values stressing co-operation and competition among members of an organization appears to be crucial for Korean society in the future. Indeed, the communal spirit-oriented new Confucian ethic, which stresses duty-consciousness, contrasts with the individual-oriented Protestant ethic, which emphasizes right-consciousness. For many Confucian-value-oriented Koreans, the development of the concept of basic human rights, especially in connection with private property, private interest, and privacy of an individual, presents challenges. It is in part because the new Confucian ethic stresses one's duty to a larger entity over individualism that Korean organizations tend to put heavy—sometimes excessive—emphasis on loyalty and patriotism.

Like traditional Confucianism, the new Confucian ethic stresses the pursuit of the highest good in 'this world' through active participation in the world as it is. Unlike world-rejecting or world-abnegating religions such as Hinduism or classical Buddhism, Confucianism is a world-affirming religion. In contrast, classical monastic Buddhism stressed the severance of all ties with friends, family, and society as a whole. Traditional Hinduism also stressed devotion to the eradication of one's bonds to 'this world'. Both religions are world-abnegating and assure the minimizing of one's interaction or concern with the 'material' world. As such, they reject the goal of material progress.

Confucianism stresses the pursuit of happiness through harmony with this world and the adaptation of oneself to the world through self-cultivation and active participation. This philosophy appears in the following statement of Confucius himself: 'Even in such a life as that relying only on vegetables and water and bent arm for pillow there can be happiness.'

Koreans by nature are known to be future-oriented people and tend to be optimistic. Koreans have also, of course, a pessimistic feeling since Korea is surrounded by large, often hostile, powers. Yong Un Kim, a scholar of Korean culture, asserts that all the famous traditional Korean dramas and novels, such as the *Story of Chunhyang*, inevitably have a happy ending, reflecting the optimism of the Korean people.[18] Because of this optimism, the traditional Koreans by nature are known to have valued pleasure highly. The historian Lee Pyung Do asserts, for example, that Koreans have traditionally been fond of singing and dancing.

This is in contrast with the Western Protestant ethic emphasizing spiritual and material asceticism, and perhaps there is a need for Koreans to adopt this aspect of Western ethics. If the emphasis on the pursuit of the highest worldly good can be combined with the Protestant emphasis on devotion to a vocation or 'calling', there can emerge a new ethic that can act as the spirit of individual enterprise for Korea.

Part II
The Internal Economic Environment and Growth

5 The Korean and Japanese Growth Patterns Compared

KOREA was one of the poorest countries in the world immediately after the Korean War. Even in 1960, after the damage inflicted during the war had been repaired, Korea's per capita GNP was still only US$80 in current prices. At that time, few, if any, observers held out much hope of improvement for Korea's poverty-stricken economy. From 1963, however, Korea entered a period of sustained high economic growth, as a result of which it developed to the level of a 'newly industrializing country' (NIC) by 1970.

The economy entered a new phase from 1986 with the onset of the 'three lows'—low oil prices, a lower dollar, and low interest rates. For the first time in the economic history of Korea, domestic savings began to exceed investment, and the international balance of payments turned from a chronic deficit position to a surplus. As a result, Korea was able rapidly to reduce her foreign debt, which had peaked at US$46.7 billion in 1985 (see Table 5.1). It was no longer necessary for Korea to worry about foreign debt and rely on advanced countries for economic assistance. By 1986 Korea appears to have achieved its earlier goal of realizing 'economic independence'.

The Korean economy appeared to reach the stage of self-sustaining growth in 1986. In that year the annual inflation rate as measured by the consumer price index stabilized at the 2–3 per cent level, and the economic growth rate exceeded 12 per cent in 1986, 1987, and 1988, recording the highest rate in the world. In 1989, Korea's per capita GNP is expected to exceed US$4,500.

In this chapter we will examine the major features of Korea's rapid growth, growth pattern, sources of growth, business cycles, and related issues. Because trade and industrial policy was such a central element in Korea's growth and structural change, however, it will be examined separately in the following chapters. Issues concerning Korea's growth strategy will be examined in relation to trade in the next chapter.

Korea's Growth Pattern

Korea's growth pattern resulted not only from Korea's outward-industrial-, and growth-oriented development strategy, but also from the choices of various economic policies. The general characteristics of the Korean growth pattern may be described as follows. The description of the Korean growth pattern in this section is based partly on the framework suggested by Chenery and Syrquin.[1]

Korea's high growth was 'ignited' by the 'expansion of exports' and sustained by the rapid growth of export industries. As the expansion of exports has been almost 'forced' by the government, export industries and the economy as a whole were 'run' by the government, in many cases beyond normal capacity.

Many Korean industries were developed on the basis of the 'export first' principle. The export-oriented growth strategy caused Korean firms to start marketing their products in overseas markets rather than in domestic markets, as in the case of the colour TV industry. As the domestic sale of colour TV sets was not allowed until 1980, colour TV firms had to sell their products in overseas markets. Other examples include industries producing such high value items as phonographs, portable telephones, and mink coats.

In contrast, Japanese firms usually started marketing their products in the domestic market. The Japanese domestic market is huge, allowing room for the growth of several large firms producing similar commodities. Any Japanese firm that could compete successfully with other Japanese firms in the domestic market could compete with foreign firms in any overseas market. Korea's 'export first' principle of industrial expansion is in direct contrast with the Japanese pattern of industrial growth based on the 'domestic market first' principle.

Because of the 'forced' nature of the growth of many industries in Korea, the share of manufacturing in the GNP has been always larger than the 'average' or 'normal' level[2] expected from other countries. Also, the shift in the production structure from agriculture to manufacturing in Korea has been faster than the pattern typically seen in other countries.

As the expansion of industrial capacity tended to be excessive, the amount of domestic investment always exceeded the amount of domestic savings. In addition, much domestic saving was diverted to real estate as a hedge against high inflation. As a result, the level of domestic savings in Korea was lower than the normal level. The gap between investment and savings was filled with foreign borrowing. This is one of the major reasons—along with the need to import oil and many other industrial raw materials—why Korea's foreign debt continued to rise until 1985. Thus, the amount of foreign capital inflow in Korea was higher than the normal level expected from other countries. Also, the debt-equity ratio of large Korean firms, which were forced to overexpand their production and export capacity, tended to be higher than that of other Asian NICs. As a result, Korean growth was characterized by low domestic savings, a high debt-equity ratio for most firms, and a large foreign debt.

Because policy priority was given to the expansion of exports and the manufacturing industries, while investment resources were insufficient and defense expenditures relatively high, investment in social-overhead capital received low policy priority and usually lagged far behind investment in directly productive activities. The government's social investment policy has been such that unless businessmen's complaints about infrastructure problems are severe, the government has been slow to expand facilities such as transportation, communications, electricity, and water and sewage systems. Thus, Korean industries grew in the face of shortages and bottlenecks with respect to airports, telephones, railroads, and so on. For instance, Kimpo international airport in Seoul was much smaller until recently than the airports in Hong Kong, Singapore, Manila, or Kuala Lumpur, not to mention Tokyo Narita Airport. Telephones in Korea have also been very expensive until recently due to the shortage of telephone lines and exchanges. In the late 1970s it cost several thousand dollars to install a telephone.

The share of GNP allocated to social-overhead investment has been smaller in Korea than is typical for countries at a similar level of development. The Korean economy, to borrow Hirshman's terms, has been a 'social-overhead capital-shortage economy' and its growth has been led by investments in directly productive activities rather than social-overhead facilities. Recently, however, Korea's social capital expenditure has been expanded sharply as a result of the preparation for the 1988 Olympics.

The expansion of industrial capacity in Korea was achieved

Table 5.1 Major Indicators of Korean Economic Growth

	GNP Per Capita (US$)	GNP (billion US$)	GNP Growth Rate (%)	Inflation Rate (%)	Interest Rate (%)	Rate of Private Savings (%)	Trade Balance (million US$)	Exports (million US$)	Foreign Debt (million US$)	Rate of Unemployment (%)	Foreign Exchange Rate (won/US$)
1960	80	1.95	1.1	10.5	10.0	2.9	−310	33	—	11.7	65.0
1961	82	2.10	5.6	12.2	15.0	4.7	−242	41	—	12.2	130.0
1962	87	2.31	2.2	15.4	15.0	4.8	−335	55	—	9.8	130.0
1963	100	2.72	9.1	22.7	15.0	9.1	−410	87	157	8.2	130.0
1964	103	2.88	9.6	23.0	15.0	8.3	−245	119	177	7.7	256.0
1965	105	3.01	5.8	5.8	26.4	5.7	−240	175	206	7.4	272.1
1966	125	3.67	12.7	12.7	26.4	9.1	−430	250	392	7.1	271.5
1967	142	4.27	6.6	13.5	26.4	7.3	−574	320	645	6.2	274.6
1968	169	5.23	11.3	13.8	25.2	9.0	−835	455	1,199	5.1	281.5
1969	210	6.63	13.8	12.9	22.8	12.9	−992	623	1,800	4.8	304.5
1970	243	7.99	7.6	13.5	22.8	12.2	−922	882	2,245	4.5	316.7
1971	285	9.37	9.1	13.9	20.4	11.2	−1,046	1,132	2,922	4.5	373.2
1972	316	10.57	5.3	16.1	12.0	15.1	−574	1,676	3,589	4.5	398.9

Year										
1973	396	13.50	14.0	13.4	12.0	19.8	−566	3,271	4,260	4.0	397.5
1974	535	18.55	8.5	29.5	15.0	18.4	−1,937	4,515	5,937	4.1	484.0
1975	591	20.85	6.8	25.7	15.0	15.5	−1,671	5,003	8,456	4.1	484.0
1976	800	28.65	13.4	20.7	16.2	19.1	−591	7,715	10,533	3.9	484.0
1977	1,028	37.43	10.7	15.7	14.4	22.3	−477	10,047	12,648	3.8	484.0
1978	1,406	51.96	11.0	21.9	18.6	24.1	−1,781	12,710	14,871	3.2	484.0
1979	1,662	62.37	7.0	21.2	18.6	22.4	−4,396	14,705	20,287	3.8	484.0
1980	1,589	60.30	−4.8	25.6	19.5	18.0	−4,384	17,214	27,170	5.2	659.9
1981	1,719	66.20	6.6	15.4	16.2	17.9	−3,628	20,671	32,433	4.5	700.5
1982	1,773	69.30	5.4	6.7	8.0	17.9	−2,594	20,879	37,083	4.4	748.8
1983	1,914	76.0	11.9	3.9	8.0	20.7	−1,764	23,204	40,378	4.1	795.5
1984	2,044	82.40	8.4	3.8	10.0	23.2	−1,036	26,334	43,053	3.8	827.4
1985	2,150	83.70	5.4	4.1	10.0	23.7	−19	26,442	46,729	4.0	890.2
1986	2,300	95.30	12.3	2.7	10.0	27.8	4,206	33,913	44,500	3.8	861.4
1987	3,098	118.6	12.8	3.7	10.0	29.9	7,659	26,244	35,600	3.1	792.3
1988	4,040	169.2	12.2	4.3	10.0	30.1	8,848	60,649	31,500	2.5	684.1

Note: GNP and GNP per capita are in current prices. The rate of inflation is based on GNP deflator. The rate of interest is the bank interest rate on time deposits for the period of one or more years.

Sources: Computed from The Bank of Korea, *Economic Statistics Yearbook,* various years. Economic Planning Board, *Major Statistics of the Korean Economy,* various years, and *The First Five-Year Economic Development Plan, 1962–1966,* Seoul, 1961.

through the expansion of existing firms rather than through the creation of new firms. This pattern has persisted for over two decades and has resulted in the growth of a small number of very large firms and business conglomerates (*jaebol* in Korean), causing a large gap between large and small firms. A related pattern is that the market concentration ratio in Korea has been much higher than in either Japan or Taiwan. The Japanese pattern, in contrast, has been based on the growth of both a significant number of very large firms as well as a large number of small firms. The Korean economy may be called 'a large firm economy', in contrast to the 'small firm economy' of Taiwan or the 'bi-polar economy' of Japan.

Korean economic growth has been accompanied by extensive investment in human resources, which has been facilitated by— and has also greatly facilitated—Korea's rapid modernization. The amount of total expenditure, both public and private, on education has regularly exceeded ten percentage of GNP, the highest level among all the developing countries.[3] The percentage of high school graduates advancing to colleges or university in Korea is now the second highest in the world after the United States.[4] This is even higher than in Japan (see Table 10.6). Indeed, Korea together with the United States may be the world's leaders in human capital formation.

Government-driven industrialization resulted in the excessive concentration of industries and population in large cities, especially in Seoul and the Seoul region. The level of urbanization in Korea has been generally higher than the norm observed in other countries. As a result, such urban problems as housing shortages, lack of educational facilities, and poor public services have been serious domestic issues since the 1970s.

Because of Korea's 'growth first' development policy, stability was given a rather low priority. As a consequence, the Korean economy has experienced more year-to-year fluctuations with its overall high growth than the Japanese economy. For instance, Korea's economic growth rate was 12.7 per cent in 1966, but dropped to 6.6 per cent in the following year; the rate again went up to 13.8 per cent in 1969, followed by a drop to 7.6 per cent in 1970 (see Table 5.1). Since the scale of the Korean economy was quite small well into 1970s, the growth rate was susceptible to large fluctuations caused by construction phases in large investment projects. The economy's outward-orientation also exposed it to fluctuations from oil price hikes and other external influences. The inexperience of policymakers, especially during the 1960s, also contributed to economic fluctuation. Rapid but sharply fluctuating growth has been a prominent characteristic of Korean development.

Korean growth has been accompanied by a high level of income equality that remained relatively unchanged in the course of development. In Japan, income distribution improved somewhat during rapid growth, but deteriorated in the 1970s. The relatively moderate change in income distribution in Korea followed the U-curve described by Kuznets. That is, income distribution worsened slightly during 1972–80, but improved thereafter. Since the magnitude of change was not large, however, the shape of the U-curve in Korea's case is quite flat.

Labour's share of income rose only slightly in Japan during high growth, but rose significantly in Korea. This may be due to the rapid increase in Korea in the absolute number of salaried workers and professional managers. The management class in Korea was very small and poor at the beginning of development, but developed continuously during the high growth period. The Korean pattern of income distribution is in contrast with the Taiwanese pattern which can be characterized as 'growth with increasing equality.'

Korean growth was accompanied by a balance-of-payments deficit until 1985 (see Table 5.2). This was caused to some extent by Korea's resource poverty, but was principally due to the policy of allowing exporting firms to import raw materials, parts, and machinery required for the production of export goods on a large scale. This has been called a 'negative import substitution policy'. Because exporting firms tried to import as much as possible, the growth rate of imports was very high. From 1986, however, the international balance of payments turned positive and Korea changed from 'a young debtor nation' to 'a mature debtor nation'.

High economic growth in Japan was accompanied by very gradual inflation, but in the case of Korea both wholesale and consumer prices rose sharply and fluctuated widely. This was especially so when the economy was hit by oil price hikes, poor harvests, changes in government, and other shocks. Until 1983 the Korean economy could be described as having 'high growth with high and highly fluctuating inflation'. The high inflation was due mainly to the excessive expansion of demand associated with

Table 5.2 The Balance of Payments, 1962–1988 (in million US dollars)

	1962	1965	1970	1975	1980	1988
Trade balance (1)	−335	−241	−922	−1,671	−4,384	11,445
Exports	55	175	882	5,003	17,214	59,648
Imports	390	416	1,804	6,674	21,598	48,203
Service balance (2)	43	46	119	−442	−1,386	1,267
Receipts	108	114	497	881	5,363	11,252
Payments	65	68	378	1,323	6,749	9,985
Transfers (net) (3)	236	203	180	227	449	1,448
Current account balance (4) (1+2+3)	−56	9	−623	−1,887	−5,321	14,161
Long-term capital (net), (5)	8	37	449	1,178	1,857	−2,732
Basic balance (4+5), (6)	−48	46	−174	−709	−3,464	11,428
Short-term capital (net), (7)	−7	−23	122	680	1,944	1,336
Errors and omissions	−2	−2	16	−122	−370	−589
Overall balance (6+7)	−57	21	−36	−151	−1,890	12,175
Foreign exchange reserves	167	138	584	1,550	6,571	12,378
(Exchange rate, Won/US$)	130	272	317	484	660	684

Sources: The Bank of Korea, *Economic Statistics Yearbook*, various years; *Economic Indicators of Major Countries*, March 1989; and Economic Planning Board, *Major Statistics of Korean Economy*, various years.

rapid expansion of industrial capacity and the abnormal, compulsory expansion of exports.

The macroeconomic linkages between growth and inflation are not very clear-cut in the Korean case. Judging from the Korean experience, developing countries may grow at high real rates despite high rates of inflation. None the less, the microeconomic impact of inflation appears to have been to harm social justice in Korea by hurting creditors, savers, fixed-income earners, and pensioners. As the majority of Korean workers were savers, they were hurt by rapid inflation. Korean workers, who do not generally own private housing, were especially hurt by the rapid increase in real estate prices. High inflation together with numerous large investments in transportation and land development projects caused a rapid change in land prices and encouraged widespread land speculation. Shrewd speculators, and even not-so-shrewd speculators, if well connected with policy makers, could earn large windfall profits in the 1960s and 1970s. The windfall profits associated with changes in land values have been a major complaint of ordinary citizens. On the basis of the Korean experience, we can say that management of unearned gains from real estate speculation is one of the most potentially sensitive social equity issues.

Sources of Economic Growth

Factors contributing to the growth of the Korean economy can be divided into demand-side factors—such as inter-industry demand, final consumption, investment, export and import—and supply-side factors—such as labour, capital, advances in knowledge, improvement in resource allocation, economies of scale, and so on. In this section we attempt to examine the contribution of these various demand and supply factors to Korea's economic growth since 1963.

Demand-side Sources of Growth

In a previous study I estimated the contribution of demand factors to the economic growth of Korea between 1963 and 1973 and found that the largest absolute change in Korea's sectoral production was caused by exports (33 per cent) rather than domestic final demand (31 per cent).[5] Using a somewhat different metho-

Table 5.3 Demand-side Sources of Growth in Manufacturing Output (per cent)

Demand Expansion	1970–5	1975–80	1980–3	1983–7
Consumption	54.8	48.1	45.8	41.7
Investment	15.5	21.1	19.8	21.6
Export	27.3	27.3	32.9	34.2
Import	−1.3	1.7	3.7	4.1
Changes in input-output coefficient	3.7	1.8	−2.2	−1.6
Total	100.0	100.0	100.0	100.0

Note: Figures for 1970–83 are the World Bank estimates. See World Bank, *Korea—Managing the Industrial Transition. A World Bank Country Study*, Vol. II, Selected Topics and Case Studies, 1987. Figures for 1983–7 are those updated by the author.

dology, the results of a recent World Bank estimate of demand-side sources of growth indicate that exports contributed 32.9 per cent to output growth in manufacturing during the 1980–83 period. This is much larger than the contribution of investment (19.8 per cent—see Table 5.3), confirming that economic growth has been export-led rather than investment-led.

These findings provide interesting contrasts with the pattern of Japanese growth during the period 1914–54. Firstly, trade was clearly more important to Korea than to Japan. Moreover, changes in technology accounted for a smaller percentage of total growth in Korea (12 per cent) than in Japan (40 per cent). In the case of Japan, positive import substitution occurred during this period—reflected by the less-than-proportional increase in imports.[6] In Korea, however, there was 'negative import substitution' during the 1963–75 period. This trend reflects an opening up of the economy up until 1980, as indicated by the increase in imports in Korea shown in Table 5.4.

Supply-side Sources of Growth

The methodology for analysing supply-side sources relies on the growth accounting approach suggested by Edward F. Denison of the Brookings Institution. Using the Denison method to break down the factors contributing to GNP growth yields interesting

Table 5.4 Changes in Demand Structure

	1970	1975	1980	1985	1988
Consumption	83.7	82.0	76.6	68.9	62.1
Investment	26.4	27.5	31.2	30.6	29.8
Exports	14.7	30.3	33.7	36.2	40.8
Imports	−24.8	−39.8	−41.5	−35.7	−32.7
Total	100.0	100.0	100.0	100.0	100.0

Sources: The Bank of Korea, *Economic Statistics Yearbook*, various years.

results. It shows that the most important source of Korean growth during both the 1963–73 and 1973–86 periods was the growth of labour input (see Table 5.5). The relative importance of labour input was lower in the later period, however, due partly to the shift, around 1977, in the Korean economy from a labour-surplus economy to one with a labour shortage.

Overall, the growth in inputs contributed more to GNP than did increases in productivity. In particular, the study of K.S. Kim and J.K. Park[7] indicates that the rise in productivity contributed relatively little to GNP growth from 1972 to 1982—a result of the excessive investment in the capital-intensive heavy and chemical industries in the late 1970s. Thereafter, however, the relative importance of improved productivity appears to have increased.

International comparisons indicate that the rise in productivity is the principal source of GNP growth in advanced countries (see Table 5.5). In the cases of Japan and the United States, for example, advances in knowledge have contributed more than labour to GNP growth. As the Korean economy grows further, the relative importance of productivity is similarly likely to exceed the contribution made by the growth in inputs.

Growth and Structural Transformation

Simon Kuznets, a Nobel laureate economist, theorizes that modern economic growth is accompanied by the following three types of structural change: change in production structure, increase in the size of production units, and rapid urbanization.[8] In this

Table 5.5 Supply-side Sources of Growth (in percentage points per annum)

	Korea		Japan	West Germany	USA
	1963–73	1973–86	1953–71	1950–62	1948–86
Real GNP growth rate	9.54	7.82	8.81	6.27	3.2
1. Contribution of inputs	5.41	4.07	3.95	2.78	1.8
Labour	3.24	2.16	1.85	1.37	0.9
Capital	2.17	1.91	2.10	1.41	0.9
2. Total factor productivity	4.13	3.75	4.86	3.49	1.4
Advances in knowledge	1.36	1.67	1.97	0.87	1.0
Improved resource allocation	0.98	0.62	0.95	1.01	0.4
Economies of scale	1.78	1.46	1.94	1.61	

Note: Kwang Suk Kim and Joon Kyung Park, 1985, estimated the sources of growth of the Korean economy for the period 1963–82. The results show that out of an income growth rate of 7.61 per cent, total factor input explains 5.12 per cent and total factor productivity (TFP) 2.49 per cent. Their estimate of TFP appears to be much lower than my estimates shown here.

Sources: Estimates for Korea for 1963–73 are from Byung-Nak Song, 1984, and for 1973–86 were those re-estimated by the author. Estimates for Japan and West Germany are from E.F. Denison and William K. Chung, 1976. The figures for the USA are from Paul Samuelson and William Nordhaus, 1989. These figures were originally from E.F. Denison, 1985.

section we examine Korea's structural transformation from this perspective.

The pattern of change in production structure in the process of development is characterized by the continuous decrease in the relative importance of the agricultural sector and the corresponding rise in the importance of the non-agricultural sectors—mainly manufacturing and services. And in the non-agricultural sector, the importance of services continues to increase relative to manufacturing.

The share in GNP of agriculture in Korea decreased from 37.6 to 10.8 per cent between 1965 and 1988, while the corresponding share of the non-agricultural sector increased from 62.4 to 89.2 per cent. During the same period the share of industry in GNP increased from 24.1 to 43.2 per cent, and is still increasing.

With the rapid growth of the economy, the number and size of firms have also increased—Kuznets' second type of structural change. The number of manufacturing firms with over 5 employees increased from 18,310 to 44,037 between 1973 and 1985. Because of the rapid economic growth, the number of non-manufacturing firms also increased rapidly. According to the Establishment Census, the total number of non-manufacturing establishments increased from 1.07 million to 1.46 million between 1981 and 1986.[9]

Rapid urbanization, Kuznets' third component of structural transformation, has also been pronounced in Korea. The proportion of Koreans living in urban areas with a population of over 50,000 increased from 28.5 to 68.7 per cent during the period 1960–87 as already indicated (see Table 2.4). If the definition of urban area is broadened to include places with over 20,000 inhabitants, nearly three-quarters of all Koreans now live in large and medium-sized cities and towns. The number of cities and towns also has increased substantially (see Table 2.4).

In my study with Edwin Mills on Korea's urbanization, I have found that Korea was more urbanized than is generally the case for countries at a comparable level of income.[10] This appeared to be due to the fact that Korea's international sector, and especially its manufactured exports, have been much larger than the 'world-average' norm established by Chenery and Syrquin. Korea's manufacturing industry is more concentrated in urban areas with access to international ports than is true in many developing countries. This fact appears to have contributed greatly to rapid urbanization. Other factors such as education, Korea's high overall population density, and the necessity of face-to-face contact with public officials also contributed to the growth of cities in Korea.

Growth and Fluctuations

The pattern of 'high growth with high fluctuation' is one of the most distinctive characteristics of Korean economic growth, and contrasts with the case of Japan or Taiwan. Economic fluctuations in Korea in the 1950s were not extreme, in part because year-to-year fluctuations in the largely agricultural economy reflected only variations in crop yields due to such things as the weather. In some countries agricultural yields fluctuate widely, but in Korea such fluctuations appear to be less extreme because of a more stable climate and extensive irrigation. With the decrease in the relative weight of agriculture, and the rise in the proportion of the manufacturing and service industries in GNP, the nature of the fluctuations changed and tended to become larger and more unpredictable.

When the scale of the Korean economy was still small, it was readily susceptible to internal and external shocks. Even huge construction projects such as the Seoul-Pusan expressway, Pohang iron and steel mill, and the Ulsan petrochemical complex could cause the entire economy to fluctuate in the early 1970s.

The economic forecasting team of the Korea Development Institute, of which I was a member, found that the Korean economy experienced seven business cycles between 1953, the year when national income data were prepared for the first time in Korea, and 1988. The periods of these seven cycles are shown in Table 5.6. The cycles are measured from trough to trough, that is, between the lowest points in each cycle.

In Korea, the lowest point of the business cycle traditionally came in the months of March or June—the bottom of the agricultural production cycle. Before Korea developed her agriculture, the period of food shortages and even starvation—known as the 'barley ridge'—came at this time. The term refers to the uphill struggle for survival between the time when the previous year's rice harvest ran out and when the winter barley crop ripened in late spring. But with the continous decline in agriculture's share of GNP, the troughs in Korea's business cycles are

Table 5.6 Business Cycles in Korea from 1953 (from trough to trough)

Cycle	Period
First	March 1953–March 1957
Second	March 1957–June 1960
Third	June 1960–June 1964
Fourth	June 1964–June 1972
Fifth	June 1972–March 1975
Sixth	March 1975–June 1981
Seventh	June 1981–

Note: These cycles coincide roughly with those identified by the Bank of Korea, except for different beginning months. They are based on a method developed by U.S. National Bureau of Economic Research.

Source: Byung-Nak Song, *The Korean Economy*, second edition, Backyoungsa Co., 1984.

expected to become 'season-free', that is, a trough can occur in any month.

Growth and Inflation

From the early 1960s until 1981 Korea had the highest inflation rate among Asian NICs. In this section we examine the causes and consequences of high inflation rates in Korea during this period.

The basic philosophy of President Park Chung Hee was 'exports first' or 'nation building through export promotion'. In President Park's eyes, setting highly ambitious export targets and then exceeding those targets was regarded as the height of achievement for businessmen and public officials in charge of export promotion. Under President Park's government, larger Korean firms were assigned annual 'export targets' by officials in the Ministry of Trade and Industry. The export targets were seen by firms as virtual 'orders' or assigned 'missions'. If they succeeded in fulfilling their export goals, they obtained numerous benefits reserved for exporters, including preferential credit and loans, administrative support, and tax and other benefits. Thus, Korean exporters saw the over-fulfilment of their 'export targets'—usually determined jointly with the government—as the keystone of their business strategy.

This type of aggressive export promotion and growth policy necessitated that the economy consistently perform far beyond normal capacity, resulting in the 'forced' expansion of investment and output by businessmen. Overly ambitious investment plans caused the inflationary financing of investment. The excessive investment demand created by this type of policy provided one of the links between the forced export growth strategy and high inflation which persisted until 1982.

The negative consequences of this inflation were considerable. Firstly, it is widely believed that high inflation harmed social justice by redistributing wealth from creditors to debtors. Many Koreans tend to think that creditors (especially small savers) are ordinary citizens, while debtors (especially large business) tend to be rich speculators. Frequent political scandals involving large bank loans have made ordinary Koreans believe that they are the losers and big businessmen are the gainers.

Secondly, the high inflation rate often outstripped the government-set bank interest rates, resulting in negative real interest rates. This caused ordinary Koreans to lose trust in the credibility of banks and thereby in the government itself.

Thirdly, although available estimates indicate that capital flight out of Korea has not been a serious problem, many Koreans have diverted savings from financial institutions to real estate. This is one of the main reasons why the savings rate in Korea has been quite low until recently. Moreover, government intervention in business to promote exports became heavy-handed and real bank interest became negative. Business firms also hid their money in real estate, further working to divert savings away from financial institutions.

Fourthly, high inflation contributed to the expansion of the unorganized credit market or 'kerb-market', which in turn came to have a major role in mobilizing and allocating investment funds. The unorganized credit market can play an important economic role in that it can act as a safety valve for organized markets and also as retailer of small loans among friends, relatives, and small contractors. But in the case of Korea this informal credit market grew too large and unregulated—reaching about half the size of the organized credit market in the 1960s, and remaining important until the early 1980s.

Price stability was finally achieved in Korea from 1982. Inflation was reduced from over 20 per cent per year in the late 1970s to 7 per cent in 1982 and about 2 per cent in 1986 (see Table 5.1). The control of inflation after 1982 was due to both domestic and foreign factors. Several factors appear to have been particularly important. Firstly, import costs fell due to the 'three lows', namely, low energy and raw materials prices, depreciation of the US dollar, and low interest rates. Secondly, the government's systematic efforts to reduce inflationary expectations began to gain public credibility as the government held to its announced intention to shift the direction of development from growth to stability. Lastly, productivity rose faster than wages (see Table 5.7).

The Economic Take-off and Turning Points

The rate of Korea's economic growth has been very rapid, and so also has been the rate of structural transformation.

Walt W. Rostow, former economic adviser to Presidents Kennedy and Johnson, has suggested that the Korean economy entered the 'take-off stage' with sustained growth in 1961.[11] He estimates that take-off was completed in Korea in the seven years from 1961 to 1968. Rostow also estimates that the 'drive to technological maturity' will be accomplished by the end of the 1980s, that is, in about 20 years from the beginning of the take-off stage—about one-third of the time Rostow estimates it took for the old developed countries that industrialized before 1914.

For his part, Rostow believes the following factors accounted for the rapid growth of the Korean economy since the early 1960s: the adoption of a sound growth strategy; the development of growth-promoting institutions and public policies; high quality workers and entrepreneurs; a technological backlog available to Korea as a latecomer; proper use of public resources for infrastructure development and education; population control; the capacity of entrepreneurs and policy makers to adjust rapidly and flexibly to external shocks; maintenance of relatively equitable income distribution; and, finally, the avoidance by economists and policy makers of the 'intellectual trap'—the assumption that an economy can be managed adequately using only such macro-economic tools as the regulation of the money supply, interest rates, and so on.

Table 5.7 Productivity and Wages, and Debt Ratio and Capacity Utilization of Manufacturing Industries, 1968–1988

	Labour Productivity		Nominal Wages	
	Index	Growth Rate	Index	Growth Rate
1968	29.8	—	6.0	—
1969	31.6	6.0	7.3	21.6
1970	35.2	11.4	9.3	27.4
1971	39.9	9.6	11.3	16.2
1972	43.4	8.8	12.9	13.9
1973	47.2	8.8	15.2	18.0
1974	52.5	11.2	20.6	35.3
1975	58.6	11.6	26.2	27.0
1976	62.8	7.2	35.2	34.7
1977	69.6	10.8	47.2	33.8
1978	78.0	12.1	63.3	34.3
1979	90.3	15.8	81.5	28.6
1980	100.0	10.7	100.0	22.7
1981	118.1	18.1	120.1	20.1
1982	127.3	7.8	137.8	14.7
1983	144.6	13.6	154.6	12.2
1984	159.8	10.5	167.2	8.1
1985	171.1	7.1	183.8	9.9
1986	201.4	17.7	200.8	9.2
1987	228.1	13.3	224.1	11.6
1988	262.0	14.9	268.2	19.7

Sources: Computed from the data in Economic Planning Board, *Major Statistics of Korean Economy*, 1988 and 1989, *Economic Survey*, January, 1989, and The Bank of Korea, *Financial Statement Data*, 1987, and *Monthly Bulletin*, February 1989.

Key Milestones

As economists, we often ask ourselves what the most important milestones in the Korean economy's development are. It is generally agreed that the following are among the most important.

1960 Postwar reconstruction and early stage of import substitution completed.

1961 The economy enters the take-off stage

Real Wages		Average Debt Ratio	Capacity Utilization Ratio (%)
Index	Growth Rate		
—	—	201.3	—
37.9	14.6	270.0	—
44.0	16.2	328.4	—
45.0	2.3	394.2	61.0
45.9	2.0	313.4	64.0
52.5	14.4	272.7	67.0
57.1	8.8	316.0	66.6
57.9	1.4	339.5	64.3
67.6	16.8	364.6	71.9
82.2	21.5	350.7	74.3
96.5	17.4	366.8	80.3
104.9	8.7	377.1	74.6
100.0	−4.7	487.9	66.9
99.0	−1.0	451.5	67.6
105.9	7.0	385.8	66.8
114.9	8.5	360.3	72.9
121.5	5.7	342.7	77.6
130.4	7.3	348.4	76.3
138.5	6.2	350.9	79.4
150.6	8.4	340.1	82.2
167.8	11.8		80.3

1963 A firm basis for export-oriented industrialization, and high economic growth is established.

1965 Normalization of economic relations with Japan provides momentum for growth acceleration through the expansion of market size, inflow of foreign technology, and promotion of innovation and the entrepreneurial spirit.

1970 Korea reachs NIC (Newly Industrializing Country) status.

As Chenery and Syrquin also indicate, Korea reached the semi-industrial stage by 1970.

1977   The national economy shifts from a labour surplus to a labour shortage. Labour shortage begins in rural areas about 1975. Nation-wide labour shortage started about 1977.

1983   As specified in the Revised Fifth Five-Year Plan, 1984–1986, economic policy shifts from growth first to growth with stability.

1986   Economy simultaneously achieves the triple economic targets of high economic growth (12.3 per cent), price stability (wholesale prices dropped to minus 2.2 per cent), and a net balance-of-payments surplus (current account surplus of US$4.6 billion). The national savings rate also increased to 33.6 per cent, exceeding the rate of investment (29.5 per cent) for the first time in Korea's history. Economy appears to have entered the self-sufficient stage.

The 'turning point' in a narrow sense implies the point in time at which an economy changes from a labour surplus to a labour shortage. According to Ryoshin Minami, the turning point in Japan took place around 1960.[12] In the case of Korea, Fei and Ranis argue that the turning point was reached in 1966–7.[13] Mason and others indicate that 'by the middle of the 1960s, South Korea had ceased to be a labour-surplus economy.'[14] But judging from the labour market conditions in Korea and the difference in development between Korea and Japan, we believe that this transition point was reached in Korea around 1977 rather than a decade earlier, as Fei and Ranis and the others claim.

From 1977 the farm labour force started to decrease and farm mechanization started to spread in rural areas. Vending machines for coffee, cigarettes, and other products were popularized from around 1977. Real wages also started to increase rapidly around this time. From 1977, Korea became a labour-scarce economy.

For most observers, the temptation to compare Korean and Japanese development is irresistable. Many people, both Koreans and foreigners, try to estimate the number of years Korea is behind Japan. In this regard, there is an interesting coincidence: Korea was opened to foreign trade 23 years later than Japan— 1876 versus 1853. Similarly, Korea hosted the Olympics 24 years after they were held in Japan in 1964. And finally, in terms of major economic indicators many Korean economists say that Korea is also behind Japan by about 20 to 25 years.

Lawrence Klein projects that if the Korean economy could continue to grow at 6 per cent or more per year between 1980 and 2000, Korea will reach advanced-country status by the year 2000.[15] Walt.W. Rostow also has predicted that Korea will become an advanced country shortly before the year 2000.[16]

The average annual growth rate of the Korean economy from 1981 (up to 1987) was 8.9 per cent, greatly exceeding the minimum 6 per cent level assumed by Klein. If the current growth trend continues, Korea could reach advanced-country status by the middle of the 1990s.

Economic Growth in Korea and Japan

The economic growth of Korea can be best understood through comparison with Japan's. The framework in this section is that applied to Japan by Yutaka Kosai and Yoshitaro Ogino.[17] Table 5.8 shows the nine characteristics (items 3 to 11) of Japan's high-growth period as outlined by Kosai and Ogino, but rearranged to suit our purposes. In this section we will examine the general features of Korea's high-growth-rate period, with comparisons with the Japanese case.

Korea's economic development has been characterized by high growth continuing over a long period. In Japan, as well, the development process was characterized by high growth rates, but this period itself was relatively short—some 15 years, from 1955 to 1970. In the case of Korea, however, high growth started in 1963 and still continues (as of 1988). According to World Bank statistics, the average annual growth rate for per capita GNP in Korea was 6.4 per cent for the 1965–87 period, the second highest after Singapore among 58 middle-income economies.[18] This far exceeded Japan's growth rate of 4.3 per cent over the same period.

Korea's high growth slumped badly only once—in 1980—due to the socio-political unrest following the assassination of President Park in 1979. The economy recorded a minus 4.8 per cent growth rate in that year, aggravated by the worst harvest since 1963 and the second round of oil price hikes. Except for 1980, Korea's economic growth rate exceeded five per cent every year

Table 5.8 Characteristics of Economic Growth in Korea and Japan During their Periods of High Growth

	Korea	Japan
1. High economic growth period	1963–present (1989)	1955–1970
2. Average annual growth rate	8.7 per cent	10.2 per cent
3. Change in growth rate	Growth rate accelerated until 1977, but slowed down until 1982, and then accelerated again.	Acceleration of growth rate as the period progressed.
4. Distribution of income	Improved during 1965–72, worsened slightly until 1980, but improved gradually thereafter.	Improved during the high growth period.
5. Labour's share of income	Significant rise from about 30 per cent to 55 per cent from 1963 to 1988.	Very slight rise.
6. Prices	Both wholesale and consumer prices rose rapidly and fluctuated wildly until 1981, but stabilized thereafter.	Almost constant wholesale prices and gradually rising consumer prices.
7. International balance of payments	Trade deficit rose until 1980, but decreased thereafter until 1985. Trade surplus realized from 1986.	Gradual change from a deficit to a surplus.

8. Rate of personal savings	Remained at a relatively low level until 1971. Average 8.9 per cent during 1963–71, but increased to 16.5 per cent for 1972–76 and 20.0 per cent thereafter until 1985.	Rose very rapidly.
9. Investment	Increased rapidly, to very high levels. The ratio of investment to GNP increased from about 10 per cent in 1963 to 33.9 per cent in 1986.	Increased rapidly, to very high levels. The ratio of investment to GNP rose from 21.2 per cent during the 1955–60 period to 34.4 per cent during the 1965–70 period.
10. Capital coefficient (the ratio of capital to output)	Remained at a relatively low level (average 2.5) until 1978, but increased to an average level of 3.7 between 1979 and 1986.	Remained low at the 1.3–1.6 level.
11. Government budget	Budget deficit rose until 1982, but decreased thereafter until 1987.	Budget was balanced until 1965.

Table 5.9 The Per Capita GNP of Korea, Taiwan, Japan, and the United States (in current US dollars)

Year	Korea	Taiwan	Japan	USA	US GNP Deflator	
					(1980 = 100)	Growth Rate (%)
1953	67		224	2,290	32.9	
1954	70		245	2,250	33.3	1.2
1955	65	128	267	2,411	34.1	2.4
1956	66	142	298	2,497	35.1	2.9
1957	74	160	336	2,582	36.3	3.4
1958	80	172	346	2,571	37.0	1.9
1959	81	131	385	2,744	37.8	2.2
1960	80	153	457	2,803	38.5	1.9
1961	82	151	559	2,856	38.8	0.8
1962	87	162	615	3,029	39.5	1.8
1963	100	178	702	3,153	40.1	1.5
1964	103	202	821	3,323	40.7	1.5
1965	105	217	917	3,557	41.6	2.2
1966	125	237	1,056	3,846	43.0	3.4
1967	142	266	1,225	4,024	44.3	3.0
1968	169	303	1,436	4,352	46.2	4.3
1969	210	343	1,670	4,658	48.6	5.2
1970	243	387	1,947	4,841	51.2	5.3
1971	285	441	2,181	5,189	53.7	4.9
1972	316	519	2,841	5,650	56.0	4.3
1973	396	691	3,807	6,259	59.2	5.7
1974	535	913	4,162	6,707	64.4	8.8
1975	591	956	4,466	7,173	70.4	9.3
1976	800	1,122	4,955	7,879	74.1	5.3
1977	1,028	1,288	6,031	8,710	78.4	5.8
1978	1,406	1,555	8,383	9,721	84.2	7.4
1979	1,662	1,892	8,621	10,743	91.5	8.7
1980	1,589	2,310	8,907	11,560	100.0	9.3
1981	1,719	2,627	9,684	12,855	109.6	9.6
1982	1,773	2,597	8,947	13,242	116.7	6.5
1983	1,914	2,743	9,905	14,127	121.2	3.9
1984	2,044	3,091	10,469	15,908	125.9	3.7
1985	2,150	3,191	11,176	16,690	129.6	3.6
1986	2,300	3,841	16,173	17,419	133.1	2.0
1987	3,098	5,075	19,642	18,567	137.1	3.0
1988	4,040	6,053	23,358	19,760	141.0	2.8

throughout the period, the maximum growth rates significantly exceeding the highest rates in Japan.

Average growth was higher in Japan during its rapid-growth period because Japan experienced no slumps and, in fact, growth accelerated in the course of this period in Japan.

The capital coefficient, the ratio of capital to output or capital requirement per unit of output, remained low in Japan throughout the years of rapid growth, but in Korea the capital coefficient increased. In Japan, the growth in the capital coefficient was offset by increases in productivity, keeping the capital coefficient low. In the case of Korea, however, excessive investment in capital-intensive heavy industries in the late 1970s and the relatively slow increases in productivity in these industries during the 1980 downturn caused the capital coefficient to rise.

Note: The Korean data are those computed by Byung-Nak Song on the basis of the Bank of Korea data which show different time-series data for the three different time periods, namely, 1953–67, 1971–80, and 1980–8.

Sources: IMF, *International Financial Statistics*, various years. Republic of China, Council for Economic Planning and Development, *Taiwan Statistical Data Book*, Various Years.

6 Foreign Trade and the Incentive System

Overview

FROM the end of the Korean War to the early 1960s, there was no well-articulated or clear-cut trade strategy in Korea. President Syngman Rhee's main interest was in politics and in directing the attention of the Korean people to issues such as unification of the country. Economic growth was given a very low priority throughout his era (1948–61). Growth of industries and thereby the economy as a whole then was based upon import substitution, foreign assistance, and over-valued exchange rates. Access to foreign exchange, the securing from the government of subsidies of various types, and quantitative restrictions on imports were the key determinants of business success during President Ree's tenure.

As most industries in Korea were consumer-goods industries such as food and textiles, import substitution took place mainly in these industries. By the early 1960s, the possibility of easy import substitution in these industries had almost been exhausted. Also, by this time a group of capable entrepreneurs emerged, and a base for further industrialization into the next phase of development was laid by them.

Korea switched, according to Gustav Ranis of Yale, from import substitution to export substitution (the so-called 'switching point') around 1963.[1] Exports from Korea expanded rapidly from 1963 with the adoption of an export-oriented industrialization strategy and the subsequent reform of various trade and economic policy measures.

Trade-oriented industrialization has been the basic growth strategy of Korea since the early 1960s, making foreign trade inseparable from industrialization in Korea. When the first Five-Year Economic Plan (1962–6) began, the total value of Korean exports amounted to only US$55 million, but by 1988 this had increased to US$55 billion. This rapid expansion of exports and its interrelationship with Korea's growth strategy, policy instruments, incentive systems, and institutional arrangements such as general trading companies, are examined in more detail in this chapter.

Korea's Growth and Trade Promotion Strategy

Growth Strategy

Growth strategies, whether in developing or developed countries, must be compatible with the country's resource endowment, population size, economic system, and other characteristics. The adoption of a correct growth strategy appears to be crucial to initiating as well as maintaining economic growth. Choosing an appropriate strategy is a 'necessary condition' for development. Korea's sustained growth since the early 1960s is due largely to the identification of, and adherence to, a growth strategy that was right for the country, namely, an outward-, industry-, and growth-oriented (or 'OIG-oriented') strategy.

The most important choice for any development-oriented country is between an 'internal policy' emphasizing efficient mobilization and reliance on domestic resources and an 'external policy' stressing the promotion of foreign trade. Many developing countries tend to choose the internal path because they think it is the correct one, as well as easier to travel. It is also compatible with strong nationalism, and was widely—and erroneously—advocated in much of the early development literature. Only a few countries like Korea appear to have recognized the advantages of the outward-looking industrialization strategy—and to stick to it.

Resource-rich countries such as Malaysia tend to grow at least initially on the basis of their resources. In these countries economic development typically starts from resource-based activities. But resource-poor countries like Korea do not have the option to choose a primary sector-oriented growth strategy. By necessity, they must grow by developing manufacturing.

Population size also influences the pattern and course of growth, especially for such industries as automobiles, colour televisions, iron and steel, and petrochemicals, which require large-scale investments and economies of scale to be efficient. According to H. Chenery's criteria, Korea is large in terms of population (42.6 million in 1988), greatly exceeding the dividing line of the 20-million mark which Chenery and Syrquin use to separate small countries from large ones.[2] As a relatively 'large country', Korea is in a better position than smaller countries such as Taiwan—or city-states like Hong Kong or Singapore—to develop scale-economy industries. For instance, there are more than 10 million households in Korea, making the domestic market large enough to support scale-economy industries producing such consumer durables as colour televisions, air conditioners, refrigerators, automobiles, and so on, on an internationally competitive scale of production. There are more than four large firms producing these commodities on an international scale in Korea. Small countries such as Singapore or Hong Kong have far fewer households than Korea and therefore have difficulty in promoting such scale-economy industries. One of the reasons Korea is ahead of Taiwan in the automotive industry probably is because Korea's domestic market is far larger. Taiwan and other small Asian NICs have rightly relied much more on small-scale industries in expanding their industrial output.

Chenery and Syrquin categorize development strategies on the basis of the choice between inward- and outward-oriented policies, resource endowment, and population size. This yields the following four strategies.[3]

1. Inward-oriented economies.
2. Outward-, primary-oriented economies.
3. Outward-, industry-oriented economies.
4. Neutral economies.

I have recently developed a more practical framework extending the Chenery and Syrquin framework to East and South-east Asian Countries (see Table 6.1).

According to Chenery and Syrquin (see Table 6.1), Korea, Japan, and Yugoslavia are the only three large countries which pursue an outward-, industry-oriented strategy. Taiwan also has chosen an outward-, industry-oriented economy, but differs from Korea by being a small country.

Korea is also different from Japan and Yugoslavia. Chenery and Syrquin say Japan reached developed country status as of 1970, whereas in that year Korea had only reached NIC status. Previously, Chenery, Shishito, and Watanabe claimed Japan's economic structure had reached the level of an advanced country as early as 1954,[4] but it seems more reasonable to assume, like Patrick and Rosovsky, that Japan was still a semi-industriaized country in 1954.[5] Lawrence Klein, however, argues that Japan reached advanced country status in 1963.[6]

Table 6.1 Proposed Typology of Development Strategies for the East and South-east Asian Countries

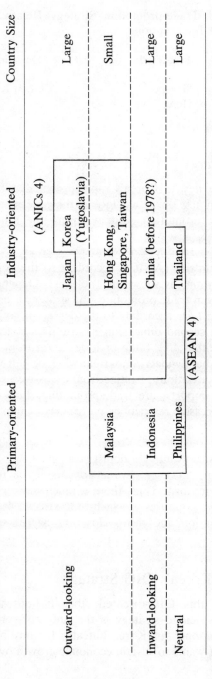

	Primary-oriented	Industry-oriented	Country Size
		(ANICs 4)	
Outward-looking		Japan | Korea (Yugoslavia)	Large
		Hong Kong, Singapore, Taiwan	Small
Inward-looking		China (before 1978?)	Large
Neutral	Malaysia	Thailand	Large
	Indonesia		
	Philippines		
	(ASEAN 4)		

Note: This typology extends the Chenery-Syrquin method. See Hollis Chenery and Moshe Syrquin, 'The Semi-Industrial Countries', in H. Chenery, S.R. Robinson, and M. Syrquin, *Industrialization and Growth: A Comparative Study*, Oxford University Press, 1986.

Table 6.2 Typology of Trade-promotion Strategy Relative to Government Intervention

Type	Free Trade	Deviation
Interventionism	Singapore	Taiwan, Korea
Laissez-faire	Hong Kong	

Trade Promotion Strategy

We have seen that the key to Korea's rapid growth has been export promotion. From now on we will look at the government's role in Korea's export promotion strategy, using the schema suggested by Lawrence Krause.[7]

Krause classifies export promotion strategies among Asian newly-industrialized countries (ANICs) according to the degree of government intervention, as shown in Table 6.2. Depending on the style of government trade promotion, the strategy is either interventionist or *laissez faire* according to the degree of government intervention. The second dimension Krause uses concerns the pattern of trade—either free trade or a deviation from free trade. Deviations can be divided, into right-wing or left-wing deviations. Right-wing deviations resulting from excessive export subsidies or tariffs on imports, are trade-promoting. Left-wing deviations, entailing excessive restrictions on exports or imports, are trade-reducing.

According to the Krause schema, Korea, like Taiwan, follows a right-wing deviationist and interventionist strategy. Compared with Japan and Taiwan, however, Korea appears to be more deviationist and interventionist. Thus, there is much more room for Korea than these two countries in which to lessen the degree of government intervention and move closer to a free trade position.

Major Features of Korea's OIG Strategy

I am convinced that this OIG-oriented, that is, outward-, industry-, and growth-oriented strategy is the only correct development strategy, not only for Korea but also for any other developing country that wants to sustain economic growth over a long period of time. This has become more true, not less true, with the increasing globalization of national economies. Regardless of the development strategy chosen, most countries may develop rapidly to a certain level—perhaps to a per capita GNP of US$2,000 (in 1980 prices)—but cannot sustain the rapid development beyond this level.

There are three aspects to Korea's growth strategy. Firstly it is growth-oriented rather than equity-oriented. Driven by the urgent need to compete successfully with North Korea in the 1960s and to escape from the vicious circle of unemployment and poverty, Korea adopted a strongly growth-oriented strategy.

High economic growth appears to be the best remedy for numerous socio-economic diseases of underdevelopment. The same thing may be said in the case of developed countries as well. When economic growth slows down, even such developed countries as the United States and the United Kingdom face many serious socio-economic problems. In fact the so-called 'advanced country disease' is associated closely with economic stagnation or slow growth. One of the most important countributions of rapid economic growth is the positive impact it has on the modernization of attitudes, ways of thinking, and the behaviour of the population. Rapid economic growth forces tradition-bound and change-resistant people to continuously modernize their attitudes and may be the best way of eliminating behavioural barriers to growth and the negative psychology of underdevelopment. As stressed by the British economist Sir Roy Harrod,[8] 'economic growth is the grand objective. It is the aim of economic policy as a whole.'

Secondly, Korea's strategy has been industry-oriented rather than resource- or service-oriented. Lacking in natural resources, Korea was not in a position, as already mentioned, to adopt a primary or resource-oriented development strategy. No matter how well Korea develops the primary sector, the Korean people cannot survive with what they produce from their own land. Also, because Korea is not a compact city-state like Singapore or Hong Kong, Korea was not in a position to emphasize a service-oriented strategy as they did in their early stages of development.

An industry-oriented strategy has various advantages over a primary- or resource-oriented strategy. For example, countries pursuing a resource-oriented strategy are vulnerable to severe economic cycles due to fluctuations in primary commodity prices.

Or the primary resource base may run out or face competition from more efficient producers or synthetic alternatives.

As the engineer and economist Mihail Manoliescu has demonstrated, 'labour is far more productive of value in industry than in agriculture.'[9] Surprisingly, there are indeed few people in developing countries who truly understand the principle of economic development by industrialization. The industry-oriented strategy is also preferable because it is compatible with the need of a developing country to continuously transform its production structure from simple products towards those requiring more capital, technology, and skilled labour. After a certain stage of development, even resource-rich countries pursuing a primary-oriented growth strategy need to shift to an industry-oriented or service-oriented strategy. The sooner the reorientation begins the better, since there appears to be a limit to the potential for growth under a primary-oriented strategy alone.

Thirdly, Korea's approach has been outward-looking rather than inward-looking or neutral. The need to import food and other raw materials impels Korea to earn needed foreign exchange through the export of manufactured goods. Ohkawa and Rosovsky indicate the fact that Japanese leaders in the past thought that international trade was 'a necessary and sufficient condition for bringing about economic development.'[10]

All of the countries that have relied upon a closed, inward-looking economic strategy have experienced relatively slow growth and the problems that accompany it. Peter Drucker has targeted a fundamental, but widespread, misconception on this point: according to Drucker:

prevailing economic theory—whether Keynesian, monetarist, or supply-side—considers the national economy, especially that of the large developed countries, to be autonomous and the unit of both economic analysis and economic policy. The international economy may be resistant and a limitation, but it is not central, let alone determining. This macroeconomic axiom of the modern economist has become increasingly shaky. The two major subscribers to this axiom, Britain and the United States, have done least well economically in the last 30 years and have also had the most economic instability.[11]

Drucker notes that planners in West Germany and Japan never accepted this axiom and have given competitiveness in the world economy the highest priority in their economic policies. As a result, these two countries have done far better than the United States and Britain in recent years. The same can be said about Taiwan, Hong Kong, and Singapore. Policymakers in these economies realized early in the development process that their economies are part of the global economic system and set their policies accordingly.

Korea's economic policies, especially its industrial growth policies, also have been designed in a global economy context and aimed at strengthening Korea's international competitive position. As a consequence, Korean policy makers need to be increasingly global in outlook as the economy itself becomes increasingly global.

As Korea's trade expanded, the imbalance in the growth between the trade and non-trade sectors also widened. As a result, this strategy generated severe criticism about Korea's growth strategy among Korean intellectuals, including some economists. In spite of well-intended but misguided criticism by economic journalists and others, Korea has been able to maintain its trade-oriented growth strategy. It is fortunate that today many Koreans understand that Korea's growth strategy fits our national characteristics, including resource endowment, population size, and so on.

The Philosophy behind Korea's Export-oriented Growth Strategy

During the rule of President Syngman Rhee, 1948–60, there was no well articulated growth strategy other than the general promotion of domestic production to replace imports. President Rhee's main interest was in politics, and his government's economic policies centred on import substitution based on an over-valued exchange rate and reliance on massive foreign assistance. Access to government-controlled foreign exchange, bank credit, and foreign assistance increasingly involved corruption and favouritism. Business success involved, in part, obtaining government protection for domestic production by securing favourable quantitative restrictions on imports. Businessmen who became wealthy under these circumstances were widely suspected of corrupt dealings. When Syngman Rhee was ousted by the so-called 'April 19 Student Revolution' in 1960, public sentiment demanded that such wealth be confiscated and the malefactors punished.

When General Park Chung Hee took power through the 16 May military coup in 1961, he was in a position to deal as he wished with those businessmen. General Park soon reached an understanding with the business community: the essence of the arrangement was that the government would exempt them from legal punishment and they in return would pay off their obligations by devoting themselves fully to 'nation building through industrialization'. This is how President Park enlisted the support of businessmen and the reason he was able to control businessmen during the rapid expansion of trade and industrial growth from 1961 to 1979.

When President Park took power, the Korean economy was in dire straits. Most Koreans were poverty-stricken, and per capita GNP in 1961 was less than US$100. South Korea lagged behind North Korea both in terms of per capita income and industrial production capacity (see Chapter 12).

The South also was behind the North in military strength as well as in the technological level and production capacity of the defense industry. There were many intellectuals who at the time proclaimed that Korea was wrongly adopting the capitalist economic system, which they believed to be inferior to the socialist economic system in the North. This added to social instability.

President Park tended to regard politicians as no more than libertines, and at first heavily suppressed political activities. Discussions concerning economic affairs were encouraged, however. Park's philosophy can be found in his often quoted remark that 'for such poor people like the Koreans, on the verge of near starvation, economics takes precedence over politics in their daily lives and enforcing democracy is meaningless.'[12]

This became the basic philosophy behind Korea's trade and industrial policy in the early 1960s, which assumed that the higher, the faster, and the more the economy grows, the better. National efforts were to be directed as much as possible away from politics and toward economic growth. *Suchul ipguk* ('nation building through exports') was President Park's favourite maxim. 'Exports first' was another favourite expression of his, and was well accepted by Korean businessmen. This phrase appeared officially in the Second Five-Year Plan (1967–71) document, and buttressed the basic philosophy behind Korea's trade and industrial policies while Park was in power.

The urgent need to catch up with and out-perform the North,

and to escape from poverty, necessitated the maximum possible growth or 'growth at any cost' and became the basic cause for the 'forced expansion' of exports and investment throughout the Park era. The export targets agreed upon between the government and individual firms were taken by businessmen as equivalent to compulsory orders. Firms which failed to achieve their export targets without a plausible excuse ran the risk of heavy administrative sanctions from the government. During the 1960s, the export promotion strategy was dominated by the government, which was the primary decision-maker in 'Korea, Inc'.

Because the measure of success for firms was their export capability, firms tended to increase production and export capacity as much as possible. This forced expansion of output and exports resulted in a high debt-equity ratio, as well as distortions in the firms' internal decision making. Large firms were in a better position than small firms to expand export capacity, and the government also favoured a small number of large firms over a large number of small firms because this meant a narrower span of administrative control. One of the reasons why large firms were in a better position than small firms in expanding export capacity was that the government banks preferred large firms to small ones in allocating bank credit. The other reason may be that large firms may be able to handle complicated red tape involving many government departments with more facility than small firms. The Federation of Korea Industries (FKI) known as the spokesman for conglomerates, used to complain as late as 1985 that one needed to process 312 documents in order to establish a firm. Small firms may not be able to compete with large firms in handling such complicated red tape.

Bong-Shik Shin of the FKI stated that, as of December 1987, there were 55 laws related to the manufacturing industries and the number of approvals by the government associated with these laws was as many as 310.[13] The number of all the permissions and approvals given by the Korean government to the Korean people was, according to him, 3,618 as of December 1977.

Gains from Export Orientation

A recent World Bank country study on the Korean economy indicates that the contribution of export growth to GNP growth has increased significantly since the 1950s. Before 1960, export

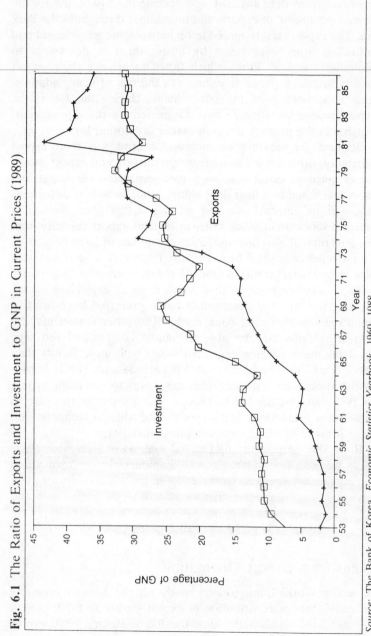

Fig. 6.1 The Ratio of Exports and Investment to GNP in Current Prices (1989)

Source: The Bank of Korea, *Economic Statistics Yearbook*, 1960–1988.

Fig. 6.2 The Ratio of Exports and Investment to GNP in 1980 Prices

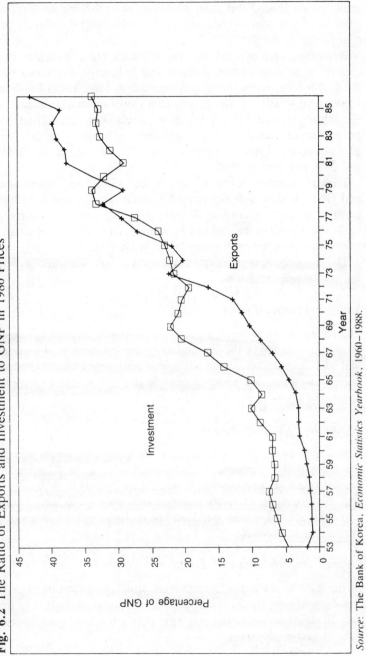

Source: The Bank of Korea, *Economic Statistics Yearbook*, 1960–1988.

growth contributed less than 10 per cent to GNP growth. This grew to 25 per cent in the early 1970s and to slightly over 33 per cent in the late 1970s.[14]

Regarding employment growth, Wontack Hong indicates that exports were responsible, directly and indirectly, for about one third of total manufacturing employment in 1966, rising to about 45 per cent in 1980.[15] The results of my own estimation based on the input-output table for the Korean economy show that the proportion of manufacturing employment created by exports was 27.8 per cent in 1968, 29.6 per cent in 1970, 44.7 per cent in 1980, and 52.5 per cent in 1985.

The relationship between exports and GNP, and investment and GNP, is shown in Figures 6.1 (current prices) and 6.2 (1980 constant prices). According to these data, the ratio of exports to GNP was less than the ratio of investment to GNP until the early 1970s, but grew to exceed the latter in later years.

The linkages between export promotion and economic growth fall into three categories.

Static Efficiency Gains

The change in growth strategy from import substitution to export promotion results in the correction of the substantial distortions that are typically associated with an import-substitution strategy. Such static gains are realized only in the first stages of export-generated growth.

Dynamic Efficiency Gains

A major dynamic gain from trade is the competitive pressure on the firms that it fosters. Dynamic gains also include expanded market size and economies of scale, improvements in technology, and development of skills among both employees and entrepreneurs. Such dynamic gains tend to be long-lasting but may be impossible to measure.

Overall Improvement of Economic Policies

In the case of an import-substitution strategy, government policies fight against the normal dynamics of the market. But in the case of an export-oriented strategy, policy tends to complement natural market forces.

Government officials can also take advantage of the policy lessons learned in advanced countries, which have typically adopted pro-trade strategies.

Policy tools of the New protectionism in Korea

Policy Instruments and the Incentive System

In this section we attempt to discuss several policy instruments and the incentive system which have been particularly important in Korea's trade and industrial development.

Credit Allocation

Due to the government's policy of rapidly expanding the production and export capacity of manufacturing firms, businessmen were obliged, because of limited internal savings, to rely on bank loans to finance the expansion of their firms. The government encouraged them to borrow, and because the officially set real interest rates were kept close to zero or even negative, businessmen tended to borrow as much as they could from banks—often in excess of the amount needed to finance planned investments. This heavy borrowing created a dependency relationship between the government and the businessmen. The excess borrowing frequently was used for land speculation. There was a saying in the 1960s that when businessmen defaulted and declared bankruptcy, they could start their businesses all over again with the money they could get from selling their land.

Such heavy borrowing from the banks owned or controlled by the government put businessmen, in effect, under tight government control, making the control of bank credit a key policy instrument. David Cole and Yung Chul Park stated that 'government control of the banking institutions has been a principal means for guiding and regulating private enterprise.'[16] The very low real interest rates on government-controlled bank loans ensured that there was always excess demand for bank credit. This created a need for credit allocation and room for the government to exercise command procedures through its control of the amount borrowed, the interest rate, and the renewal terms. A similar situation prevailed in the allocation of foreign credit, putting the government in an excellent position to wield wide discretionary control over firms.

Taxes

A second important policy instrument was the tax structure and administration. Firms were exempted from indirect taxes on income earned from export sales, and there was also a 50 per cent exemption from corporate and personal income tax on export earnings during 1961–72. Equally or more important was the discretionary use of tax investigations to enforce government directives. Because of the many informal transactions concerning the allocation of bank and foreign credit, as well as land speculation, dual accounting in bookkeeping was common among firms that borrowed heavily from the banks, putting the firms in an even more vulnerable position if threatened with a tax investigation. Not a few firms folded as a result of tax investigations, and the punishment for tax fraud included penalty taxes as well as criminal prosecution.

Administrative Support

Administrative support for business also served as an effective supplemental policy instrument. Until the early 1970s, laws and regulations concerning trade and industry had largely been inherited from the Japanese colonial period. Regulations enacted during the Japanese period were mainly intended to control—not promote—business activities, especially by the native Korean population. Thus, the red tape involved in arranging exports was virtually impenetrable. It is still very extensive as indicated above in this chapter. Administrative support, as also appropriately emphasized by Yung Whee Rhee and others,[17] was critical for Korea's trade and industrial development. When I attended an official export-promotion conference in 1972, a high ranking official from the Ministry of Trade and Industry reported that the number of approvals required to fully complete export procedures had been reduced to 'only' 43—whereas the number had previously exceeded 100.

The monthly export-promotion conference, established in December 1962, was itself one of the most important administrative support mechanisms because it was always attended personally by President Park Chung Hee. The meeting served as a forum for revising and extending administrative support of various sorts, and was also attended by all important public officials and private experts concerned with trade. It also served as an excellent forum for exchanging information among policymakers, businessmen, and economic experts. The attendees included the president's chief economic secretary, the Minister of the Economic Planning Board, the Minister of Trade and Industry, the Director of the Korea Trade Promotion Agency, and the Chairman of the Korea Traders Association. The President himself checked the progress of exports and the performance of exporting firms. Moreover, almost every month the President recognized successful businessmen with medals and citations. Personally, I believe that such presidential citations and the social recognition that went with them were very effective motivators in a traditional country like Korea where people value loyalty to the President and country very highly. Such non-monetary rewards as citations were valued just as much as monetary rewards—if not more so. The cost of such medals and awards was very low, but its social value to the recipient was often immense. Also, the ability to tell one's problems directly to the President and cut through all that red tape was very important.

Industrial Zones and Wage Controls

Selecting a site and building a plant are among the most serious decisions a manufacturing firm must make. To support firms in this regard, the government developed export industrial estates in Seoul, Masan (near Pusan), and Kumi (hometown of President Park, near Taegu) in the 1960s and continued the programme into the 1970s. In 1969 the government enacted the Regional Industrial Development Law and developed at least one regional industrial estate in every provincial capital. Through this industrial-estate development policy, the government provided export firms with an opportunity to purchase industrial sites at greatly discounted prices. User fees for electricity, water, transportation, communications, and other services for export manufacturers were also kept under government price controls. So were the prices of other services.

The government also helped control wages of workers at the exporting firms and also restricted labour union activities. Exporting firms in Korea have apparently benefited from the low wages that helped maintain international competitiveness and from enforced freedom from labour unrest.

Favourable Exchange Rate

With the adoption of the export-oriented strategy in the early 1960s, the government normalized the highly over-valued exchange-rate system and unified the complicated multi-tier exchange-rate system into a single-rate system. The reform of the exchange-rate system together with monetary and fiscal policies during the 1964–7 period, facilitated greatly the growth of Korean export industries. The maintenance of the effective exchange-rate system contributed to maintaining the international price competitiveness of Korean exports throughout the period of rapid export expansion and high GNP growth.

Rationalization of Imports

Because Korean manufactures rely heavily on foreign raw materials and machinery, the import of these items was crucial for manufacturing firms. Through an export-linked system of import privileges, the government allowed exporting firms to freely import raw materials, capital goods, and parts required for the production of exports, up to the amount of export earnings.

Table 6.3 presents a typology of these various policy tools. Overall, the government made extensive use of both incentive systems and command procedures, some of which were discretionary while others were non-discretionary measures. The government generally used direct intervention on a highly selective and short-run basis, and, fortunately, rather effectively; this was especially true during the early years of President Park's administration. With the growth of firms and the accumulation of experience by both the government and the business community, a different style of policy implementation was needed. Under the Fifth Five-Year Plan (1982–6), for example, the government came to rely more on the free market mechanism, and now relies more on non-discretionary measures than on discretionary measures and uses incentive mechanisms more than command procedures.

General Trading Companies

The legal framework for the creation of general trading companies (GTCs) in Korea was established in 1975 by the Ministry of Trade and Industry to speed up export expansion. The first

Table 6.3 Typology of Instruments of Trade and Industrial Policy

	Incentives	Command Procedures
Non-discretionary	Special tax measures Financial subsidies and export credit Effective exchange rate Effective rate of interest including interest rate subsidies Tariff rate adjustment or exemptions	Administrative support including the enactment of laws and acts Price and wage controls (control of prices of electricity and water for industrial uses. Control of labour unions and wages of industrial workers. Industrial estate development and location policy. Provision of infrastructure facilities. Tax inspection (automatic audits). Deferment of trade and capital liberalization measures. Export-import link system permitting the use of export earnings for imports.
Discretionary	Rationing of credit including the allocation of foreign loans (the amount of borrowing, interest rate, loan period, and time of renewal, etc.) Decisions concerning subsidies	Government persuasion and 'window' guidance of various types. Upward adjustment of controlled prices. Allocation of export targets. Tax inspection (selective audits). Co-ordination of investment in plant and equipment. Promotion of scale economies and efficiency by encouraging mergers.

Korean GTC was established when the government designated Samsung Trading Company as a GTC in May 1975. By 1976 the government had designated 13 GTCs, four of which have since lost their GTC status due to bankruptcy or poor performance. Since 1985 only nine companies have been performing GTC functions. In the first year 13.6 per cent of Korea's exports was handled by the ten largest GTCs, but by 1983 the share had increased to 51.3 per cent.[18] This compares with Japan a decade earlier: in 1972 the ten largest Japanese GTCs had handled 51 per cent of exports and 63 per cent of imports.[19]

Trading companies in Korea were designated a GTC if they could meet the following requirements: minimum paid-in-capital of approximately US$2.1 million, annual exports of US$50 million, ten overseas branch offices, public stock offerings, and other qualifications. On the basis of these requirements, five GTCs—Samsung, Daewoo, Hanil, Kukje, and Ssangyong—were designated in 1975. Three years later the total number of GTCs had risen to thirteen. The eight other companies were Bando, Hyundai, Hyosung, Koryo, Kumho, Samwha, Sunkyong, and Yulsam.

The most important aspect of using the GTC system to promote exports was that the government continuously pressured GTCs to expand exports by regularly raising the minimum export value requirement. For instance, the government raised the export value criterion from US$50 million in 1975 to US$301 million in 1979—the latter amounting to two per cent of total Korean exports. As a result, two GTCs, Yulsan and Samwha, lost their accreditation when their respective exports fell short of this minimum requirement. Since 1985 there have been nine GTCs in Korea.

Although the government raised the export value criterion for GTCs, it also provided GTCs with various benefits, including cash subsidies tied to export volumes. Because the total value of these various benefits exceeded, at the margin, the marginal costs of expanding exports, the GTCs had a clear incentive to increase exports as much as they could, making the GTC system and the accompanying incentive system a powerful engine of export expansion. The Korean GTCs were modelled after the Japanese GTCs and are recognized as the world's most successful adaptation of the Japanese system.

Compared with the Japanese GTCs, however, Korea's GTCs still lag far behind in terms of size, intelligence-gathering networks, marketing strength in global markets, ability to raise capital, and organizational capability. The entrepreneurial 'technology' associated with GTCs is 'soft technology', and Korea still has a clear need to promote it.

Implications Concerning the Korean Incentive and Disincentive Systems

The monetary incentives in particular and the market system in general have been proved to be very powerful in mobilizing the efforts of the Korean people towards the goal of rapid economic growth. Moral persuasion based on loyalty also has been a very powerful supplement to monetary incentives in Korea.

Because of the long tradition of Confucianism, Koreans, like other East Asians, respond strongly to moral persuasion based on a sense of loyalty to family, firm, and country. One of President Park Chung Hee's maxims, 'loyalty to the country through export', has been very effective in enlisting the support of Korean entrepreneurs and the people generally. Moral persuasion appears to be one of the most important policy instruments in Korea and other East Asian countries.

The Korean government also used 'sticks' or the 'threat system' such as tax inspections, withdrawal of financial support, and legal punishment to enforce policies—but generally it has relied more on the carrot than on the stick. Following Korea's experience, other developing countries should consider making extensive use of non-monetary rewards, such as citations or presidential awards, to mobilize commitment to development policies. Negative incentives of some sort may be crucial for developing countries to discipline businessmen. Businessmen in advanced countries are disciplined largely through competition in the market-place, but businessmen in developing countries, where the market system is poor, need to be disciplined in different ways.

Under the Park Chung Hee government, with its primary objective of expanding export capacity, Korean businessmen were expected to maximize exports rather than profits. From the government's perspective, profit was generally considered to be a secondary objective for Korean firms. Under the government's export promotion strategy, 'survival of the fittest' among competing firms was not determined in the market-place, but through discretionary government actions. 'Fitness' was judged in terms of the ability to expand exports, rather than based on profitability. If determined 'unfit', firms were likely to face bankruptcy. Such firms were under constant threat of tax investigations and other punitive sanctions. On the other hand firms that efficiently used their government-backed loans to expand exports were implicitly considered fit and favoured with even further support. In many cases, this included special privileges to start new lines of business with new government loans borrowed at negligible interest rates. Indeed, the terms of government support were the major factors in the success of many Korean firms which had not accumulated much business expertise of their own. This kind of government support was very effective in motivating firms to expand their export capacity in accordance with the government's development strategy.

7 Industrial Structure and Policy

Changes in Trade Structure

Changes in Korea's export structure have led to related changes in its industrial structure as a result of the export-oriented industrialization strategy. Pronounced shifts in the composition of exports have occurred on a regular basis since the beginning of the First Five-Year Plan in 1962. One gauge of this changing export structure is the following list of Korea's top ten exports[1] in different years, and the percentage shares shown in Table 7.1.

Top Ten Exports, 1962–1986

1962 Silk, tungsten, fish and fish products, animal oil and fat, plywood, miscellaneous products, textile fabric, machinery, clothing, chemical products.

1974 Clothing, electronics products, ships, textile fabrics, sweaters, plywood, footwear, steel plate, cotton goods, synthetic resin products.

1984 Textiles and garments, ships, electronics products, steel products, footwear, synthetic resin products, metal products, petroleum products, electric products, tires.

1986 Textiles and garments, electronics products, steel products, footwear, ships, automobiles, fish and fish products, general machinery, electric products, synthetic resin products.

Exports in the early 1960s were dominated by primary commodities such as silk, tungsten, and fish and fish products. Exports of manufactured goods ranked lower. But as industralization proceeded, manufactured goods emerged as the dominant export commodities. The proportion of primary commodities (agricultural, marine, and mineral products) in the export total was 73 per cent in 1962, but fell to less than 10 per cent by 1974. By 1987 the figure has dropped further to about 5 per cent (see Table 7.1).

Along with the rising proportion of manufactured goods in export, the leading types of manufactured exports also changed. During the 1960s the major manufactured exports were such

Table 7.1 Exports by SITC Group and Major Commodities (per cent)

SITC Commodities	1960	1965	1975	1987
0. Food and live animals	30.4	16.1	11.9	4.4
Fish and fish/marine products	8.0	10.2	7.1	1.6
1. Beverages and tobacco	1.4	0.5	1.3	0.2
2. Unfinished materials, inedible	49.7	21.2	3.0	1.0
Raw silk	3.1	3.9	0.4	—
Textile fibres	4.5	4.4	0.8	0.2
3. Mineral fuels	3.6	1.1	2.1	1.6
4. Animal and vegetable oils and fats	0.6	—	—	—
5. Chemical products	1.3	0.2	1.5	2.7
6. Manufactured goods classified by material	12.4	37.9	29.1	21.6
Plywood	0.1	10.3	4.1	0.1
Textile yarn and fabrics	7.7	15.0	12.8	7.1
Iron and steel	1.5	7.3	4.6	4.6
7. Machinery and transport equipment	0.3	3.1	13.8	35.7
Electrical machinery	0.0	1.1	8.7	18.3
Transport equipment	0.0	0.6	3.6	9.1
8. Miscellaneous manufactures	0.3	19.7	37.1	32.5
Clothing	0.0	11.8	22.0	15.9
Footwear	0.0	2.4	3.8	5.8
9. Others n.e.s.	—	0.2	0.2	0.3
Total export value (US$ million)	(22)	(175)	(5,081)	(47,280)

Sources: The Bank of Korea, *Economic Statistics Yearbook*, 1962, 1968, 1978, and 1988.

labour-intensive goods as plywood, wigs, sweaters, and so on—all of which depended on relatively simple technology. In the 1970s the major export commodities shifted to textiles, ships, steel plate, and the like, which relied on capital and somewhat more complex technology, as well as labour. By the early 1980s, export commodities had become even more capital-intensive. The year 1986 may have been a turning-point at which manufactured exports shifted decisively to skill-intensive goods such as computers, semi-conductors, colour television sets, and automobiles.

These changes reflected Korea's resource endowment and other conditions, and largely retraced the Japanese pattern as outlined by Lawrence Krause and Sueo Sekiguchi.[2] That is, the predominant export manufactures shifted over time from (1) labour-intensive goods to (2) other capital-intensive goods, (3) capital-intensive and skill-intensive goods, (4) capital-and-technology-intensive and high-wage goods, and (5) research-, capital-, and high skill-intensive goods.

The structure of imports reflects Korea's specific conditions as well as Korea's trade promotion policies. Korea's lack of natural resources required for industrialization led to their share in imports being very high. So, too, is the proportion taken by food-stuffs (Table 7.2).

The intensive promotion of heavy industries in the 1970s—and technology-intensive industries more recently—caused a rapid rise in machinery imports needed to support this development, since Korea's own machinery industry was not well developed. Consequently, machinery and transport equipment amounted to about a third of total imports by 1987, as shown in Table 7.2.

The Impact of Foreign Trade on Industrial Structure

As the export structure changed from labour-intensive to capital-and-technology-intensive goods, the proportion in the manufacturing sector of such goods as textiles and wood products decreased, while the proportion of capital-intensive industries—basic metals, machinery, for example—became larger (see Table 7.3). After 1980 the proportion of heavy and chemical industries began to exceed that of light industries in the manufacturing sector.

One interesting point regarding Korea's manufacturing structure is that due to the premature and excessive expansion of heavy industry, which usually emerges late in the development

Table 7.2 Import Structure by SITC Group and Major Commodities (percentage distribution)

SITC Commodities	1960	1965	1975	1987
0. Food and live animals	9.6	13.7	13.0	4.0
Cereals and preparations	6.2	11.7	9.5	2.1
1. Beverages and tobacco			0.2	0.1
2. Crude materials, inedible	19.9	23.7	15.4	14.4
Textile fibres	14.1	12.9	4.6	2.5
Metalliferous ores		1.1	2.4	2.7
3. Mineral fuels	7.1	6.7	19.0	14.7
Coal	0.2	0.5	0.7	2.4
Petroleum and products	6.9	6.2	18.4	2.7
4. Animal and vegetable oils and fats	0.8	0.8	0.7	0.3
5. Chemical products	23.1	22.3	10.9	11.2
6. Manufactured goods classified by material	14.3	15.4	11.9	15.2
Leather	—	—	0.9	1.1
Textile yarn and fabrics	5.5	5.8	3.5	3.1
Iron and steel	4.5	5.3	4.7	5.0
Non-ferrous metals	1.0	1.9	0.9	2.4
7. Machinery and transport equipment	12.2	15.8	26.2	33.9
Electrical machinery	3.2	2.7	7.0	12.4
Transport equipment	0.4	5.4	7.5	3.5
8. Miscellaneous manufactures	1.8	1.6	2.6	5.2
Professional and scientific instruments	1.2	0.8	1.2	2.1
9. Unclassifiable	11.2	—	0.1	1.0
Total export value (US$ millions)	(329)	(463)	7,274	41,020

Sources: The Bank of Korea, *Economic Statistics Yearbook*, 1961, 1968, 1978, and 1988.

Table 7.3 The Structure of the Manufacturing Industry (per cent)

	1960	1965	1970	1975	1980	1986
Total	100.0	100.0	100.0	100.0	100.0	100.0
1. Food and beverages	36.5	26.1	29.3	23.1	20.2	15.3
2. Textiles and leather	25.2	28.3	20.8	20.9	17.7	15.1
3. Wood products	3.4	3.2	3.3	2.1	1.5	1.2
4. Paper products	5.8	7.6	5.1	4.4	3.7	4.1
5. Non-metallic mineral products	4.9	4.4	4.8	4.7	5.0	4.3
6. Chemical products	9.7	13.9	18.1	19.8	23.1	20.7
7. Basic metals	2.7	3.9	1.0	2.9	6.4	7.5
8. Metal products and machinery	10.3	11.3	14.4	19.3	20.5	29.6
9. Other manufacturing	1.5	1.3	3.2	2.8	1.9	2.2
Light industry						
Early industry	61.7	54.4	50.1	44.0	37.9	30.4
Middle industry	14.1	15.2	13.2	11.2	10.2	11.8
Heavy industry						
Late industry	22.7	29.1	33.5	42.0	50.0	57.8

Note: Early industries = (1–2), middle industries = (3–5 and 9), and late industries = (6–8).

Sources: The Bank of Korea, *National Income in Korea*, various years; *New National Accounts*, 1986; and *Economic Statistics Yearbook*, 1989.

cycle, the proportion of middle industries appears to be relatively small. According to Chenery and Taylor,[3] 'early industries' such as foods and textiles are closely associated with the satisfaction of basic needs, and their share in GNP generally stops growing once per capita income reaches about US$600 (in 1983 prices). 'Middle industries' such as wood products, rubber products, and chemicals continue to expand until per capita income reaches the US$1,200–1,500 level (1983 prices). 'Late industries', such as machinery, metal products, and printing and publishing, begin to grow in importance only after per capita income reaches US$900 (1983 prices). According to this schema, Korea virtually jumped directly from the early-industries stage to the late-industries stage as a result of the government-driven expansion of late industries in the 1970s.

Overall, Korea's industrial structure reflects the country's poor resource endowment and export-oriented growth strategy. The need to export manufactured goods, in order to buy intermediate capital goods as well as raw materials needed for exports and domestic consumption, caused the proportion of manufacturing output in total industrial output to be higher in Korea than the global norm. The proportion of manufacturing in gross domestic product (GDP) was 31.6 per cent in Korea in 1987 (see Table 7.4), much higher than the average 23 per cent level observed in advanced countries. Among advanced countries, however, those with unusually large manufacturing sectors are West Germany (32 per cent) and Japan (30 per cent).[4] Both have more manufacturing than expected in large part because of their own resource poverty. The USA (20 per cent) represents the opposite case, where manufacturing is based on a relatively rich natural resource endowment.

Korea's industrial structure in terms of employment is shown in Table 7.5. From 1965, the total labour force grew at a rate of about 3 per cent, whereas the non-farm labour force grew at a rate of about 6 per cent. The share of industrial employment in total employment in 1980 was 28.7 per cent, higher than the average of 23.0 per cent for middle-income countries.[5] At the same time, however, there is still a relatively large number of Koreans living in the rural areas of Korea. In terms of gross domestic product, the share of agriculture was 10.8 per cent, but in terms of employment, the share of agriculture was 20.6 per cent in 1988.

Table 7.4 The Structure of Production (percentage distribution in current prices)

Sector	1960	1965	1970	1975	1980	1987
1. Agriculture	39.9	41.0	31.1	27.8	14.6	10.8
2. Industry	18.6	24.1	28.4	33.1	41.4	43.2
Mining	2.3	2.0	1.3	1.5	1.4	0.7
Manufacturing	12.1	17.3	19.1	25.3	29.6	31.6
Construction	3.5	3.6	6.4	4.9	8.2	8.1
Utilities	0.7	1.2	1.6	1.4	2.1	2.8
3. Services	41.5	34.9	40.5	39.1	44.0	46.0
Total (GDP)	100.0	100.0	100.0	100.0	100.0	100.0

Note: Sector classification is based on the World Bank method suggested in World Bank, *World Development Report*, 1987, 1988.

Sources: The Bank of Korea, *Economic Statistics Yearbook*, 1978, 1989, and *New National Accounts*, 1986.

Table 7.5 Employment by Industry (in percentages)

	1965	1970	1975	1980	1988
1. Agriculture	58.6	50.4	45.9	34.0	20.6
2. Industry	13.3	17.3	23.4	28.7	34.6
Mining	1.0	1.2	0.5	0.9	0.8
Manufacturing	9.4	13.2	18.6	21.7	27.7
Construction	2.9	2.9	4.3	6.1	6.1
3. Services	28.1	32.3	30.7	37.3	44.8
4. Total	100.0	100.0	100.0	100.0	100.0
Number ('000)	8.206	9.745	11,830	13.706	16.870

Source: The Bank of Korea, *Economic Statistics Yearbook*, various years.

The Number and Size of Firms

The number of manufacturing firms did not increase much until the early 1980s, partly because of the Korean government's policy of promoting the expansion of production capacity in existing firms. The creation of new firms was given rather low priority, particularly in the 1970s when the government adopted the policy of promoting heavy and chemical industries (HCI). As a consequence the number of firms with 5–49 employees actually decreased from 21,013 to 19,844 during the 1966–76 period.

The emphasis on promoting the HCI was built into Korea's first Long-Term Perspective Plan (1972–81).[6] The decade of the 1970s was the decade when HCI businesses were encouraged and even forced to do their best to achieve the plan's targets by expanding their firms. When the Korean economy started to experience a construction boom in the Middle East in the late 1970s, the government urged businessmen to further accelerate the expansion of existing heavy and chemical industrial complexes. Moreover, the government was directly involved in establishing large-size heavy industries such as the Pohang Iron and Steel Mill and the Korea Heavy Industry Company.

Although the number of manufacturing establishments increased by less than one-tenth between 1966 and 1976 (see Table 7.6), the average size of firms increased from 25 to 69 employees during this decade. The number of factories in Taiwan, however, increased rapidly from 27,437 to 43,829 during the same years. It was only after 1981 that the number of firms started to increase rapidly in Korea.

As heavy and chemical industries grew in the 1970s, the gap between large and small firms increased and emerged as a new economic and political issue. On the one hand, there was a growing need for small sub-contracting firms to supply components and services to large firms. There was also an increasing number of young Koreans who aspired to go into business on their own. On the other hand, bureaucratic regulations made it almost impossible to establish new firms. One had to obtain 312 signatures from government agencies in order to establish a single firm. Bong-Shik Shin of the Federation of Korean Industries estimated that in the 1970s it took more than 350 days just to get the required signatures.[7] The need to simplify these procedures was repeatedly publicized in newspapers in the early 1980s, and finally were greatly simplified from the mid-1980s.

The promotion of small manufacturing industries emerged as one of the major policy issues in the mid-term revision of the Fifth Five-Year Plan. In the revised plan document covering 1984–6, a separate section was devoted to the promotion of small manufacturing industries. The efforts to promote the growth of new businesses resulted in the enactment in 1986 of a special law to support the creation of small firms.

Table 7.6 The Number of Manufacturing Establishments and Employees by Firm Size, 1966–1985

	Number (and percentage) of Establishments			Number (and percentage) of Employees ('000)			Value Added (billion won)		
	1966	1976	1985	1966	1976	1985	1966	1976	1985
1–49	21,013	19,844	35,676	223.7	276.5	570.1	38.8	323.6	3,137.9
	(92.5)	(79.5)	(81.0)	(39.5)	(16.1)	(23.4)	(24.9)	(7.9)	(11.7)
50–99	874	2,094	4,273	59.5	147.5	300.3	13.4	262.8	2,198.9
	(3.8)	(8.4)	(9.7)	(10.5)	(8.6)	(12.3)	(8.6)	(6.5)	(8.2)
100–299	593	1,990	3,001	92.3	332.6	497.2	26.0	635.8	4,722.4
	(2.6)	(8.0)	(6.8)	(16.3)	(19.4)	(20.4)	(16.6)	(15.6)	(17.7)
Over 300	238	1,029	1,087	191.2	960.6	1,070.4	78.0	2,852.9	16,677.4
	(1.1)	(4.1)	(2.5)	(33.7)	(55.9)	(43.9)	(49.9)	(70.0)	(62.4)
Total	22,718	24,957	44,037	566.7	1,717.3	2,438.0	156.2	4,075.1	26,736.6
	(100.0)	(100.0)	(100.0)	(100.0)	(100.0)	(100.0)	(100.0)	(100.0)	(100.0)

Sources: Computed from Economic Planning Board, National Bureau of Statistics, *Mining and Manufacturing Census*, 1966, 1976, and 1985.

Thereafter, the number of manufacturing establishments increased rapidly. Establishments with over 5 employees increased from 24,957 in 1976 to 44,037 in 1985, according to the census of manufacturing. However, the Establishment Census of the National Bureau of Statistics puts the number of manufacturing establishments with more than 5 employees at a much higher figure—76,042 in 1986 (see Table 7.7). When the value-added and employment figures are correlated with the national income statistics, it appears that the higher figures given in the Establishment Census are more realistic. It appears that many firms underreported the number of their employees to manufacturing census enumerators. Thus, the number of firms with over 5 employees in the manufacturing census turned out to be smaller than the actual number.

Compared with Japan, Korea has relatively fewer manufacturing establishments. Japan has roughly three times the population of Korea, but has about four times the number of manufacturing establishments. Moreover, in Korea, firms with more than 300 employees contribute relatively more to total employment than do smaller firms. In the case of Japan, however, small firms with between 5 and 49 employees are relatively more important. Despite these differences, one surprising similarity is that the average size of all manufacturing establishments in 1986 was about 15.0 employees in both Korea and Japan.

Concentration and Market Power

The government's policy of promoting fast-growing firms and rewarding them with preferential access to credit and other incentives, as well as the promotion of heavy and chemical industries in the 1970s, has resulted in a tendency for industrial concentration to increase. Also, because of economies of scale in the government administration of credit and taxation, government officials preferred a small number of large firms to a large number of small firms.

Enterprise concentration can be measured by 'market concentration'—defined as the sales share of the largest 3 to 4 firms in a single commodity market—or by 'aggregate concentration' which is indicated by the sales share of the largest 5, 10, 50, or 100 manufacturing firms across several markets.

Market concentration measured by the 3-firm concentration

Table 7.7 Comparison of Manufacturing Establishments and Employees in Korea and Japan, 1986

Size of Establishment (employees)	Number (and percentage) of Establishments		Number (and percentage) of Employees (1000)	
	Korea	Japan	Korea	Japan
1–4	142,910 (65.3)	448,193 (51.2)	287.5 (8.7)	1,073 (8.0)
5–49	66,259 (30.3) (87.1)	385,657 (44.1) (90.4)	897.7 (27.3) (29.9)	5,116 (38.3) (41.7)
50–99	5,134 (2.3) (6.8)	23,263 (2.7) (5.5)	357.4 (10.9) (11.9)	1,597 (12.0) (13.0)
100–299	3,394 (1.6) (4.5)	13,255 (1.5) (3.1)	563.8 (17.1) (18.8)	2,136 (16.0) (17.4)
Over 300	1,255 (0.6) (1.6)	4,219 (0.5) (1.0)	1,183.6 (36.0) (39.4)	3,429 (25.7) (27.9)
Total	218,952 (100.0) (100.0)	874,587 (100.0) (100.0)	3,290.0 (100.0) (100.0)	13,351 (100.0) (100.0)

Note: Figures in parentheses are the ratios only for establishments with more than 5 employees.

Sources: The Korean data are from Economic Planning Board, National Bureau of Statistics, *Establishment Census,* 1986. The Japanese data are from Ministry of General Affairs/Bureau of Statistics, *Establishment Census,* 1986, as reported in *Statistics of Japan,* 1987.

Table 7.8 The Change in the Conglomerates' Share in Manufacturing Sales and Employment, 1977–1985

Conglomerates	Sales			Employment		
	1977	1980	1985	1977	1980	1985
Top 5	15.7	16.9	23.0	9.1	9.1	9.7
Top 10	21.2	23.8	30.2	12.5	12.8	11.7
Top 20	29.3	31.4	36.4	17.4	17.9	15.5
Top 30	34.1	36.0	40.2	20.5	22.4	17.6

Sources: Kyu Uk Lee and Sung Soon Lee, 'Business Integration and Concentration of Economic Power,' Korea Development Institute Research Report 85–02, September 1985. The data for 1985 are from the Korea Development Institute.

ratio averaged 62.0 per cent of total manufactured goods in Korea in 1982, higher than the Japanese figure of 56.3 per cent in 1980.[8] According to the World Bank, aggregate concentration measured by the sales share of the largest 100 firms in the manufacturing sector in Korea was 40.6 per cent in 1970, 44.9 per cent in 1977, and 46.8 per cent in 1982. The same figure for Japan was 28.4 per cent in 1975 and 27.3 per cent in 1980.[9] The Korean figures are clearly much higher than the Japanese figures. Leroy Jones also emphasizes the high degree of concentration in Korea as follows: 'Korea has an extremely high level of aggregate concentration by the standards of industrialized non-communist nations, particularly when adjusted for the size of the economy.'[10]

One of the most important aspects of industrial concentration in Korea is the market power exercised by the business conglomerates called *jaebol*, the Korean counterparts of the Japanese *zaibatsu*. There were altogether 32 *jaebol* in Korea as of 1987. But in 1989 the number increased to 43 as the total assets of all the companies belonging to the next 8 large groups in 1988 exceeded the criterion of 400 billion *won* (about US$500 million) which is the official dividing line between *jaebol* and non-*jaebol*.[11] The 43 *jaebol* comprise altogether 672 industrial companies. Conglomerates in Korea encompass almost all large private corporations. Conglomerate-affiliated firms grew faster than non-conglomerate firms, as indicated by the formers' continuously

Table 7.9 The Conglomerates' Share in Manufacturing Capacity and GNP, 1985

Conglomerates (Group)	Manufacturing Value Added	Sector Fixed Capital	Share in Total GNP	Number of Subsidiaries
Top 5	18.7	20.4	5.5	94
Top 10	24.2	27.9	7.1	147
Top 20	29.5	34.4	8.6	218
Top 30	33.1	39.6	9.7	270

Note: The share of conglomerates in GNP was estimated using the data in the following sources: Kyu Uck Lee, 'Concentration of Economic Power in Korea', Unpublished Paper, Korea Development Institute; and Bank of Korea, *Economic Statistics Yearbook*, 1987.

increasing share of total sales since 1977, as shown in Table 7.8. The largest 30 conglomerates control 270 firms and contributed about 10 per cent of Korea's GNP in 1985 (Table 7.9).

There are arguments for and against the expansion of conglomerates in Korea. One critical argument, especially by non-economists, is the increasing disparity between conglomerates and non-conglomerates, especially smaller firms. The main point of their argument is that conglomerates tend to engage in predatory or exclusionary activities and exploit small industries. Another is the danger that powerful conglomerates will exert too much control over the economy and the government.

On the plus side, some people argue that conglomerates need to continue to grow to keep Korea competitive with Japan and other advanced countries. One can argue that today's markets for Korean conglomerates are global markets, and their market concentration should be judged on this basis, not simply with regard to the domestic market. Other advantages of conglomerates may be that they import foreign technology and provide training to both workers and entrepreneurs. They are also mobilizers and repositories of managerial and entrepreneurial talent. It could be that conglomerates are, as emphasized by Joseph Schumpeter, dynamically more efficient than small firms. In the final analysis, the merits and demerits of Korean conglomerates must be judged in terms of dynamic efficiency, not static efficiency. Their growth has deep roots in the country's need to escape grinding poverty, to overtake and out-perform North Korea, to import foreign technology, and to overcome the lack of natural resources—all in a short period of time. They obtained special favours from the government which small firms did not, so that their growth became in some sense artificially high. Fortunately, all Korean firms—conglomerates and non-conglomerates alike—have been fully utilizing their production capacity since 1986, and, with the global scope of the markets in which Korean conglomerates compete, the arguments against the expansion of conglomerates appear to be losing ground.

Nevertheless, the promotion of a competitive market environment is essential for Korea's free-enterprise, market-economy system. Policy makers and businessmen are only gradually realizing the importance of free and fair competition. In fact, the laws regulating monopolies and enforcing fair trade have a short history in Korea. The Monopoly Regulation and Fair Trade Law was enacted for the first time in Korea in 1980. The Fair Trade Commission was established in the Economic Planning Board in 1981 according to this law. The purpose of the Law is stated in Article No. 1, as follows. 'This Law shall be aimed at encouraging fair and free competition and thereby stimulating creative business activities and protecting consumers as well as promoting a balanced development of the national economy.'[12] Stated as it is, the purpose of the Korean Fair Trade Law is rather broad and comprehensive. This law has perhaps been regarded as the most useful law in Korea by both policy makers and the ordinary people.

Through my service as Fair Trade Commissioner with the Economic Planning Board, I have observed that Koreans are highly group-oriented and have a strong tendency to form cartels of various kinds in order to control markets. It is important to educate the general public about the importance of free and fair competition, and instill an understanding of the Fair Trade Law. The government also needs to change, as stated by Masu Uekusa of Tokyo University, 'the basic thrust of public policy toward industry from a strong regulatory policy to a pro-competition policy.'[13] Policy makers at the Economic Planning Board increasingly realize the importance of the Fair Trade Law in improving the quality of products, productivity, and structure and organization of Korean industries.

Table 7.10 The Status of Korean Public Enterprises, 1988

Type of Public Enterprise	No. of Enterprises	Employment ('000)	Assets (trillion won)	Sales (trillion won)
Government enterprises	4	73.4	9.51	2.68
Government-invested enterprises	26	160.4	55.97	10.10
Subsidiary companies of GIEs	67	75.2	8.02	5.82
Other government-backed enterprises	6	31.1	27.93	3.95
Local public enterprises	119	25.1	5.35	0.47
Total	222	365.3	106.78	23.02

Note: Assets and sales are as of the end of 1986.

Sources: Dae-hee Song, September 1988, and Economic Planning Board, *White Paper on Public Enterprise*, Seoul EPB, 1988.

Public Enterprises

Public enterprises or PEs have played crucial roles in the economic development of Korea. When the First Five-Year Plan (1962–6) began, there were only 52 PEs, but the number increased to 103 by 1988. If local PEs are included, the total number of PEs rises to 222, as seen in Table 7.10. Out of these PEs, 4 are government enterprises, 26 are government invested enterprises (GIEs), 67 are subsidiary companies of GIEs, 6 are government-backed enterprises, and 119 are local PEs. Government enterprises are those staffed and operated by government officials and take the form of government offices. Examples are the Office of Railroads and the Office of Monopoly (in charge of cigarettes and ginseng). When the government owns more than 50 per cent of an enterprise it is called a government-invested enterprise. Examples are the Korea Electric Power Corporation, the Korea Development Bank, the Korea Highway Corporation, the Korea Trade Promotion Corporation, the Korea Broadcasting Corporation, the Korea Tourism Corporation, and the Korea Land Promotion Corporation, among others.

Subsidiary companies of GIEs are those indirectly invested in

Table 7.11 The Public Enterprise Sector

	1963	1970	1975	1980	1986
Number of enterprises	52	119	116	111	107
Sectoral value-added					
Billions of won	31.8	262.1	848.5	6,680	6,859
As percentage of GDP	7.0	9.2	8.3	9.1	9.1
Sectoral employment					
In thousands				280	341.9
As percentage of total employment				1.9	2.0
Sectoral investment					
Billions of won	21.6	216.3	918.6	3,253.7	3,897.3
As percentage of total investment	31.7	18.9	33.2	27.6	15.6

Note: Local public enterprises are excluded.

Source: Jones, Leroy P., and Il Sakong, 1980, Dae-hee Song, 1986, Shin-il Kang, 1988, and Soo-il Kwack, 1988a.

by the government. The activities of these companies are closely related to those of GIEs. Local PEs are those providing local services related to water, health, and so on, supported by the local governments. The number of local PEs was only 7 in 1969, but increased rapidly to 119 by 1988 due to the rise in the standard of living of local people.

PEs in Korea expanded with the beginning of rapid economic growth in the early 1960s. In terms of the share in total investment, PEs reached a peak in the middle of the 1970s (see Table 7.11). The investment in PEs accelerated especially with the beginning of the Development Plan for Heavy and Chemical Industries (1972–81) in 1972. But since the middle of the 1970s, the share of total investment by PEs appears to have declined. The declining trend accelerated somewhat in the 1980s with the beginning of the privatization policy which was one of the key policy directions of the Fifth Five-Year Plan (1982–6).

PEs in Korea before 1960 were largely confined to public utilities: basic necessities such as salt, monopolised high-value consumer products such as ginseng and cigarettes, and banking. But with the beginning of the five-year development plans in the 1960s, the boundary for PEs was dissolved. The government established PEs in whatever areas that were considered appropriate by the government. From the 1980s, many PEs took the form of development corporations such as the Agriculture and Fishery

Development Corporation, the Korea Land Promotion Corporation, the Industrial Site and Water Resource Development Corporation, the Petroleum Development Corporation, the Korea Trade Promotion Corporation, the Overseas Development Corporation, and the Korea Development Bank.

The government PE policy in the 1960s and 1970s was to establish PEs in any area if they were essential in expanding Korea's export capacity and could not be properly handled by private enterprises. Thus, the government established PEs to handle even such items as iron and steel, petroleum and chemicals, and tourism, that are normally considered to be traditional areas of private businesses. But the government PE policy in the 1980s changed greatly. The government attempted to privatize PEs as much as possible. The chief reason for this is simply that the private sector can operate PEs at least as efficiently as the government.

The Contrast between Korean and Japanese Industrial Policy

There is no standard definition of the term 'Industrial policy'. Leading textbooks on economics in Western industrial countries do not deal with industrial policy as such. The United States and other industrial countries in the West do not have industrial policies comparable to those in Japan and Korea, and this absence of an explicit and effective industrial policy is, according to Robert Heilbroner and Lester Thurow, a major reason for the recent decline in productivity in the United States.[14] In the past, public policies related to industries in the Western industrial countries were chiefly related to industrial organization in each sector or were designed to help efficient industries and discourage or redirect declining industries.

The most apparently successful case of a deliberate industrial policy can be seen in Japan. According to Miyohei Shinohara, the Japanese industrial policy equates to 'policies adopted by the Ministry of International Trade and Industry (MITI)' that have been 'designed to bring about an overall strengthening of international competitiveness of various modern industries'.[15]

Korea has adopted a similar industrial policy since the beginning of the First Five-Year Plan (1962–6). Masu Uekusa of Tokyo University states that 'Korea's Ministry of Trade and

Industry has adopted a Japanese type of industrial policy in order to realize rapid macroeconomic growth.'[16] The major characteristics of industrial policies in Korea and Japan will be examined, using the framework of Japanese industrial policy outlined by Shinohara.[17]

In Japan the promotion of industrial development was a co-operative effort between business and government—an approach foreigners have frequently referred to as 'Japan, Inc.'—in which the main government organization was MITI. In the case of Korea, however, the main government organization was not the Ministry of Trade and Industry (MTI), but the President himself, supported by the Economic Planning Board and the MTI. Because the role of government was much stronger in Korea than in Japan, especially during the 1961–79 period, it may be proper to call it 'Korea, Inc.,' a co-operative effort in which government took the lead and business followed, whereas the opposite was perhaps the case in Japan.

In Japan, moreover, large, privately-owned banks were important partners in the industrial promotion system. In Korea, however, banks were small, and government-run, and as such played only a subordinate, largely implementing, role in the process.

The objectives of the Korean and Japanese industrialization policies have also been different. Japan's goal was to catch up with the advanced nations, but in Korea it was to expand export manufacturing capacity as much as possible. In addition, catching up with North Korea's initial lead in industrialization was also an important policy target in the early 1960s. Industrial policy in Japan did not focus on selecting and intensively promoting promising infant industries. Rather, it sought to promote the entire modern manufacturing sector on an overall basis. Korea's policy was also broadly directed, but since virtually all of the industries were of infant status, the net effect was to promote the most promising industries at any given stage.

 Import substitution in Japan was closely linked to export promotion. But in the case of Korea, export promotion was accompanied by 'import promotion' of needed inputs. Firms were allowed to freely import raw materials, parts, and machinery required for export production, up to the limit of the value of their export earnings. This is the main reason why imports expanded rapidly with the rise in exports, and why the trade deficit grew sharply between 1962 and 1985, as shown in Table 5.2. Import substitution, as such, was not considered an explicit policy objective after the adoption of the export-oriented growth strategy.

Japan's huge domestic market of over 100 million people facilitated export promotion in Japan. Any firm that could succeed in competition with other large firms in the domestic market was well positioned to compete successfully with foreign firms in overseas markets. In the case of Korea, many firms started up as competitors in the global market because of the smallness of the domestic demand base; this was especially true for heavy industrial goods. After firms had succeeded in overseas markets, they started marketing to the pent-up domestic demand that had been preserved for them by tariff and other barriers against non-essential consumer imports. Examples include colour televisions, personal computers, semiconductors, and high quality garments.

The feedback relationship between the expansion of exports and domestic demand was very strong in Japan and facilitated high economic growth. Because a large proportion of parts and machinery required for the production of export commodities could be produced domestically by Japanese firms, the inter-industry linkages among Japanese industries were very high. But in the case of Korea, most parts and capital goods needed for export industries had to be imported because of low inter-industry linkage and limited domestic market size. As a consequence, the feedback relationship between export and domestic demand was rather weak. When I computed the proportion of total imports to the total output of all industries using the input-output tables for the Korean and Japanese economies for 1985, I found that the figure for Japan was 6.9 per cent, much lower than the Korean figure of 28.1 per cent for the same year. This implies that to produce one unit of output, Korea needs to import 28.1 per cent of input, but Japan needs to import only 6.9 per cent of input. This is based only on direct input requirements. If indirect requirements are included, import requirements could be much higher. When I computed import requirements for manufacturing output per US$100 for Korea, the results turned out to be as follows. If only direct requirements are included, the amount of imported input requirements per US$100 worth of output were

$20.10 in 1970, $22.30 in 1980, and $18.50 in 1985. When indirect requirements are also included, the same figures increase to $26.20 in 1970, $35.40 in 1980, and $30.60 in 1985.[18]

The high growth in Japan was not merely export-led, but was also, to a large extent, investment-led. In Korea, where the domestic market was relatively small, the investment-led aspect has been weaker. Also, in Japan, large firms developed in parallel with small and medium-sized firms, whereas, in the case of Korea the major emphasis was placed on promoting large firms until the early 1980s.

It is worth noting that all the industries promoted by the Korean government turned out to be successful by 1986. Korea's massive investment in heavy and chemical industries in the late 1970s was, at the time, harshly criticized by many economists as misguided. In fact, some of the machinery firms were very costly. However, most of those heavy industries have been operating almost at full capacity since 1986 and have turned out to be very successful. One typical example is Pohang Iron and Steel. Most Koreans vehemently opposed the mill's construction with borrowed money, as they thought Koreans lacked the needed production technology and management and marketing skills. Even economists from the World Bank expressed their opinion that the project was unlikely to be profitable and recommended that the Korean government cancel the plan. Ironically, it is now often cited by World Bank economists as a successful case of industrial promotion.

The key lesson appears to be that major industrial facilities can be developed successfully even in poor developing countries, if promoted on a selective basis. Because the development of such industries facilitates technological learning, enhances the quality of human resources, and provides linkage effects to other industries, it can have a profound impact, mostly favourable, on economic structure and growth. The conceptual framework to be used in judging the feasibility of these industries is not the principle of static gain or comparative cost under the misleading assumption of an unchanging environment. Such national-scale projects have to be evaluated on the principle of dynamic gain or what Miyohei Shinohara calls the 'comparative technical progress criterion' or the 'dynamized comparative cost doctrine' which puts the project in a long-term dynamic economic context.[19]

Managing the Transition to Maturity

Korea's per capita income rose, as already mentioned, above US$2,000 (1980 prices) in 1985, thereby passing Arthur Lewis's threshold between 'development economies' and 'developed economies'. The Korean economy has begun to resemble a mature advanced economy more than a poor, underdeveloped economy. But Korea is still undergoing rapid transformation industrially, financially, and socially.

Industrially, the major export industries of Korea have changed from traditional, labour-intensive ones to capital-intensive, and now to technology-intensive ones. As a result, Korea's exports and industrial structure have been fundamentally transformed.

Financially, Korea became a trade-surplus country and mature debtor nation in 1986, so she is no longer a young debtor nation. She also became self-sufficient in savings and domestic investment in 1986. The foreign debt also started to decrease rapidly after 1985. Socially, democratization is underway in almost every Korean organization and in other corners of society. The future of Korea and her economy depend upon how she manages her transition to maturity. In this regard, three issues appear to be especially important.

Managing Trade in the Global Context

Continuous expansion of trade is crucial for the Korean economy to mature. However, the expansion of Korean exports is likely to face increasing trade friction with trade partners. First of all, Korean export markets are highly concentrated: more than half of the total exports go to the United States (35.3 per cent in 1988) and Japan (19.8 per cent in 1987) and more than half of the total imports come from these two countries (from the United States 24.6 per cent and Japan 30.7 per cent in 1988) (see Table 12.5). Secondly, Korea's major export items such as colour televisions, automobiles, and computers have become increasingly competitive with those of the United States and Japan. Thirdly, the main source of Korea's trade surplus is the United States. As Korea's trade pattern becomes increasingly similar to Japan's, Korea will need to diversify her export markets to avoid sanctions and restraints in concentrated markets. This is one of the reasons

President Roh Tae Woo is trying hard, through this *Bukbang* (northern frontier) *Jeongchaek* (policy), to expand trade with socialist countries—especially the Soviet Union, Eastern Europe, and China. None the less, the United States will remain the most important market for Korean exports, especially for newly emerging, high-technology industries. Accordingly, Korea's ability to maintain a favourable trade relationship with the United States is crucial. Korea needs to adjust her trade policy to find a long term, mutually beneficial, and harmonious relationship with the United States, including the liberalization of Korea's markets without stunting the growth of Korea's new industries. Korea also needs to establish a more balanced trade regime with Japan, which now maintains a large net surplus with Korea. These issues are examined in more detail in Chapter 12.

Institutional Reform

The reform of various institutional arrangements is crucial at this stage of industrial development to further promote Korea's trade and growth and also to assure the vitality of society. Reform is particularly needed in the financial sector whose growth lags somewhat behind other sectors: other areas include land use and the public sector. The financial sector in Korea has been under strict government controls and has been directly or indirectly involved in some important policy failures. For instance, the premature over-expansion of heavy and maritime industries by the government on the eve of the second oil crisis resulted in a heavy loss for the banks, which has been forced by the government to provide these industries with tremendous loans. In addition, Korea's business conglomerates are, in contrast to Japan's, not backed by their own banks and have depended heavily on government approved loans. As such, Korean conglomerates are in a much weaker position than Japanese conglomerates in world markets. So far the function of the Korean financial sector has been associated more with the determination of the direction of investment than the mobilization of domestic resources.

Land use in Korea is also heavily controlled by the government. According to urban planner Yung-Hwi Roh, in the past some types of land were subject to more than 100 laws or regulations. One consequence is a severe shortage of land for industrial and residential use. Upward surges in the price of land and housing in Korea have been due in large measure, as stated already in Chapter 2, to extensive regulation of land use. In the future the efficient use of Korea's scarce land resources will be crucial to the maturation of the Korea economy and the maintenance of an equitable distribution of wealth. Lawrence B. Krause emphasizes that 'a misallocation of land can become a serious barrier to growth, as is now becoming evident in Japan.'[20]

As might be expected, the public sector in Korea, where the government has led the growth of the economy, is relatively large. Although the public sector's overall level of efficiency appears to be quite good, it must be operated still more efficiently. To this end the privatization of the public sector needs to be promoted.

The government itself also needs to be reformed. Virtually no major event takes place in Korea without government involvement, and the government is responsible for both the successes and the failures of almost every large project in Korea. When a project fails, it is the government that is blamed by the people. Generally, the Korean people tend to blame the government for whatever does not function well or turns out badly. This contributes to the alienation of the people from the government and has added to popular discontent in recent years.

Balancing Equity and Efficiency

Equity recently has emerged as a crucial socio-economic issue. With the rise in incomes, people's expectations and sense of relative poverty has increased even more rapidly. Also, the government can no longer ignore the people's demands for better housing, pollution control, improved urban transportation, better educational facilities, and improved quality of the environment. Expenditures on these objectives are not directly related to the increase in productivity of the economy, especially in regard to the current democratization policy. However, as the number of people dissatisfied with the existing levels of regional, personal, and industrial inequality rises, pressures to sacrifice efficiency for greater equity will also rise. Balancing equity and efficiency in the egalitarian society of Korea will probably become an increasingly important domestic issue in the future.

Table 7.12 Major Statistics of the Samsung Group

	1953	1960	1965	1970	1976	1980	1986
Employment ('000)	0.267	1.87	4.80	9.08	25.8	75.0	147.2
Sales (billion won)	0.113	2.7	7.0	36.5	455.3	2,385.5	14,615.8
Domestic sales	0.112	2.7	5.7	33.8	237.6	1,136.8	7,241.1
Exports	0.001	—	1.3	2.7	217.7	1,248.7	7,374.7
Capital (billion won)	0.016	0.7	3.1	10.0	50.9	392.3	1,101.9
Fixed assets (billion won)	0.004	0.43	3.0	22.7	110.3	697.1	2,948.4
Long-term liabilities (billion won)		0.13	2.0	20.5	72.8	782.0	5,168.4
Net profit after tax (million won)	3	45	13	130	10,370	10,850	161,150
Tax (billion won)	—	—	—	—	68.1	254.5	717.1
R&D expanditure (billion won)	—	—	—	—	1.9	9.8	163.1
Training expenses (billion won)	—	—	—	—	—	—	10.9
Exchange rate (won/US$)	18.0	65.0	272.1	316.7	484.0	659.9	861.4

Source: The Office of the Secretary to the Chairman, Samsung Conglomerate, *Samsung Osipnyonsa (A 50-Year History of Samsung)*, Seoul, Samsung Group, 1988.

The Samsung Business Group — A Representative Korean Conglomerate

Samsung conglomerate, sometimes referred to as *Samsung guroop* (group) by Koreans, consists of 37 companies as of 1988.[21] This group owns the country's largest general trading company (Samsung GTC), the largest electronics company (Samsung Electronics), the largest semiconductor company, and also some of the country's largest hotels, department stores, daily newspapers, airplane companies, insurance companies, and recreational facilities. Its sales totalled 14.6 trillion won (US$17 billion) in 1986. As Table 7.12 indicates, the GNP of Korea in that year was US$118.6 billion. Samsung has grown much faster than the economy as a whole since the early 1960s. For instance, its total sales were only US$25.7 million (equivalent to about 0.9 per cent of GNP) in 1965, but increased to US$17 billion (about 14.3 per cent of GNP) in 1986. Its total sales volume is expected to soon exceed the total volume of government revenue, which was US$18.6 billion in 1986. The amount of tax paid by the Samsung *jaebol* was about 5.0 per cent of the total tax revenue of the government in 1986. Compared with other large corporations in the world, it was 42nd in sales volume in 1985 according to *Fortune* magazine. But in 1986, it moved up to 35th in the world.

Until 1960 most of Samsung's businesses were domestic-market oriented. For instance, the proportion of exports to total sales was less than 0.1 per cent in 1960, as shown in Table 7.12. But with the beginning of the export drive of the government in the early 1960s the figure increased rapidly. Exports increased to 18.6 per cent in 1965 and to over 50 per cent in 1980. The Samsung group now sells more than 50 per cent of its total production in overseas markets.

Samsung *jaebol* started its business as a trading company. Samsung Trading Company, established in 1951, is the largest of its kind in Korea. Since 1986, it has been the largest company in Korea in terms of sales volume.

In the 1960s, the main lines of business for the Samsung group were such 'early' industries as textiles, sugar, and the like. But in the 1970s, 'middle' industries such as petrochemicals, paper products, and so on, became the main lines of business. In the 1980s, however, the main lines of business shifted again to such 'late' industries as electronics, computers, and semiconductors. Sam-

sung is very well known for its emphasis on manpower training
and timely and foresighted restructuring of its industrial structure. To many Koreans, the word 'Samsung' means efficiency and
organizational capability. As the growth of the Samsung group
represents the growth of Korean industries, it is important to
understand the growth of the Samsung group to better understand the Korean economy.

8   Korean Economic Planning and
Policy Formulation

Economic Plans and the Objectives of Government Economic Policy

Effective formal economic planning in Korea started with the First Five-Year Economic Development Plan (1962–6). Earlier plans had been drafted, but they had not been implemented because of the political changes in 1960, when the Student Revolution toppled the Syngman Rhee government, and in 1961, when a new five-year plan was shelved by Park Chung Hee's military government. President Park's new government then drafted its own First Five-Year Plan (FFYP), which was carried through to completion. Korea has completed five five-year planning cycles, and is now in the middle of the Sixth Five-Year Plan (1987–91).

The objectives of Korea's successive five-year plans, as shown in Table 8.1, have changed over time with the rise in income, shifts in economic structure, and changes in economic issues and priorities. The changes in the objectives of the government's economic policy may be examined in relation to four major government economic functions:[1]

(a) Creating the economic and legal framework (that is, the constitution, rules of the economic game, and economic laws). The constitution of Korea has been almost totally revised nine seperate times since liberation in 1945.
(b) Ensuring stability—macroeconomic functions.
(c) Promoting efficiency—microeconomic functions (industrial policy, trade policy, agricultural policy, and social infrastructure policy)
(d) Promoting equity (personal, regional, and industrial equity)

The main objectives of Korea's FFYP (1962–6) were to break the vicious circle of poverty and to build a foundation for self-sustaining growth. These were closely related to the first of the above functions of government, namely the establishment of an economic and legal framework.

The function of establishing an economic and legal framework

Table 8.1 An Overview of Korea's Five-Year Plans

Plan	Period	Growth Rate	Objectives	Major Policy Directions
First FYP	1962–6	7.1[a] (7.9)[b]	1. Breaking the vicious circle of poverty. 2. Establishing the foundations for self-sustaining economic development.	1. Securing energy supply sources. 2. Correcting structural imbalances. 3. Expanding basic industries and infrastructure. 4. Effective mobilization of idle resources. 5. Improving the balance of payments position. 6. Promoting technology.
Second FYP	1967–71	7.0 (9.7)	1. Modernization of industrial structure. 2. Promotion of self-sustaining economic development.	1. Self-sufficiency in food, development of fisheries and forestry. 2. Laying the foundation for industrialization. 3. Improving balance of payments position. 4. Employment creation, family planning and population control. 5. Raising farm household income. 6. Improving technology and productivity.
Third FYP	1972–6	8.6 (10.2)	1. Harmonizing growth, stability, and equity. 2. Realizing a self-reliant economy.	1. Self-sufficiency in food staples. 2. Improving the living environment in rural areas. 5. Development of national land resources and efficient spatial distribution of industries.

3. Comprehensive national land development and balanced regional development.

3. Promotion of heavy and chemical industries.
4. Improving science, technology, and human resources.

6. Improving the living environment and national welfare.

| Fourth FYP | 1977–81 | 9.2 (5.7) |

1. Achievement of self-sustaining economy.
2. Promoting equity through social development.
3. Promoting technology and improving efficiency.

1. Self-sufficiency in investment capital.
2. Achieving balance payments equilibrium.
3. Industrial restructuring and promoting international competitiveness.
4. Industrial restructuring and enhancing international competitiveness.

5. Employment expansion and manpower development.
6. Improving living environment.
7. Expanding investment for science and technology.
8. Improving economic management and institutions.

Table 8.1 (*continued*)

Plan	Period	Growth Rate	Objectives	Major Policy Directions
Fifth FYP	1982–6	7.5 (8.7)	1. Establishing foundations for price stability and self-sustaining economy. 2. Technology improvement. 3. Improving quality of life. 4. Restructuring government's economic functions.	1. Eradicating inflation-oriented economic behaviour. 2. Increasing competitiveness in heavy industries. 3. Improving agricultural policy. 4. Overcoming energy constraints. 5. Improving financial institutions. 6. Readjusting government functions and rationalizing fiscal management. 7. Solidifying competitive system and promoting open-door policy. 8. Manpower development and promotion of science and technology. 9. Establishing new labour relations. 10. Expanding social development.
Sixth FYP	1987–91	7.3	1. Establishing socio-economic system. Promoting creative potential and initiative.	1. Expanding employment opportunities. 2. Solidifying foundation for price stability. 6. Improving national welfare through improved social equity. 7. Promoting market economic system and

readjusting government functions.

2. Industrial restructuring and improvement of technology.
3. Improving national welfare through balanced regional development and income distribution.

3. Realizing balance of payments surplus and reducing foreign debt.
4. Industrial restructuring and technology improvement.
5. Balanced regional and rural development.

Note: Prepared from the successive five-year plans formulated by Economic Planning Board. Goals and major policy issues of the *Fifth Five-Year Plan (1982–6)* are those of *Revised Five-Year Plan (1984–6)*. See Economic Planning Board, 1961, 1966, 1971, 1976, 1981, and 1986.
a: planned growth rate.
b: achieved growth rate.

transcends economics and may be the most important task for the poorest countries just starting their economic development. The legal framework determines the scope of property rights, regulations governing business activities, and the nature of contracts. These define the nature and scope of the economic system and the economic environment in general.

The objectives of the second plan (1967–71) aimed mainly at vitalizing the microeconomic functions of the government— namely, promoting the efficient allocation of resources through agricultural, industrial, trade, and social infrastructure policies.

The rapid growth of the economy caused increasing disparity between income classes, between export and domestic industries, between firms of different sizes, and between regions. As a consequence, the promotion of equity emerged as an important policy issue in the third plan (1972–6). The promotion of a more equal distribution of income was given even higher priority among the policy objectives of the fourth plan (1977–81).

Before 1963, when Korea's per capita income was less than US$100 a year, there was little excess income to redistribute from the better off and to the less fortunate. Accordingly, the distributive function of the government was largely restricted to providing the very poorest with food and other basic necessities. At the time there were no systematic income transfer programmes in Korea, such as food stamps, national health insurance, or social security, and the government tried chiefly to expand production and income.

As Korea's rural-agricultural economy began to change into an industry-oriented economy, the economy became increasingly complex and subject to business fluctuations and inflation. In this environment, economic stability emerged as a new policy issue. The fifth plan (1982–6) specified achieving economic stability as its major policy objective.

Maintaining economic stability was not considered a very important government function until the first oil crisis in 1973. Before then, the principal source of instability in the mainly agricultural economy was weather conditions, rather than business conditions. In 1988, stability emerged as one of the most important policy objectives. Both policymakers and the Korean people consider economic stability, especially in the face of growing labour-management friction, as a key policy goal.

From the fourth plan the government's key goals shifted from the quantitative aspects of economic growth to the qualitative aspects of life. The fourth plan placed much more emphasis on social development, and was even officially named the Five-Year 'Socio-economic' Development Plan.

The relative degree of importance of the government and private sectors has also changed substantially since the first plan. During the early planning periods, the government sector played the dominant role since the market system was not well developed. It was only as the urban-industrial sector expanded that market activities and the function of the market system began to modernize. As a consequence, the function of the private sector market system expanded greatly relative to that of the government. Since the fifth plan, particular emphasis has been put on enhancing free competition. The enhancement of market economic functions and the promotion of creative potential and an innovative spirit became the major economic policy goals of the Chun Doo Hwan government inaugurated in 1980. In the sixth plan (1987–91) it was listed as the most important objective.

One point that seems to be worth noting, based on the Korean experience, is that, at the early stages of development, microeconomic policies may play a more critical role than macroeconomic policies. In many cases, microeconomic approaches to development can be more practical and appropriate in simple developing economies. For instance, the Korean economy in 1955 was so simple that only 53 manufacturing establishments had more than 200 employees. To help these firms financially, the Korean government relied on the microeconomic approach of lending money directly to the individual firms rather than on the indirect, macroeconomic approach of increasing the money supply. Moreover, because development usually takes place in the form of specific investments, the microeconomic approach emphasizing project analysis appears to be more appropriate. Developing countries, especially in their early stages of development, may need microeconomists more than macroeconomists. Later, after the financial institutions and other market mechanisms mature somewhat, macroeconomists can play a more significant role.

Major Economic Policies of the Five-Year Plans

Just as the level of income and economic circumstances have changed since the beginning of the first plan in the early 1960s, so have economic policies. In this section we review briefly Korea's major economic policies in successive five-year plans.

The First Five-Year Plan (1962–1966)

The First Plan was prepared in a hurry by the military government that took power in 1961, and is thus considered one of the worst five-year plans in Korea. It was, as stated in the Second Plan (1966–71), no more than a list of costs and outputs of major development projects to be undertaken in the future and of broad policy proposals to achieve the goal of maximum growth of exports, income, and employment.[2]

The major contents of the fiscal and financial policies as stated in the plan document were largely an enumeration of reform measures concerning various policy systems, that is, the tax, budget, and monetary systems, financial markets, and foreign exchange systems. Trade policy was, however, relatively systematic. Its aim was to expand exports as much as possible by providing export firms with cheap loans, tax benefits, export compensation schemes, and various administrative supports.

Rapid economic development, on the basis of the principle of exports first, and maximum growth during the First Plan period resulted in the rapid expansion of both exports and output, but was accompanied by a rapid increase in prices as well. Inflation became very severe towards the end of the First Plan—the rate exceeded 30 per cent in 1964. As a consequence, the government needed to take various emergency measures to stabilize prices.

The Second Five-Year Plan (1966–1971)

From 1965, the government undertook the reform of various policy measures not only to stabilize prices but also to facilitate 'sound economic growth'. The major reforms include a September 1965 financial reform assuring positive and realistic interest rates, a March 1965 exchange rate reform normalizing highly overvalued exchange rates, a 1964 trade reform allowing generous importation of parts and machinery to be used for the production of export goods, and a 1965 fiscal reform stabilizing government expenditures. All these reforms were reflected in the Second Plan and carried further throughout the Second Plan period. They resulted in the rapid growth of exports and GNP, stable prices, and higher domestic savings during the period. But as both private and public investment expanded rapidly, investment requirements greatly exceeded domestic savings. The necessity to increase domestic savings and thereby reduce foreign borrowings became ever greater.

The Third Five-Year Plan (1972–1976)

The Third Plan put major emphasis on the promotion of heavy and chemical industries (HCI), and the year 1972 marks the beginning of Korea's HCI drive. Thus, fiscal and financial policies were directed to support HC industries. Provisions for more financial loans, special depreciation allowances, low tax rates, and better public services and administrative support to HC industries constituted the core of economic policies during the Third Plan period. A great effort was made to raise domestic savings to finance the HCI drive, but the amount of domestic savings fell far short of investment requirements. As a consequence foreign borrowing expanded enormously, and management of foreign borrowing and debt emerged as a major policy issue.

As industries grew rapidly, the gap between the urban-industrial and the rural-agricultural sectors increased substantially from the early 1960s. As rural/urban disparity became a serious issue towards the end of the 1960s, the government adopted a farm-price support policy to eliminate it, beginning in 1969. Although this has been one of the major causes for government budget deficits in Korea since 1969, this policy alone was not enough to eliminate the rural/urban disparity. More systematic measures were necessary. In this context the government undertook from 1971 the New Village (or *Saemaul*) Movement (NVM) to drastically improve the income and living conditions of rural people, and thereby remove the rural/urban gap. The NVM was, together with the HCI drive, a serious nation-wide effort to increase the income and equity of the Korean people throughout the 1970s.

The first oil crisis of 1973 affected the Korean people fundamentally. The economy became highly unstable and the inflation rate exceeded 40 per cent in 1974. The control of supply-side inflation emerged as a new issue in addition to the control of previous inflation, which was largely a demand-side inflation. Growth, equity, and stability have all since become important policy issues for Korea.

The Fourth Five-Year Plan (1977–1981)

Because of high inflation caused by the first oil crisis, stability was given relatively high policy priority when the preparation of the Fourth Plan was in progress in the mid-1970s. The government adopted the monetary rule of fixing money-supply growth at a prescribed constant rate of 20 per cent per annum. This was, of course, to stabilize the money supply, prices, and the overall economy. The government also adopted a value-added tax system to modernize Korea's tax administration. The major changes in trade policy during the Fourth Plan period included the expansion of 'policy imports' (imports related to exports), maintenance of realistic effective exchange rates, expansion of export subsidies, tax benefits, and foreign loans to export firms. Indirect support related to manpower training and research and development, for example, was also expanded. The government also improved administrative supports and expanded the number of industrial estates for export firms, including industrial export estates and free export zones. The general trading company system was introduced to expand trade in the world markets.

The Fifth Five-Year Plan (1982–1986)

In the early 1980s, the Korean economy was characterized by very slow growth, rapidly expanding foreign debt, and high inflation. The necessity to speed up export-led growth became ever greater. As a result, export promotion was given the highest policy priority again.

The major changes in trade policy included intensive promotion of export goods and market diversification, reform of the export support systems, lowering of tariff rates to expand importation of goods to be used in manufacturing, and expansion of loans associated with the exportation of durable goods such as machinery and ships. Foreign-debt management was also given high policy priority. The essence of the debt-management policy was to reduce the debt-service ratio from 13.2 per cent to 11.1 per cent during the Fifth Plan period. Because of the increasing foreign debt the necessity to expand domestic savings became even greater.

The major policy goal of the fiscal and financial policies was to increase the domestic savings rate from 2.9 to 23.5 per cent during the Plan period. Fiscal policy consisted largely of reduction of fiscal expenditures, expansion of depreciation allowances and R&D-related tax benefits to export firms, and tax reform to improve income distribution. The direction of monetary policy was to adjust upward the annual growth rate of the money supply to 22 per cent and to switch from direct to indirect controls. An emphasis was placed also on the development of financial markets.

The Sixth Five-Year Plan (1987–1991)

As of 1986 the Korean economy realized high economic growth, stable prices, and a trade surplus, and thus faced a new phase of growth. The broad policy direction of the Sixth Plan was to enhance the efficiency and strengthen the international competitiveness of the Korean economy in general by reforming the free enterprise market system. Thus, the major contents of policy reforms included the drastic reduction of various government regulations constraining growth of enterprises plus extensive promotion of liberalization of finance, imports, and foreign exchange. These issues are examined further in Chapter 12.

The major changes in economic policy include the gradual reduction of various fiscal subsidies, privatization of public enterprises, a shift from direct to indirect monetary controls, reduction of foreign borrowing, and improvement of exchange-rate management.

Decision-making Machinery

Many people, inside as well as outside Korea, believe the achievement of high economic growth since the early 1960s has been mainly the work of planning by a small elite, and that the 'visible hand' of government intervention in the operation of the market system has been constant and extensive. The perception of a 'Korea, Inc.' theory is an example of this sort of thinking. But how valid is it?

The most important characteristic of the decision-making machinery involved in formulating and implementing economic plans and policies in Korea is that it is headed by the President and as such is a nationwide apparatus. If necessary, for either formulating or implementing the plans or policies, this apparatus can mobilize any institution or policy instrument in Korea to help formulate or implement plans or policies. Secondly, the apparatus has been managed by leaders who are fully committed to economic development. President Chun Doo Hwan (1980–8), like President Park Chung Hee, threw the full commitment of his administration behind economic development.

Economic decision-making has been overwhelmingly a 'top-down' process. In the 1960s many government offices, including the economic ministries, were staffed by retired army generals and colonels. Because the President himself was a retired army general, Korea's economic decision-making process was very close to a 'General Headquarters' (GHQ) style, in which the President himself made all major decisions and settled policy disputes among his senior officials. Many Koreans complained that Korean economic policy in the 1960s was managed by command. Nevertheless, the GHQ style turned out to be very effective in initiating development and achieving the Park government's top priority goal of rapid growth.

As the level of economic development increased and the economy became increasingly complicated, however, the top-down style of decision-making was accompanied by increasing disadvantages. This was especially so with the massive investment in heavy industries and the over expansion of the shipbuilding industry on the eve of the second oil crisis in the late 1970s. The narrowness of the decision-making process was heavily criticized towards the end of the Park government by both bureaucrats and businessmen. The Chun Doo Hwan government quickly proclaimed its intention to open up and decentralize the economic decision-making process in Korea.

Because of Korea's economic decision-making process, the notion of 'Korea, Inc.' gained currency among foreign observers, who saw parallels with Japan. The Japanese government organizations that made up the core of 'Japan, Inc.' are widely believed to be the Ministry of Finance, the Bank of Japan, and the Ministry of International Trade and Industry (MITI). According to Yutaka Kosai and Yoshitaro Ogino, however, this overlooks an important aspect of the Japanese decision-making process—namely that not only Japanese government organizations but also politicians and political parties have played significant roles.[3] Japan's ruling Liberal Democratic Party, in particular, has played a leading role in the policy-making process. Strong political leaders have pushed through many important policies: Hayato Ikeda was a driving force behind the National

Income-Doubling Plan (1961–70) and Kakuei Tanaka proposed reorganizing the Japanese archipelago as outlined in his book *Building a New Japan*.[4]

In the case of Korea, the influence of politicians and political parties has been rather small. Under the Park regime it was almost negligible, since Park's approach to managing the economy relied on using a handful of capable technocrats and bureaucrats. Politicians were largely despised or ignored by the President. The influence of politicians and political parties increased somewhat under the Chun Doo Hwan government, and to a much greater extent with the beginning of the Roh Tae Woo administration.

The hierarchical order in the policy-making process is from the President to the Deputy Prime Minister, who heads the Economic Planning Board, and then to the head of the concerned ministry—whether the Minister of Trade and Industry, the Minister of Energy and Resources, or the Minister of Agriculture and Fisheries. Particularly notable in the Korean decision-making process is the role played by the President's Economic Secretary. Although this post is only of vice-ministerial rank, the Economic Secretary's influence on economic policy and the staffing of various economic ministries often has been equal to or greater than the influence of the Deputy Prime Minister, especially in the 1960s and early 1970s.

The Economic Planning Board has played a central role in preparing and implementing Korea's various economic plans and policies ever since the EPB was established in 1961. As soon as Park Chung Hee took power he created the Economic Planning Board by combining the Bureau of the Budget of the Ministry of Finance, the Bureau of Statistics of the Ministry of Home Affairs, and the planning functions of the Ministry of Reconstruction. The Minister of the EPB was given the concurrent title of Deputy Prime Minister and authorized to control, co-ordinate, and adjudicate among other ministries on economic matters. The DPM presides over the fortnightly Economic Ministers' Meeting attended by eleven economic ministries and the Minister of Foreign Affairs.

The EPB has been quite successful in its planning function and generally meets the three tests of a good planning function suggested by Nobel laureate economist Arthur Lewis. Lewis states that an effective agency must: '(1) have the support of the head of the government; (2) allow all the leading decisionmakers in the economy to participate in drawing up the plan: (3) control crucial decisions at the stage of implementation.'[5] The EPB clearly has had strong support from the President, encouraged participation of important decisionmakers in the preparation and implementation of economic plans, and was able to control and co-ordinate the decisions of various economic ministries through its control of the national budget.

The Korean decision-making machinery has been particularly effective at policy implementation. In the case of trade policy, for example, the monthly Export Promotion Meeting was institutionalized by the President to implement export expansion. The personal attendance of the President, economic ministers and other high-ranking officials, representatives of trading companies and related organizations, and heads of economic research institutes and selected academic economists underscored the high priority given to trade matters. I participated several times on behalf of the Korea Development Institute, observing personally how the meeting provided a forum for government officials, businessmen, economists, and policy makers to exchange views and to examine and improve trade policy.

Korea's decision-making machinery also has been highly outward-looking in the sense that economic technocrats and bureaucrats have sought to learn from the suggestions of foreign experts and studied the experiences of other countries through Korea's involvement with international organizations such as the World Bank and the International Monetary Fund. The decision-making machinery has relied also on formal and informal communication channels. Informal channels have traditionally had an important part in bureaucratic communications in Korea, as in other East Asian countries, and provide a means of circumventing the rigidity of formal hierarchical arrangements. Informal communications are highly democratic and perhaps as influential as formal channels. Typically, technocrats and bureaucrats gather needed information, data, expert views, and public opinion through various informal meetings before formalizing their policy proposals. Once policy objectives and directions are given formal sanction by the decision-making machinery, they are officially handed down as virtual 'orders' to the economic ministries and other institutions in charge of implementation.

Decision Making for the Sixth Five-Year Plan

The economic-planning machinery in Korea has changed with the rise in income and the accumulation of planning experience by economic technocrats. In this section we will examine the planning mechanism as it functioned for the Sixth Plan (1987–91).[6]

The broad outline of the Sixth Plan was set by the Cabinet Council in the presence of the President, the Prime Minister, and the ministers of all functional ministries. Based on this broad outline, an Economic and Social Development Council was convened to determine specific guidelines for the plan. The Prime Minister served as chairman of the Council, while the vice-chairmanship was filled by the Deputy Prime Minister in his concurrent role as head of the Economic Planning Board. The Council had a total of 50 members, including all cabinet ministers and other appointed members.

One notch below the Council, the Economic and Social Development Co-ordination Committee oversaw the integration of the various sectoral plans. The Committee's 40 members included all the Vice-Ministers and other appointed members. The drafting of sectoral plans was carried out by 40 separate Sectoral Planning Committees and subordinate Working Groups. As the head of one of these Sectoral Planning Committees I had the opportunity to personally see this process at work. The sector-specific plans were, in turn, co-ordinated by nine Sectoral Co-ordination Councils. Overall, more than 500 Korean experts in various fields participated in the plan's development.

Preparatory work for the Sixth Plan started in early April 1985 and was finalized by the President in late June 1986. The planning document was published, distributed, and publicized during the four-month period from July to October 1986.

The principal institution in charge of preparing, co-ordinating and writing the actual Sixth Plan document was the Korea Development Institute, the research institute of the Economic Planning Board. The command function of the planning machinery has generally decreased with each successive plan, but it is still regarded by the Korean people as having considerable power. As development continues, directed planning is likely to further decline in importance relative to continuous economic management through macroeconomic policy instruments.

Planning Implementation

One of the most important characteristics of Korea's style of plan implementation is its extensive use of both incentive and disincentive mechanisms. Particularly during the highly centralized and growth-oriented development strategy pursued by the government of President Park, the government made extensive use of discretionary authority in manipulating incentives such as subsidies, tax differentials and loans, and in using command procedures such as tax differentials, loans, and the termination of infrastructure services. Whenever incentive procedures were not effective the government was quick to employ disincentive mechanisms or command procedures to secure compliance by private firms. These disincentive mechanisms usually took the following forms.[7]

Tax Audits

Systematic and detailed investigation of tax returns by the Office of Tax Administration were used to discipline firms which did not co-operate with government economic policies. Such audits usually were very time consuming, sometimes lasting as long as six months. Korean firms came to see these investigations as near lethal punishment, and many firms were, in fact, driven into bankruptcy by a protracted audit and investigation.

Suspension of Bank Credit or Recall of Loans

The debt-equity ratio of most Korean firms is very high, usually exceeding three-to-one as a result of massive borrowing—typically at artificially low interest rates—to finance expansion.[8] Such high levels of indebtedness made firms dependent on bank credit even for their operating funds—and hence for their very survival. If the government cut off the supply of credit to a firm or recalled its loans, it could mean a lethal blow to any highly leveraged firm.

Disconnection of Infrastructure Services

There are basic infrastructure services such as electricity, water, roads, and telephones without which most firms cannot function. The government has used the denial of such services to punish firms that do not comply with the government economic policies.

For example, the MTI (Ministry of Trade and Industry) often disconnected electricity to firms that did not comply with the export targets set by the government!

Because of these strong disincentives, Korean firms soon learned that the best way to survive and prosper was to comply with the government's directives. For this type of implementation to work, effective communication and close consultation between firms and policymakers is essential. Moreover, if policy enforcers do not understand economic principles or do not consult with firms to set realistic goals, this type of forceful implementation can lead to widespread corruption and be highly destructive to the economy.

There is no doubt that in an increasingly complex economy such as Korea's, the 'impersonal rule of law' is preferable to the 'personal rule of men'. As Gunnar Myrdal and other economic liberals emphasize, non-discretionary measures—rather than discretionary measures—should be relied on as much as possible. Such thinking has become popular among Korean businessmen since President Park's death in 1979 and has been accepted by policy makers as a more desirable approach to implementation. This has been one of the important changes in the liberalization of economic management from the early 1980s, representing a major shift towards a more purely market-directed system and the readjustment of government functions.

Contrasts with Japan

Japanese economic policies have generally been governed more by a set of rules than by such a discretionary implementation, as in Korea under President Park. Kosai and Ogino point out that the major guidelines governing Japanese economic policies during the high economic growth period (1955–70) were:[9]

(a) Maintaining a stable exchange rate of 360 yen to the dollar.
(b) Ensuring a balanced budget
(c) Keeping the tax burden below 20 per cent of national income
(d) Using monetary measures to keep the balance of payments position at the target level.

Because of these rules, there was far less room for Japanese policy-makers to use discretionary implementation mechanisms during the high economic growth period. The absence in Korea of similar overall strictures opened the way for greater use of discretionary means to enforce government economic policy. In both countries, however, excellent co-operation between government and private firms also contributed greatly to the success of economic policies.

Not all government economic policies were the right ones, however. In the case of Korea, the over-expansion of heavy industries and of shipbuilding in the late 1970s were examples of failures resulting from excessive government direction. In addition, the decision to delay development of the automobile industry in Korea on the assumption that the country didn't have a comparative advantage was, in hindsight, probably wrong. In the case of Japan, the success of the car industry was due largely to an increasingly fierce competition among various Japanese car manufacturers rather than to successful government promotion.

Other differences between Korea and Japan concern the economic roles played by small companies and the behaviour of households.[10] In Japan, small firms made a major contribution to the rapid growth of the economy, and households acted as the main suppliers of domestic savings and investment capital. In Korea, however, the government relied chiefly on large companies to achieve the goal of expanding exports. The role of small firms was clearly considered of secondary importance. And because Korean households saved very little, the government has relied on foreign sources for investment capital.

All in all, the style of policymaking and implementation used in Korea in the 1960s and 1970s is effective only if it is carried out by capable and committed policymakers, and only in relatively early stages of development when the market system still functions poorly. As the economy develops and becomes increasingly complicated, greater reliance on market forces becomes imperative, and discretionary enforcement of policy decisions carries significant negative side effects.

9 The Consumption and Savings Behaviour of Koreans

Consumption and Savings in Korean Households

Patterns of consumption and savings among Koreans are basically similar to those in advanced countries and can be largely explained by the same basic economic theories. Factors such as disposable income, total household wealth, expected future income, and the rates of inflation and interest play a major role in determining consumption and savings behaviour in Korea just as in economically more advanced countries. At the same time, however, there are substantial differences between Korea and advanced countries in the level and growth rate of income, in social structure, in the structure of the household or consumption unit, in values, and in the utilization of various financial institutions. As a result, Korean economists have identified some distinctive characteristics of consumption and savings behaviour that distinguish Korean households from households in developed Western countries.[1]

National Character and Economic Behaviour

Savings and consumption patterns are greatly influenced by culture and values. As previously noted, Koreans traditionally ranked occupations in the order of scholar, farmer, manufacturer (or artisan) and, lastly, merchant. Scholars still enjoy the most respect in Korea, and opinion surveys typically find that becoming a scholar or university professor is the top aspiration among most university students. Becoming a government official is also a highly favoured occupation among Koreans. Many high school students choose the field of law with an eye to becoming a government official. Accordingly, and as only one example of the impact of values on economic behaviour, private saving to accumulate capital for private business was traditionally given very low priority in Korea.

Because Koreans value harmonious human relationships very

highly, a 'Dutch treat' is still considered uncouth by many Koreans. They consider generosity toward friends and relatives an important virtue, and there is a tendency for Koreans to spend a great deal on treating others and on maintaining human relationships. Ceremonies such as the first birthday, weddings, celebrations of the sixtieth birthday, and funerals are often on a much larger scale than the family can comfortably afford. Koreans—perhaps even more than Japanese and Chinese—tend to spend a great deal on drinking and socializing with others. This is the reason why the proportion of consumption expenditure on the item classified as 'others' in Table 9.1 is higher than one would normally expect.

In Korea a large proportion of economic activities are, in the words of Arthur Lewis, 'governed not by desire for income maximization, but by other, "non-economic" considerations.' As Lewis indicates, 'ritual laws' based on kinship, authority, and human relationships of various sorts, greatly affect economic transactions.[2] This is a prime reason for a large proportion of donations or grants, and informal—but not illegal—transactions in Korea. The gifts of money, goods and services, and charitable donations among Koreans, especially relatives, are part of everyday life. Whenever a Korean makes some money, he or she tends to think of helping others. This is why almost all Korean firms have some sort of charitable arrangement. What Kenneth Boulding calls 'grant economics', as well as the exchange system, is very important in the case of Korea.

Moreover, Koreans seem to value the present time more than the future. One distinguished Korean expert on this issue, Professor Yong-un Kim of Hanyang University, says that Koreans are very optimistic and tend to enjoy their present life very much no matter how sad it is.[3] An explanation is that Koreans have traditionally lived in extremely difficult and unstable circumstances and they tend to put more emphasis on living in the here-and-now than on saving for the future.

The above factors would appear to have a negative influence on savings, but there are many positive influences on savings in Korean culture as well. For instance, Koreans were traditionally forced to live by cultivating small pieces of land and had to save whatever they harvested to survive the long cold winter. This has led to the traditional sentiment that Korean women are 'born savers', whereas Korean men are 'born spenders'.

The Difference between Urban and Rural Households

Another key difference between Korea and the West is that household economic behaviour varies sharply in Korea between the urban-modern sector and the rural-traditional sector. Although the urban-modern sector is increasingly dominant, and rural households are behaving more and more like urban ones, the coexistence of two different but often overlapping modes of economic behaviour—what economists refer to as a dualistic economic structure—continues to put its imprint on household patterns of consumption and savings.

The main source of income for rural households in Korea is agriculture. Rice—limited by climate to one crop a year—still dominates Korean agriculture, especially in remote rural areas. Some secondary crops such as barley and wheat are planted as well, but rice is king, amounting to 78.1 per cent of Korea's total grain tonnage in 1988. In terms of value, rice looms even larger because of the government's rice price support policy. Since the economy of rural households is closely tied to the rice production cycle, their income and consumption time horizon (or planning period) may be as long as a year. Conversely, in the case of urban wage and salary earners, the income and consumption cycle may be as short as a month.

The typical consuming unit in the rural sector is the traditional extended family, whereas in the urban sector the basic consumption unit is the modern nuclear family. In both cases, however, decisions concerning consumption and savings customarily rest almost exclusively with the family head—although in practice his wife may be the chief budget manger.

The reasons for saving also are different between urban and rural households. For instance, housing is a major goal of saving for many middle- and lower-income urban households, and expenditures on housing consititute a substantial proportion of household income (averaging 30.9 per cent for urban households in 1987—see Table 9.1) while housing expenditure constitutes only a small proportion of income for farm households (8.4 per cent in 1987). At the same time, educational and miscellaneous expenditures are relatively higher in rural areas. The reason why rural families spend a larger proportion of their income on education than urban families is that they have to send their children to urban areas for a higher education. Children's expenditure on

Table 9.1 The Consumption Expenditure of Urban and Rural Households (1,000 won)

	1965		1975		1985		1988	
	Urban	Rural	Urban	Rural	Urban	Rural	Urban	Rural
Amount (1,000 won)	117.4	100.5	783.7	616.3	4,783.8	4,690.8	6,996.3	6,031.0
Share (%)	100.0	100.0	100.0	100.0	100.0	100.0	100.0	100.0
Foods	56.7	53.0	43.6	47.3	29.8	28.4	27.9	26.2
Clothing	6.5	8.0	8.7	6.9	6.1	4.0	6.7	4.5
Housing	13.8	11.7	17.5	13.3	27.0	7.6	30.9	9.0
Education	4.4	4.5	6.5	6.2	6.2	13.0	6.1	11.1
Medical	1.2	3.0	4.0	3.7	5.7	5.2	7.6	5.8
Transportation	2.0	1.6	4.1	2.1	5.1	4.1	5.6	4.7
Others	15.4	18.2	15.6	20.5	20.1	37.6	15.2	38.7

Note: Urban household expenditure on housing includes imputed rental value of *chonsae* (or key) money and owner-occupied housing.

Sources: Computed from the Bank of Korea, *Economic Statistics Yearbook*, 1971, 1978, 1981, and 1989, Economic Planning Board/ Bureau of Statistics, *Annual Report on The Family Expenditure Survey*, 1980, 1985, 1988; and Ministry of Agriculture and Fisheries, *Report on the Results of Farm Household Economic Survey*, various years.

boarding and lodging, transportation, and communications, when away from home, tends to be also included in the educational expenditure of rural families.

Values, tastes, and habits of consumers in the rural sector are typically more traditional and less tied to the monetized economy than is the case with urban residents. Rural households tend to spend a larger proportion of their income on 'traditional activities' including large—and many critics say wasteful—ceremonies. Nobel laureate economist Arthur Lewis and others have shown that dualism in economic behaviour between the rural and urban sectors is substantial in most developing countries.[4] Recent studies on Korea have also shown that dualism in demand and savings patterns between farmers and urban workers is quite pronounced.[5]

Although the principal consumption theories and models that have been developed for advanced countries also explain consumption and savings behaviour in Korea, they appear to explain urban consumer behaviour better than rural consumer behaviour. Historically, the existing models were developed with reference to highly urbanized and industrialized countries, and they generally have limited applicability to poor developing countries—such as Korea was in the 1960s—which are only partially urbanized and have a large rural-agricultural population.

Indeed, for countries like Korea which are undergoing rapid urbanization and massive movements of rural people to the city, to include the influence of urbanization on consumption in the model may be useful in the analysis of the changing pattern of consumption and savings behaviour. The level of urbanization in Korea was merely 28.5 per cent in 1960, but increased to 68.7 per cent by 1987 (see Table 2.4) and is expected to eventually level out at about 75 per cent—the level seen in such industrialized countries as Japan and the USA. The average level of urbanization for 19 industrial market economies was 75 per cent in 1987.[6] The proportion of non-farm households to total households also increased rapidly from 46.4 per cent to 82.6 per cent between 1960 and 1988 (see Table 9.2).

In an earlier study of consumption, I proposed a consumption function model for developing countries that took urbanization into account and tested it using Korean data for the 1953–75 period.[7]

The results indicate that the propensity or tendency to con-

Table 9.2 The Change in Households and Employment Status, 1960–1987 (in thousands)

	1960	1965	1970	1975	1980	1985	1987
Total households (A)							
Number	4,378	5,184	5,857	6,754	7,969	9,589	10,513
Average size (persons)	5.7	5.6	5.4	5.1	4.6	4.2	4.1
Farm households (B)							
Number	2,349	2,507	2,483	2,379	2,162	1,996	1,826
Average size (persons)	6.2	6.3	5.8	5.6	5.0	4.4	4.2
Share (%, B ÷ A)	53.6	48.4	42.4	35.2	27.1	20.8	17.4
Total workers (C)							
Number	—	8,522	9,745	11,830	13,683	14,970	16,870
Self-employed (D)							
Number	—	3,019	3,331	4,012	4,645	4,679	5,093
Non-agricultural (E)	—	512	1,250	1,652	2,271	2,793	3,239
Share (%, D ÷ C)	—	35.4	34.2	33.9	33.9	31.3	30.1
(%, E ÷ C)	—	6.0	12.8	14.0	16.6	18.7	19.2
Farm workers (F)							
Number	—	4,810	4,916	5,425	4,654	3,733	3,319
Share (%, F ÷ C)	—	56.4	50.4	45.9	34.0	24.9	20.7

Sources: The Bank of Korea, *Economic Statistics Yearbook*, various years; Byung-Nak Song, 1984; and Economic Planning Board, National Bureau of Statistics, *Annual Report on The Economically Active Population*, 1963–88.

sume out of rural income is lower than out of urban worker income. This confirms that in Korea, as in most countries, farmers have a higher savings rate than urban workers. The propensity to consume by urban capitalists is also much lower, and the propensity to save higher than for either rural farmers or urban workers—as in advanced countries. This model can explain, separately, not only the dualistic behaviour of consumption and savings in rural and urban areas, but also the difference in consumption and savings behaviour between workers and capitalists.

Consumption Pattern and Government Policy

Equity associated with consumption overlooks all the problems of differences in taste and spending now versus saving for the future. Nevertheless, what goods people have or value are the most visible reflection of economic disparities. I have found that the following typology of goods is useful in examining disparities associated with household and individual consumption.

At an early stage of development—income levels of up to US$600–700 in 1985 prices—people most value small consumer goods, especially radios, bicycles, and sewing machines (the three 'smalls'). These are the commodities that people in poor countries such as China and India desire to possess. There may be many other goods causing consumption disparity as well. But these three may be the most important ones. The disparity Koreans felt most in the 1960s was of this sort. As Koreans' income passed the US$600–700 level in the early 1970s, they could easly afford to buy such small consumer goods and no longer feel disparity based on having or not having the three 'smalls'.

Further up the income ladder, middle-range consumer durables, namely black-and-white television sets, refrigerators, and washing machines—the three 'middles'—are popular. These are most prevalent at a per capita income level of up to US$1,600–1,700. The disparity Koreans felt most in the 1970s was associated largely with having or not having the three 'middles'. Since Korea's per capita income level passed this level in the late 1970s, most Koreans do not now focus much attention on these goods. Countries such as Thailand, Paraguay, and Turkey, still have the problem of consumption disparity associated with these three 'middles'.

Paul Samuelson, the first American Nobel laureate economist, calls a colour television set, car, and cooler (including air conditioner) 'the 3 Cs'. These three become key consumption targets as people's per capita income exceeds the US$1,600–1,700 level. The consumption disparity Koreans feel most strongly at present is associated with these 3 Cs, especially whether one can or cannot own a private automobile. There were only 16 private automobiles per 1,000 persons in Korea in 1986, much lower than the rate in advanced countries, where the figures in 1983 were 221 for Japan, 527 for the U.S and 402 for West Germany (see Table 10.6).

In the process of development the Korean government has worried about highly visible consumption disparities. The government has tried hard to discourage these by levying heavy excise taxes on so-called luxury goods. The best-known example is colour television sets. The government initially allowed Korean firms to produce colour televisions only for export. Domestic sales were strictly prohibited until 1980, when colour television broadcasting was finally allowed. Automobiles were also considered a luxurious and 'disparity-creating' item until 1987 and, thus, ownership was discouraged through heavy taxes.

Most people who supported this policy failed to recognize that it greatly handicapped the growth of colour television production. This is a good example of how the notion of trade-off between growth and equity can frequently be deceptive. The real problem seems to be that this kind of policy can result in the sacrifice of both growth and equity. That is, the policy of discouraging ownership of private automobiles and colour televisions also reduced manufacturing employment opportunities for working class families, thereby helping to increase income disparities.

Why Do the Japanese and Taiwanese Save More than Koreans?

Although Korea, Japan, and Taiwan are similar with respect to their recent rapid development, they are quite different in terms of savings behaviour. Japan is widely recognized to have the highest savings rate in the free world. Next to Japan is Taiwan. Korea has long been far behind these two countries in terms of the savings ratio, although this pattern is now changing.[8] As a consequence, Korea has relied heavily on foreign savings to finance her development (see Table 9.3).

This difference between high rates of savings in both Japan and Taiwan and the low savings rate in Korea has been of considerable interest to economists and policy makers. The rest of this section examines the factors that appear to account for this contrast in savings behaviour.

In his famous comparative study of Taiwan and Korea, Tibor Scitovsky provides several reasons why Taiwanese save more than Koreans: his explanations are presented here, but in a different order:[9]

(a) Economic growth was faster in Taiwan than in Korea.
(b) Relatively more Taiwanese save up to establish their own businesses.
(c) Bonus income in Taiwan forms a larger part of total income than in Korea.
(d) Existing firms in Taiwan save more than those in Korea.
(e) Taiwanese spend less on education than Koreans.
(f) Taiwanese generally save up more for their old age than Koreans.

In reviewing a variety of studies of Japan's world-record saving rate, Miyohei Shinohara notes that most studies give multiple reasons for Japan's exceptional savings rate.[10] The most frequently cited reasons are, in order:

(a) High growth rate of the Japanese economy
(b) The Japanese bonus system
(c) Japan's limited social welfare system
(d) Japan's national character and the 'demonstration effect'
(e) The high proportion of individual proprietorship
(f) The lack of consumer credit
(g) An assets effect
(h) The age composition of Japanese society

Several of these factors—rapid growth, large bonuses, saving for individual proprietorships, and saving for retirement—also feature in Scitovsky's explanation of Taiwan's high savings rate and provide a starting point for examining different hypotheses that may explain Korean savings behaviour.

Major Savings Hypotheses

The Growth Rate Hypothesis

Nobel laureate economist Franco Modigliani of the Massachusetts Institute of Technology and James Dusenberry of Har-

Table 9.3 National and Foreign Savings in Korea (per cent)

	National Savings				Total (C) (=A+B)	Foreign Savings (D)	Stat. Disc.	Gross Domestic Investment (E) (=C+D)	Gross Domestic Investment to GNP (A/GNP)	National Savings to GNP
	Private		(A)	Govt. (B)						
	Pers.	Corp.	Total							
1962	-3.5	41.0	37.5	-12.0	25.5	83.3	-8.8	100.0	12.8	3.3
1963	18.5	31.5	50.0	-2.0	48.0	57.5	-5.5	100.0	18.1	8.7
1964	25.0	34.0	59.0	3.3	62.3	48.8	-11.1	100.0	14.0	8.7
1965	1.2	36.5	37.7	11.4	49.1	42.6	8.3	100.0	15.0	7.4
1966	19.1	23.0	42.1	12.8	54.9	39.1	6.0	100.0	21.6	11.8
1967	6.1	27.1	33.2	18.7	51.9	40.2	7.9	100.0	21.9	11.4
1968	11.3	23.4	34.7	23.6	58.3	43.1	-1.4	100.0	25.9	15.1
1969	24.5	20.3	44.8	20.5	65.3	36.9	-2.2	100.0	28.8	18.8
1970	14.1	26.2	40.3	24.3	64.6	34.7	-0.7	100.0	26.6	17.3
1971	15.2	24.5	39.7	17.8	57.5	41.6	0.8	100.0	25.1	14.6
1972	29.0	37.1	66.1	9.1	75.2	24.2	0.6	100.0	22.2	16.5
1973	35.9	38.8	74.7	12.0	86.7	14.9	-1.5	100.0	25.7	22.8

Year										
1974	22.9	31.5	54.4	6.2	60.5	37.3	2.1	100.0	31.6	19.9
1975	22.0	30.6	52.6	8.7	61.3	37.3	1.4	100.0	30.0	19.1
1976	34.4	35.4	69.8	16.6	86.4	10.0	3.7	100.0	25.6	23.9
1977	44.3	31.2	75.5	16.3	91.8	4.5	3.7	100.0	31.2	27.5
1978	42.6	26.3	68.9	16.8	85.7	13.5	0.8	100.0	35.6	28.5
1979	34.5	20.9	55.4	18.1	73.6	24.8	1.6	100.0	31.2	28.1
1980	20.4	27.4	47.8	16.9	64.6	35.7	−0.3	100.0	31.3	21.9
1981	22.0	27.1	49.1	18.5	67.6	32.3	0.1	100.0	30.3	20.5
1982	34.7	27.8	62.5	21.5	84.1	15.9	—	100.0	27.4	23.1
1983	34.3	35.0	69.3	24.2	93.5	6.5	—	100.0	28.9	27.0
1984	38.4	34.4	72.8	22.1	94.9	5.1	—	100.0	30.8	29.2
1985	40.6	35.7	76.3	22.3	98.6	1.4	—	100.0	30.0	29.6
1986	50.8	42.8	93.6	23.0	116.6	−16.6	—	100.0	28.8	33.6
1987	42.5	44.4	86.9	23.6	110.4	−10.4	—	100.0	29.8	35.6
1988	—	—	—	—	115.7	−15.7	—	100.0	30.6	35.3

Notes: Pers. = personal savings; Corp. = corporate savings; Govt. = government savings; Stat. Disc. = statistical discrepancy. Ratios are based on current prices.

Sources: Computed from the Bank of Korea, *National Income Accounts,* 1984, *New National Accounts,* 1986, and Economic Planning Board, *Major Statistics of the Korean Economy,* 1988, 1989. Data after 1981 are from the Bank of Korea, *Economic Statistics Yearbook,* 1989.

vard University contend that consumption and savings are largely
determined by this year's income level relative to the previous
top income level.[11] This is because people tend to maintain the
consumption patterns they are accustomed to based on past income, and save most income above this former level. For people
in very rapidly growing countries like Korea in the 1960s and the
1970s, each year represents a new high over the previous peak
income level. Thus, according to the relative income hypothesis,
the difference between this year's and last year's incomes—that
is, the income growth rate—becomes the major determinant of
savings. The higher the growth rate, the higher the saving ratio.

While this hypothesis is often used to explain the high savings
ratio of Japan and Taiwan during the period of their rapid economic growth, it has also been used to explain the high savings ratio
in Korea. Jeffrey Williamson of Harvard argues that during
Korea's early growth spurt 'most of the rise in the domestic
savings rate in Korea up to 1971 or 1972 can be attributed to
successful growth.'[12]

The Transitory versus Permanent Income Hypothesis

The nature of income also influences people's decisions concerning savings and consumption. If the increase in income is of a
transitory nature, such as an irregular salary bonus, people tend
to consume less and save more. In contrast, if the increase in
income is of a permanent nature, people tend to consume more
and save less. This is the permanent versus transitory income
hypothesis—with permanent or life-cycle income defined as 'the
level of income that a person receives on average through good
and bad economic weather.'[13]

In a rapidly growing economy, the proportion of transitory
income tends to be high relative to permanent income. In addition, the related 'consumption inertia' hypothesis argues that
households take some time to adjust to changes in income,
whether these changes are temporary or permanent. Accordingly, when incomes are growing rapidly, consumption expenditure
tends to lag behind, causing savings to rise. These related hypotheses not only can be used to explain the high savings ratios in
Japan and Taiwan during the period of their rapid growth, but
also apply to Korea. Taken at face value, however, it is not

evident from these hypotheses why Korean savings behaviour until recently lagged so far behind.

The Bonus Hypothesis

According to the savings hypothesis advocated by Milton Friedman of the University of Chicago, the income of a transitory nature tends to generate a higher propensity to save than income of a permanent nature. A bonus is transitory in nature, and if it occupies a large proportion of income, it will lead to a higher propensity to save. Scitovsky and other scholars have suggested that because the proportion of bonus income is higher in Japan than anywhere else in the free world, so is the savings ratio. Along the same lines, they suggest that although bonuses are quite common among Korean firms, they account for a smaller portion of income than in either Taiwan or Japan—providing one of the reasons why Korea's savings ratio has been the lowest of the three until recently.

Another kind of transitory income worth noting in this regard is income resulting from bribery, donations, hand-outs, and the like, which are quite common in some developing countries. According to a 1986 study by the Federation of Korean Industries, such 'informal' outlays by Korean firms amounted to one per cent of total sales.[14] According to the transitory income hypothesis, this type of irregular income should lead to a higher savings rate. But in fact this does not appear to have been the case. One can perhaps hypothesize that if such income is truly unexpected and wholly a windfall gain, the propensity to save out of such income may be very low.

Family Security versus Social Security

Martin Feldstein of Harvard argues that a comprehensive social security system works to discourage household savings. According to this hypothesis, the savings ratio should be high in Korea as well as Japan and Taiwan since all three countries had virtually no social security systems until very recently. Tibor Scitovsky notes that the 'insufficiency of social security benefits, which forces people to save more for their old age, and the limited availability of consumer credit and mortgage loans' are the two simplest and most often advanced explanations of the high savings rate in Japan.[15]

People in advanced Western countries with extensive welfare programmes tend to look to the government for assistance in old age or in an economic downturn. In Asia, especially in Korea, Japan and Taiwan, most people still rely on their families for economic security. By custom and because of the general weakness of governmental social security programmes, security for an individual in these countries generally is a private or family concern. This way of thinking encourages higher savings ratios and also has worked to delay the introduction of social welfare programmes in these three countries.

The family security system is especially important in Korea, where, under the profound influence of Confucianism, the family retains its importance as the basic economic, social, educational, and welfare unit.

The Confucian ethic that stresses family relationships causes Koreans to feel strong ties and loyalties to the family, and this explains why many Korean parents sacrifice themselves for the education of their children, why Korean wives sacrifice their own happiness for the sake of their husbands and children, and why Korean sons may sacrifice their careers for the happiness of their parents. There is a practical economic aspect to this family-centred ethic as well. Since parents rely on their children for old age security, they may consciously or unconsciously invest in their children's education so that their children can increase their earning ability.

However, traditional values and relationships among family members have changed with the development of Korea's economy. These changes put pressures on Koreans to increase private savings for their old age, partly displacing sons and relatives as the source of older people's security.

The Proprietorship Hypothesis

Another theory argues that private entrepreneurs and those who want to go into business for themselves try to save more. As a result, the hypothesis goes, the larger the proportion of sole proprietors in a society, the higher the savings ratio. Some economists accordingly have explained the higher savings ratio in Japan and Taiwan on these grounds, as there are more established and would-be individual businessmen in the former two countries than in Korea.

Traditionally many bright young Korean students hoped to become high-ranking government officials. It is still the aspiration of many Koreans to enter law schools and pass the civil service examinations and end up with senior government posts. Until very recently, sole proprietorship was not a very attractive occupation to many Koreans.

As pointed out by Scitovsky, the Taiwanese development strategy has kept the size of firms small and encouraged the number of firms to multiply. But the Korean-style growth pattern, on the contrary, has relied, as already noted in Chapter 5, mainly on large firms. Thus, the entry and growth of small firms in Korea has been relatively small until very recently. In 1986 the number of manufacturing establishments in Taiwan was 76,886, proportionately much larger than the Korean figure of 76,042— even though Korea has twice Taiwan's population. Although the growth rate of manufacturing firms became faster in recent years in Korea, the diffusion of small firm ownership continues to be far greater in Taiwan. The number of manufacturing establishments per 100,000 people in Korea was 70 in 1976 but increased rapidly to 183 in 1986. But it is still much smaller than either the Taiwanese figure of 395 or the Japanese figure of 350 in the same year.

The birth and growth of small firms in Taiwan were mainly financed through the owners' own savings, but in Korea most new firms depended on borrowed capital. Consequently, the ratio of indebtedness of Korean firms typically has been very high until recently. For all manufacturing firms in Korea the debt ratio in 1987 averaged 340.1 per cent, and peaked at 487.9 per cent in the 1980s.

The Interest-rate Hypothesis

According to this hypothesis, realistic real interest rates, assuring an adequate level of return on savings, are crucial to raising the savings ratio. Surprisingly, although it would appear to be common sense that high real rates of interest would encourage savings, this assumption has been challenged by many economists. Although some supporters of the life cycle and transitory income hypotheses suggest a positive relationship between interest rates and savings, they believe that the relationship may not be very strong. More systematic empirical research on this issue is clearly essential, especially in developing countries, where currently available data are insufficient.

In the case of Korea and Taiwan, however, the relationship between interest rates and saving rates appears to be, contrary to economists' observations, far stronger than in advanced countries. One possible explanation is that people in wealthier countries usually save for the long term—namely, for their retirement years. But people in poorer countries such as Korea, especially until the early 1970s, save for the very near future. The planning horizon for savings tends to distort the relationship between interest rates and the propensity to save. Those who save for retirement will tend to do so on a regular basis regardless of the interest rate, weakening the linkage between interest rate and savings ratios. For poorer people in developing countries who save for short-term goals, however, small differences in the interest rate can make a significant difference in how much money is diverted from consumption to savings especially when interest rates are high.

This sensitivity to interest rates may explain why most poorer Koreans put their money in the informal—or kerb—financial market. The kerb market has traditionally provided a high return, although at relatively high risk (see Table 9.4). In contrast, the government-controlled rates available from the organized savings institutions frequently do not even keep up with the rate of inflation. Because of high inflation rates, official bank interest rates in Korea were negative throughout most of the 1970s (see Table 9.4). Despite the risks of loss of unsecured 'kerb market' savings, the unorganized money market apparently reached its peak during 1964–5 when kerb market lending was equal in volume to about 40 per cent of total regular bank loans.

Since 1983 Korea has adopted a high interest rate policy in the organized banking sector and has succeeded in substantially raising the level of national savings. By 1986 it exceeded 30 per cent of GNP (see Table 9.3). In the case of Taiwan, Lawrence J. Lau of Stanford indicates that the 'twin strategies of export promotion and realistic interest rates caused not only dramatic economic growth—but also a tremendous improvement in the living standards of the average citizen.'[16] It can be said that the same holds true for Korea.

Table 9.4 Nominal versus Real Interest Rates, 1962–1988 (per cent)

	Nominal Interest Rate		Rate of Inflation[2] (C)	Real Interest Rate		Household Savings Ratio[3]
	Bank[1] (A)	Kerb Market (B)		(A–C)	(B–C)	
1962	15.0	—	18.4	−3.4	—	−1.2
1963	15.0	52.4	29.3	−14.3	23.1	4.0
1964	15.0	61.4	30.0	−15.0	31.4	4.1
1965	26.4	58.8	6.2	20.2	52.6	0.2
1966	26.4	58.7	14.5	11.9	44.2	5.0
1967	26.4	56.4	15.6	10.8	40.8	1.7
1968	25.2	55.9	16.1	9.1	39.8	3.8
1969	22.8	51.2	14.8	8.0	36.4	9.1
1970	22.8	50.8	15.6	7.2	35.2	4.6
1971	20.4	46.3	16.2	11.6	30.1	4.8
1972	12.0	38.9	19.2	−7.2	19.7	8.1
1973	12.0	39.2	13.2	−1.2	26.0	11.8
1974	15.0	37.6	29.6	−14.6	8.0	9.3
1975	15.0	41.3	24.7	−9.7	16.6	8.5
1976	16.2	40.5	17.7	−1.5	22.8	11.8
1977	14.4	38.1	16.3	−1.9	21.8	16.5
1978	18.6	41.7	20.6	−2.0	21.1	17.8
1979	18.6	42.4	19.3	−0.7	23.1	16.5
1980	19.5	45.0	25.8	−6.3	19.2	8.7
1981	16.2	35.3	16.2	0.0	19.1	8.8
1982	8.0	30.6	7.7	0.3	22.9	12.9
1983	8.0	25.8	2.9	5.1	22.9	14.0
1984	10.0	24.9	3.8	6.2	21.1	16.6
1985	10.0	24.0	4.1	5.9	19.9	17.2
1986	10.0	24.3	2.3	7.7	22.0	21.1
1987	10.0	—	3.7	6.3	—	—
1988	10.0	—	4.1	5.9	—	—

Notes: 1. Nominal interest rate implies the bank interest rate on time deposits for a period of one or more years.
2. Based on GNP deflator.
3. Household savings ratio = personal savings divided by personal disposable income.

Sources: Computed from The Bank of Korea, *Economic Statistics Yearbook*, 1984, 1988 and Yung Chul Park, 1988.

Savings and the Financial System in Korea

Until recently, rural Koreans relied mainly on informal financial institutions rather than on banks or other modern formal financial institutions. There were three reasons for this. Firstly, financial institutions were not well developed or easily accessible to rural people, who found it extremely inconvenient to walk to town to do their banking. Secondly, village economic life for the most part was not 'monetized' or 'commercialized' and, thus, was largely detached from the modern financial sector. Finally, Koreans, until recently, had little confidence in formal financial institutions which were under tight government control and often handicapped by misguided policy considerations which, for example, generally kept official interest rates well below their free-market rate.

Incessant social, political, and economic unrest also undermined the credibility of banks. Koreans' distrust of formal financial institutions took root during the period of harsh Japanese colonial rule, and was made worse by the Korean War (1950–3), the 1960 Student Revolution, the 1961 military coup, and drastic economic measures such as the 1962 currency reform which froze bank deposits, and the August 1972 emergency measures that erased informal debts of all kinds.

Conversely, Korea's informal financial instutions have a long and important history. Yung Chul Park and David C. Cole calculate that 'the size of the unregulated (or informal) financial market was about half that of the deposit-taking banks in terms of the volume of credit outstanding' even in the 1970s.[17]

One of the most important informal financial arrangements in Korea is the *kay*, a form of rotating credit club. This is perhaps one of the most common and distinctive characteristics of financial activities in traditional Korea. The *kay* typically served as a social network intended to promote mutual help, co-operation, and friendship among members of the *kay* by using the *kay* money (traditionally in the form of grain) contributed by the members to capitalize collective activities. While still in junior high school, the author participated with three other friends in a simple form of the traditional *kay*. Each of the four members contributed 40 kg of unpolished rice and lent it to a villager at a real interest of 50 percent a year. This *kay* rice was expected to increase from 160 kg in the first year to 240 kg the next year, and so on. To junior high school students, such an accumulation appeared to be marvellous. At the time, a 50 percent rate of interest was very common among Korean villagers. But our *kay* folded after several rounds of accumulation when the government froze the payment of rural debts and the debtor disappeared from the village.

A more common type of *kay* among urban Koreans in recent years is operated on a financial basis rather than on the basis of social ties. Park and Cole explain the modern *kay* in the following way:[18]

A lump-sum fund (*kay* fund) composed of variable contributions, based on interest payment calculations, from each member of the *kay*, is distributed (or more properly loaned out), at fixed intervals and as a whole, to each member in order of a predetermined sequence (sequence *kay*), by auction (auction *kay*), or by lottery. As a saver-depositor, the longer the duration of a *kay* member's deposit (that is, the later his position in the sequence *kay*), the higher the rate of return on his installment deposit. As a borrower, the longer the duration of his loan (that is, the earlier his position in the sequence *kay*), the higher the rate of interest to be paid. [Their notation *kye* is replaced by *kay*.]

Participating in a *kay* was very common for income earners of all classes in the past. The amount of money saved by this means was substantial. Park and Cole found from various surveys conducted in Seoul in the 1960s and 1970s that 45–90 per cent of urban households participated in various *kay* clubs. One 1971 survey revealed that the sample households contributed up to 32 per cent of their monthly wage income to *kay* installment payments, and 40 per cent of the *kay* members lent their *kay* funds to others for non-consumption purposes, while the income from such loans amounted to about 7 per cent of household income.[19] This confirms that Koreans saved extensively through *kay* groups, and if the savings in both formal and informal institutions are combined, the savings ratio in Korea in the 1960s and 1970s might not be as low as the statistics on bank savings alone indicate.

Other Forms of Investment and Saving

Jeffrey Williamson of Harvard indicates that the marginal private savings rate in Korea during 1960–74 was only 13.8 per cent, much lower than that predicted by life-cycle models. He contends, however, that 'capital gains in land and other quasi-fixed factors may have served to deflect private saving from conventional and more socially productive channels, thus accounting for the low measured private savings rates in the past'.[20] This suggests that a large proportion of savings in Korea in the past took the form of land and other valuable assets, even while savings through formal financial institutions remained surprisingly low. This is consistent with the high value Koreans traditionally put on land. While the Chinese are said to value gold more than land, in the past Koreans considered land the only trustworthy asset. For the economy as a whole, however, savings cannot take the form of land.

Another factor that appears to affect Korean consumption and savings behaviour is the enormous—even excessive—enthusiasm for education. Virtually all parents desire a university education for their children. Entering into a first-class university is virtually a life-and-death matter for many Korean students and their parents. Enthusiasm for education leads Koreans to 'invest' in tutors and tuition—forms of human capital investment rather than normal consumption. Investing in human capital formation may be more pronounced in Korea than anywhere else in the world, and may substitute in part for other forms of saving.

Koreans' investment in the form of physical capital may be smaller than that of either the Japanese or the Taiwanese. But because Koreans expend a large proportion of their savings in human capital through education for themselves or their children, their investment in human capital may not be smaller than the Japanese or Taiwanese. If investments in both physical and human capital are added together, Koreans' savings rates may not be as low as is often assumed.

The Korean economy grew at the highest rate in the world in 1986 and 1987. Equally important is the fact that this growth was accompanied by a high savings ratio, a trade surplus, and very stable prices. Many people think that this remarkable growth was due in large measure to Koreans' massive investment in human capital in earlier years.

10   Equity of Income and Economic Life

For to every person who has something, even more will be given, and he will have more than enough; but the person who has nothing, even the little that he has will be taken away from him. (Matthew 25:29)

Equity is a multi-dimensional issue with deep roots in values, culture, and psychology. This makes it one of the most difficult issues facing Korea at the present time. Koreans appear to have changed their views on equity due to the rise in incomes as the economy has developed. When they were very poor, especially immediately after the Korean War, their major concern about equity was associated with obtaining basic human needs, and many people survived on materials provided by domestic and foreign welfare organizations. As the economy improved to the stage where most problems of absolute poverty could be solved, the 'equity' issue shifted to the question of 'relative wealth' and, more broadly, the whole question of the quality of life.

Some changes in real and perceived shifts in relative equity reflect transitional phases of the growth process. Simon Kuznets hypothesized that the pattern of income equality in the course of development follows a U-shaped curve. That is, the degree of equality of income distribution is likely to be very high at early stages of development as most people come to enjoy higher incomes, more wealth, better employment opprotunities, and the benefits of advanced social-security systems. Between these stages, however, inequality can first worsen after development takes off, and only begin to lessen some years later. The historical pattern of income distribution in Korea appears to have followed this pattern.

This chapter examines equity with respect to income, wealth, and the quality of life. Consumption reflects the amount of goods and services actually consumed and, thus, indicates the actual level and distribution of material welfare. Equity with respect to consumption was discussed in the preceding chapter. Income, however, indicates potential consumption—including present consumption and future consumption, that is, savings. Wealth represents the potential to increase income and thereby consumption in the future. It is worth noting that regardless of the change in people's concern with equity, policy makers have placed the emphasis mainly on income. GNP and per capita GNP have so far been the dominant yardsticks in measuring growth as well as welfare in Korea.

Korea is known to have a relatively high degree of income equality, for reasons that are both historical and structural. Measuring economic equity is fraught with difficulties, however.

Although the distribution of wealth is perhaps the most comprehensive measure of economic equality and inequality, its measurement is especially difficult because market values of various assets that comprise wealth—especially land—have changed rapidly in Korea. Because of the rapid changes in land prices and associated capital gains, even owners themselves may not know the exact value of their assets. The change in the value of financial assets has also been very rapid. For instance, the average market price of stocks of 502 firms listed on the Korean stock market as of 1989, have more than tripled since 1986. The overall stock price index increased from 227.8 to 693.2 between 1986 and 1988.[1] The other reason that makes the measurement of wealth difficult is that owners hide assets to avoid taxes and problematic publicity.

Measuring equality in terms of income is also hard in Korea, where the population is highly mobile and income keeps changing. This makes consistent sampling of representative households a serious problem, thus undermining the quality of a key data base.

Moreover, as with wealth, people also tend to underreport their incomes. This is especially so when the income results from underground or informal economic activities or abuse of power and position. Also, family members or even the income earners themselves may not know the exact amount of their household's monthly income since business accounting is usually settled on an annual basis. Conceptual or definitional differences in income between surveyors and surveyees also make the measurement of income and wealth difficult. For these reasons there can be big differences between the estimated total of household income based on household surveys and that estimated from national income statistics. My own efforts to project total farm and urban household income from household surveys gave a result that was some 21 per cent less than the total household income figures based on national accounts for the year 1985.

Income and Equity

Incomes among poverty-stricken Koreans were at the bare-subsistance level and very equal in the 1950s because of the destruction of the Korean War (1950–3). The chief objective for most Koreans then was how to survive. The economic base, other than agriculture, was mostly destroyed by the War, and agriculture itself was very poor—virtually unmechanized and subject to flood, drought, and other natural disasters. Foreign aid provided the margin of survival for many Koreans.

The main goal of national development policy in the 1950s was to rehabilitate the war-ravaged economy, with the emphasis placed on developing its agricultural foundation. This development policy did not have any noticeable impact on equity, although it helped somewhat to raise incomes. Until 1963, when per capita income still stood at only US$100, neither the level nor distribution of income changed greatly.

It was only after 1963 that inequality started to be a significant important economic issue because of accelerating income growth. In 1963, Korea switched its national development strategy from an inward, agriculture- and rehabilitation-oriented focus to an outward, manufacturing- and export-oriented focus. The new development strategy immediately fostered disparities between agriculture and industry—that is, between the rural and urban sectors. As the industrial sector expanded rapidly in the late 1960s, the income disparity between rural and urban households emerged as the most important inequality issue. As shown in Table 10.1, rural and urban household incomes were about equal as of 1965, but by 1970 rural household income had declined to only 67 per cent of the average urban household income. As the rural/urban income gap increased, more people tried to move out of rural areas to seek better economic opportunities in urban areas. By the late 1960s, 'over urbanization' or 'over concentration' of population in the largest cities, especially Seoul, had emerged as a major social issue. Squatter settlements in Seoul also expanded rapidly due to the continuous inmigration of poor rural people.

To tackle this problem, the government started the *Saemaul Undong*, or New Village Movement,[2] in 1971. Its purpose was to enhance the household incomes and living conditions in rural areas to encourage people to stay on the farm. Through this

Table 10.1 Comparison of Rural and Urban Households

	Share of Agriculture in GNP (%)	Farm Population (million)	Share of Farm Population in Total Population (%)	Household Income ('000 won)		
				Rural (A)	Urban (B)	Ratio A/B
1955	43.9	13.3	61.9	—	—	—
1960	36.5	14.6	58.3	—	—	—
1965	37.6	15.8	55.8	112.3	112.6	99.7
1970	26.8	14.4	45.9	255.8	381.2	67.1
1975	24.7	13.2	38.2	872.9	859.3	101.6
1980	14.4	10.8	28.9	2,693.1	3,205.2	84.0
1985	13.5	8.5	21.1	5,736.2	6,046.4	94.9
1986	12.3	8.2	19.7	5,995.0	6,735.0	89.0
1987	11.7	7.8	18.5	6,535.3	6,740.1	97.0
1988	11.0	7.3	17.4	6,996.3	6,031.0	116.0

Note: Urban household income is averaged for salary and wage-earning households.

Sources: Economic Planning Board, *Major Statistics of Korean Economy*, various years, and the Bank of Korea, *Economic Statistics Yearbook*, various years.

movement the government expanded its investment in rural areas. In the mid-1970s as much as 10 per cent of the total national investment was allocated each year to rural areas through this movement. This was in addition to private investment in agriculture and government investment in agricultural infrastructure, such as irrigation and flood control. As a result of these programmes and an extensive price-support system for rice, rural household income was raised to almost the same level as urban household income by 1975. The rapid emigration of surplus farm labour also contributed to the rise in per capita rural income and thereby reduced the rural/urban disparity. The share of farm population in the total population decreased to about 30 per cent by the late 1970s, as shown in Table 10.1.

As more people moved into cities, the inequality of incomes within the urban sector emerged as a new equity issue. The new inequality within the city is associated with the rise in wages and the accumulation of wealth, including housing. To prevent the 'over expansion' of large cities, including Seoul, the government adopted various policies. One was to establish a green belt along the administrative boundary of Seoul city. This artificial restriction on the expansion of Seoul created a land shortage and forced up the price of land and housing. This worsened the sense of disparity between wage earners and property owners—that is, between workers and capitalists—in the late 1970s.

The other important disparity that emerged in the 1970s was between large and small firms. When the government adopted an export-oriented industrialization strategy in the early 1960s there were few manufacturing firms, and most were very small. To compensate for their inexperience in international trade and their small size, the government tried to expand the scale of operation by providing firms with tax subsidies, financial loans, site-selection privileges, and other benefits. As a result, many firms have grown to the point where they are competitive with large companies in advanced countries. The gap in assets and income between large and small firms has grown remarkably since the early 1970s. This gap was also widened by the government's aggressive promotion of heavy and chemical industries in 1972 and the creation of general trading companies soon afterwards, as described above in Chapter 6.

Since the beginning of rapid growth in the early 1960s the income of all Koreans has increased rapidly. Table 10.2 shows that average per capita income increased at an average annual rate of 6.9 per cent between 1965 and 1985. The average income of the poorest 40 per cent of the population also increased at the slightly lower, but still remarkable, rate of 6.4 per cent per year.

The overall level and trend of income distribution in Korea since 1965 can be summarized as follows.

Firstly, income distribution between rural and urban households improved from 1965 to 1970, chiefly due to the farm price-support policy.

Secondly, from 1970 to 1980 income disparity increased somewhat and is reflected consistently in several separate measures of income distribution (see Table 10.2). The reasons include the increasing disparity between wage-income and property-income receivers and between large and small firms.

Thirdly, since 1980 income distribution appears to have improved somewhat, perhaps due to the reduction of disparity in income between wage earners and property-income receivers, thanks to more stable housing and real estate prices. As indicated by Richard J. Szal, extensive promotion of small industries also contributed to the improvement of income distribution since 1980.[3]

An international comparison of income distribution indicates that the equality of income distribution in Korea is far higher than in India, Sri Lanka, Argentina, and the United States, but lower than in Taiwan, Japan, and West Germany (see Table 10.3).

It is surprising to find that the rise in income in Taiwan was accompanied by a rise in equality of income distribution, while this was not the case in Korea. Lawrence J. Lau indicates that Taiwan is the most successful case of high growth with equity. Taiwan's success is, according to him, due to the fact that 'the nation's leaders have explicitly aimed to enhance the 'people's livelihood,' that is, the standard of living of the average citizens, under their ideology of 'Three Principles of the People' (first proclaimed by Sun Yat-sen).[4] Although of more recent vintage, President Roh Tae-Woo's declaration of 'An Economy for Ordinary People' provides a similar ideological basis for putting higher priority on enhancing ordinary people's livelihoods in Korea.

One study on income distribution in Taiwan by three well-known specialists on development economics makes the important conclusion that 'it is possible for economic growth to be

Table 10.2 Changes in Income Distribution and the Poverty Level in Korea, 1965–1985

	1965	1970	1975	1980	1985
Income shares of quintiles					
Lowest 20% (A)	5.7	7.4	5.7	5.1	6.1
Second quintile (B)	13.6	12.3	11.1	11.0	11.6
Third quintile (C)	15.5	16.3	15.5	16.0	16.2
Fourth quintile (D)	23.3	22.4	22.4	22.6	22.4
Highest 20% (E)	41.9	41.6	45.3	45.3	43.7
Highest 10%	25.8	25.4	27.5	29.5	28.3
DDR (Decile distribution ratio) (A+B)/E	46.1	47.4	37.3	35.5	40.5
Gini coefficient	0.34	0.33	0.39	0.39	0.36
Mean income per capita, monthly ('000 won, 1985 prices)					
1. Average	34.7	46.9	70.7	105.0	137.7
2. Lowest 40 per cent	16.8	23.1	29.7	42.3	60.9
3. Average consumption	31.9	41.3	59.0	75.0	89.9
Poverty income (minimum acceptable standard)					
1. Per capita monthly ('000 won, 1985 prices)	33.5	47.1	57.9	69.9	84.9
2. Percentage of households below poverty-income level	—	81.8	80.6	60.7	44.5
Poverty class designated by government					
1. Disabled ('000)	287	306	330	282	282
2. Persons supported by government ('000)	3,917	2,338	934	1,676	1,995

Note: Exchange rate: 1 US dollar = 890.2 Korean won in 1985. Poverty income was computed by the author. 'Poverty class' designated by the government consists of those protected by the Livelihood Protection Act.

Sources: Computed from Byung-Nak Song, *The Korean Economy* (in Korean) second edition, Backyoungsa, Co., Seoul 1984; Economic Planning Board, *Social Indicators in Korea*, 1987, 1988 and *Major Statistics of Korean Economy*, 1987, 1989; The Bank of Korea, *Economic Statistics Yearbook*, 1987, 1988.

Table 10.3 Comparison of Income Distribution by Country

	Lowest 20 Per Cent (A)	Second Quintile (B)	Third Quintile (C)	Fourth Quintile (D)	Highest 20 Per Cent (E)	Highest 10 Per Cent	Decile Distribution Ratio (F)=(A+B)/E
Korea (1985)	6.1	11.6	16.2	22.4	43.7	28.3	40.5
Taiwan (1964)	7.7	12.6	16.6	22.0	41.1	—	49.4
Taiwan (1970)	8.4	13.3	17.1	22.5	38.7	—	56.0
Taiwan (1976)	8.9	13.7	17.5	22.7	37.2	—	60.7
Taiwan (1980)	8.8	13.9	17.7	22.8	36.8	—	61.7
Taiwan (1985)	8.4	13.6	17.5	22.9	37.6	—	58.5
Japan (1979)	8.7	13.2	17.5	23.1	37.5	22.4	58.4
USA (1980)	5.3	11.9	17.9	25.0	39.9	23.3	43.1
W. Germany (1978)	7.9	12.5	17.0	23.1	39.5	24.0	51.6
India (1976)	7.0	9.2	13.9	20.5	49.4	33.6	32.8
Argentina (1970)	1.4	9.7	14.1	21.5	50.3	35.2	28.0
Sri Lanka (1981)	5.8	10.1	14.1	20.2	49.8	34.7	31.9

Sources: Statistics for Korea and Taiwan are from The Economic Planning Board, *Social Indicators in Korea 1986*, and Republic of China Council for Economic Planning and Development, *Taiwan Statistical Data Book, 1987*. Statistics for other countries are from The World Bank, *World Development Report 1987, 1989*

compatible with an improved distribution of income during every phase of the transition from colonialism to a modern developed economy.'[5] This statement is supported by the Taiwanese income distribution data shown in Table 10.3. In the case of Korea—notwithstanding a similar export-oriented development path—income distribution measured in terms of the decile distribution ratios first improved (1970–5), then worsened (1975–80) and then began to improve again (since 1982) as shown in Table 10.2.

Wealth and Equity

In the 1950s arable land was the most important and usually the only asset of the majority of Koreans then dependent on agriculture. Arable land was fairly equally distributed because of the land reform conducted in the late 1940s, and was the key factor in the relative equality of incomes into the 1960s.

Land and housing remained the dominant assets for most Koreans in the 1960s. According to the 1968 National Wealth Survey, the total value of non-land assets held by all Korean households amounted to only US$2.0 billion—merely 10.5 per cent of the total value ($20.4 billion) of all physical capital in Korea. At the time, the value of land accounted for 23 per cent of total privately held assets. In the 1970s the relative importance of non-land assets increased substantially. According to the 1977 National Wealth Survey, the value of total non-land assets held by Korean households was US$21.7 billion, equal to 18.5 per cent of total physical capital.[6]

Conversely, ownership of stock has remained narrow, and the Korean stock market has been slow to develop. In 1968 the total market value of the stock of the mere 34 listed companies was only US$230 million, about one-tenth of all household non-land assets. In the second National Wealth Survey, taken in 1977, the stock of 323 listed companies had a market value of US$4.86 billion, some 22.3 per cent of total household non-land assets. By 1988, publicly traded stock was valued at US$88 billion, amounting to 60.8 per cent of GNP, with 62.5 per cent being held by individuals. Now, however, the government is actively promoting wider public ownership of the stock of both private and public corporations.

As indicated above, the relative importance of non-land assets is still small. And except for the wealthiest tenth of the population, household assests consist, at most, of a home. According to the 1985 Population and Housing Census the ratio of total housing units to total households was 69.2 per cent, falling to 58.9 per cent in cities and towns (see Table 10.5). Since some households own more than one housing unit, the proportion of households which do not own housing units exceeds 50 per cent. For those who do not own a home, this aggravates the perception of poverty and economic inequality.

Factors Influencing Equality in Korea

Notwithstanding the equity problems identified in the previous section, World Bank economists point out that 'the distribution of income in Korea is among the best in the developing world.'[7] Hak-chung Choo, a Korean expert on income distribution, also indicates that income distribution in Korea, especially in the 1960s, was highly favourable relative to most other countries.[8] What factors contributed to this pattern? The following appear to be particularly important.

Land Reform

Immediately after its establishment in 1948 the Korean government legislated a Land Reform Act in close co-operation with the former US Military Government. This resulted in one of the most thoroughgoing and successful land reforms in the world. The land of former Japanese landlords was held in trust by the US military government, while Korean landlords were few in number and also in no position to resist, since many of them had accumulated land under Japanese colonial rule.

Before land reform the ownership of arable land was extremely unequal. Only 14 per cent of farmers were owner-cultivators, about 39 per cent of arable land was cultivated under conditions of tenancy, and a small number of landlords (about 4 per cent of the rural population) took about half the main crop from their tenants in lieu of rent.[9]

Landlordism is still prohibited in Korea by law. There is a 3-*chongbo* (about 7.35 acres) limit on farm land ownership, contributing to very equal income distribution within the agricultural sector.

The Korean War

The Korean War destroyed virtually all physical infrastructure and production facilities. Irma Adelman and Kim Mahn-Je assumed in their econometric model of the Korean economy that the value of capital stock in Korea in 1953 was zero due to wartime destruction.[10] All Koreans were forced to begin again from scratch. The war clearly worked to make income and wealth more equal, but only by making Koreans equally poor.

Regional and Cultural Homogeneity

Koreans have always been influenced by the same cultural, climatic, and geographical factors, and are not divided by religious and racial differences such as exist between, say, Malay and Chinese Malaysians.

Korea is small and the weather and soil conditions are everywhere similar. This has helped increase social mobility, reduce regional differences in wages, and create a high degree of equaltiy in the regional distribution of income. Remy Prud'homme of the University of Paris states that in Korea 'interregional disparities are not large relative to what they are in most other developing countries.'[11] Edward Mason and others also indicated the same thing.[12]

Korea's relatively good marks for regional balance notwithstanding, regional disparities still appear to have increased since the beginning of industrialization. This is mainly because of differences in industrial location factors. Heavy and chemical industries became concentrated near Pusan and Inchon, which had good port facilities.

There is no 'underclass' as such in Korea, and no substantial segregation of Korean cities into poor and wealthy areas. Korea's largest cities, such as Seoul and Pusan, have had squatter settlements since the end of the Korean War. Many of these have disappeared in the process of rapid growth, and in Korea's social life and educational system, status is determined by merit and achievement more than by family background.

Equal Educational Opportunities

Koreans have strong aspirations for education and have generally equal opportunities for schooling. This is true especially in primary education. When the labour-intensive industries started to grow rapidly with the beginning of industrialization in the 1960s, the required skill level for these industries was relatively low. People who had received only primary education were able to find employment opprotunities and thereby share in the economic fruits of Korea's development. Primary schooling in Korea promoted both growth and equity, especially in early stages of development.

There are many Koreans who make enormous sacrifices for the education of not only their children, but even of their brothers or sisters. When Koreans become wealthy and think of repaying society, one of the first things they think of doing is establishing fellowships for poor students.

Korea's educational system puts a premium on competitive selection, not family wealth. No student has ever entered Seoul National University, the most competitive in Korea, for reasons other than academic perfomance. Throughout the long history of the university, only one student, a son of President Syngman Rhee's protégé and chief advisor, circumvented these standards —and he was shortly driven out by the other students.

Growth Strategy

There are two aspects worth noting about the relationship between growth strategy and equity. The first is that creating and providing productive jobs through a growth-oriented strategy for the unemployed or under-employed population is generally the surest way to increase the income of lower-class households and reduce inter-class income disparities. The second is that Korea's strategy of developing labour-intensive industries in the early stage of development created numerous employment opportunities for workers having only a primary school education. In this way, too, Korea's growth strategy helped enhance equity rather than worsen it.

Equality-oriented Policies

The Korean government has emphasized equity as well as growth in many of its development policy decisions. Examples include the farm price-support policy, a very low tax rate on farm income, and price controls on such daily necessities as coal briquettes and bus fares. In addition, limits on agricultural land ownership, tax disincentives to discourage owning more than one housing unit, measures against conspicuous consumption of consumer durables, and other policies all have helped to increase egalitarian attitudes as well as actual income equality.

The Extended Family System

The Korean family system also appears to be contributing to the high level of equity in Korea. As in other East Asian countries, including Japan and Taiwan, the extended Korean family system is the basic unit for consumption and social welfare. Traditional Koreans consider welfare a private or family matter, and they tend not to rely on state or public institutions for economic assistance. Korean parents tend to rely on their children for economic support after retirement, and Korean children accept this responsibility. As a consequence, there are a large proportion of multi-generation households in Korea. In 1980, 87 per cent of all households contained two or more generations, while single-person households made up only 5 per cent—much lower than the Japanese figure of 21 per cent in 1985.

Equity and Social Class Consciousness

The proportion of Koreans who see themselves as poor, that is, as belonging to the lower class, was 56.4 per cent in the 1980 Social Statistics Survey (see Table 10.4). This figure decreased to 42.6 per cent in 1985. The proportion of population falling below the poverty line can be seen from the figures in Table 10.2.

I have computed the poverty income level, or minimum acceptable standard income, on the basis of the cost of subsistence food budget for a typical Korean household. According to the results, 60.7 per cent of households in 1980 and 44.5 per cent of households in 1985 fell below this line. The poverty income approach, the social statics surveys, and the housing ownership ratio approach all yield about the same ratio of estimated population belonging to the lower income class.

At the same time, the number of Koreans who claim to feel that they belong to the middle class appears to have increased in recent years. According to the Social Statistics Survey[13] conducted in 1980, 41 per cent of the sample identified themselves as middle class. In 1985 the same figure was 53 per cent. If the

Table 10.4 Subjective Class Consciousness of Koreans (per cent)

	1980	1985
Upper class	2.6	4.4
Middle class	41.0 ⎤	53.0 ⎤
Upper lower class	14.0 ⎦ > 55.0	13.9 ⎦ > 66.9
Middle lower class	23.9	16.4
Lower lower class	18.5	12.3

Source: Economic Planning Board/National Bureau of Statistics, *Social Statistics Survey*, 1981, 1986.

proportion of people saying they belong to the upper lower-income class is included, these proportions rise to 55 per cent in 1980 and 67 per cent in 1985. Similar results can be found from other surveys. For instance, the annual *Joong-ang Daily News* 'Survey of Opinions on National Social Life', covering a sample of 1,500 adult Koreans, found that the proportion of people who feel that they belong to the middle class stood at 58 per cent in 1985 and increased to 60 per cent in 1986, and again to 61 per cent in 1987, indicating a steady growth in middle-class consciousness.[14]

Welfare and the Quality of Life

The economic well-being—broadly speaking, the quality of life of the average Korean—has improved substantially since economic growth began to accelerate in the early 1960s. To measure the quality of life in Korea, the Economic Planning Board has compiled social indicator data every year since 1979.[15] The most recent social indicator survey covers 243 terms, some of which are presented in Table 10.5. Collectively, these show that rapid economic growth has brought about substantial improvement in economic welfare and the quality of life.

Koreans live much longer now than they did twenty years ago. Their life is more urbanized, and they enjoy a wider and better range of consumer goods. The share of household income spent on basic necessities has sharply declined. For instance, the proportion of the household budget spent on food and beverages decreased from 62.3 per cent to 38.7 per cent between 1965 and

1988. The quality of the Korean diet also has improved significantly. Koreans now eat more meat, fish, dairy products, and
fruits. More people now drink piped water and are covered by
medical insurance. Koreans drive or ride more, and on better
roads; and they study for longer periods of time at better schools.
The average period of schooling for Koreans over age six increased from 5.0 years in 1965 to 8.6 years in 1985, as shown in
Table 10.5.

The areas which have not improved much are housing and
leisure. Korea continues to be a country of hard workers, with a
long work week. Leisure hours (weekly non-working hours) have
not increased since 1965. The improvement in housing conditions
in Korea, moreover, has been rather disappointing. Although
there has been some improvement in terms of housing space per
person and in terms of the number of housing units, the housing-
supply ratio—total housing units to total households—has deteriorated. This is due to the rapid increase in the number of
nuclear or core families and the concentration of population in
urban areas.

As Korea reached the stage of a NIC (newly industrializing
country), the country started to face such typical problems of
industrialized countries as pollution, environmental deterioration, crime, and industrial and traffic accidents. Although precise
data are not available, increasing environmental pollution, in
particular, detracts substantially from improvements in the quality of life due to increased physical consumption.

International comparisons, as shown in Table 10.6, indicate
that Korea lags behind Taiwan and the industrialized countries
in most aspects of welfare, except education. In terms of education, however, Korea is far ahead of Taiwan and at a level equal
to some industrialized countries such as the United Kingdom,
France, and West Germany. Indeed, in terms of the proportion
of the population aged 20–24 enrolled in higher schools, Korea
ranks higher than Taiwan, Japan, West Germany, France, and
England, as seen in Table 10.6.

Overall, the most important points about economic growth and
the quality of life in Korea are the following:

Firstly, higher per-capita GNP has resulted in higher welfare
for most Koreans. The severe criticism of Korea's growth pattern
by some domestic critics is not supported by social indicator
statistics. These belie the contention that the government has

Table 10.5 Social Indicators for Korea, 1965–1987

	1965	1970	1975	1980	1985	1987
1. Income						
GNP (US$ billion)	3.0	7.8	20.2	56.5	83.7	118.6
Per capita GNP (US$)	105	248	591	1,605	2,047	3,098
2. Food						
Share in total consumption (%)	62.3	56.4	53.5	47.4	40.0	38.9
Daily calorie intake (cal)	2,189	2,370	2,390	2,485	2,687	2,815
Daily protein intake (gm)	57.1	65.1	71.1	73.6	86.6	88.6
Daily rice consumption, urban household (gm)	359	404	329	343	323	324
3. Housing						
Average space per person (m^2)	—	6.3	7.9	9.5	9.6	9.7
Housing units ('000)	3,912	4,360	4,734	5,463	6,274	6,449
Households ('000)	5,057	5,857	6,754	7,968	9,575	10,264
Housing/household ratio (%)						
National average (%)	81.3	77.8	74.4	71.2	69.7	69.2
Cities and towns (%)	—	—	67.8	58.4	56.8	58.9
4. Education						
Average education (years)	5.0	5.7	6.6	7.6	8.6	8.6[a]
Total students ('000)	6,694	7,986	9,204	10,568	11,152	11,222
Students/population (%)	22.1	25.4	26.5	27.7	27.6	26.4
High school graduates enrolling in higher schools (%)	—	35.9	31.0	43.3	49.6	46.1

5. Health						
Life expectancy (years)	55.2	57.6	60.6	66	69	69
Population per physician	2,609	1,773	1,801	1,485	1,230	1,077
Medical insurance coverage						
Number ('000)	—	19	67	9,113	17,879	21,257
Coverage ratio (%)	—	0.1	0.2	23.9	43.5	50.5
6. Culture & Leisure						
Households having T.V. (%)	—	6.4	30.2	86.7	99.1	99.6
Telephone subscribers ('000)	221	476	1,058	2,705	6,517	8,625
Phones per 100 persons	0.8	2.0	4.0	8.9	19.3	29.4
Total automobiles ('000)	39.1	126.5	193.9	527.8	1,113.0	1,611
Passenger cars ('000)		60.7	84.2	249.1	556.7	844.4
Vehicles per 100 persons	0.06	19	24	65	1.35	2.0
Weekly non-working hours	—	116.4	118.0	116.7	116.1	116.1
Average travel distance per person per year (Km)	529	962	1,493	2,298	2,603	2,755
7. Public safety						
Numbers of crimes ('000)	443	301	387	595	810	946
Crimes per 100,000 population	1,371	953	1,098	1,561	1,974	2,276
Traffic accidents ('000)	14.9	37.2	58.3	120.2	146.8	175.7
Coverage of industrial accident insurance (%)	8.5	26.3	45.1	66.1	59.4	59.8
Deaths due to accidents	2,276	3,548	4,087	5,460	—	8,164
8. Social environment						
Share of urban population (%)	34.3	43.1	50.9	60.1	65.4	68.1
Population growth rate (%)	2.7	2.2	1.7	1.6	1.2	1.2

Table 10.5 (*continued*)

	1965	1970	1975	1980	1985	1987
Labour force participation rate						
Average (%)	55.6	57.6	58.3	59.0	56.6	58.3
Female (%)	36.5	38.5	39.6	41.6	40.6	40.0
Total divorces ('000)				21.7	25.9	31.3
Poverty population ('000)	3,851	2,423	1,234	1,782	1,928	2,103
Labour union participation						
ratio (%)	22.2	19.8	22.8	20.0	15.7	17.3
Economically disabled ('000)	355	346	330	282	282	284
Unemployment rate (%)	7.4	4.5	4.1	5.2	4.0	3.1
Government officials ('000)	333	417	479	596	671	692
9. Physical environment						
Medical institutions ('000)	9.7	10.3	11.1	11.8	18.3	19.6
Piped-water supply per person						
per day (litres)	106	158	216	256	282	295
supply ratio (%)	21.4	32.4	42.4	54.6	66.2	68.1
Road pavement ratio						
All roads (%)	5.7	9.6	22.3	33.2	49.9	54.2
National highways (%)	17.7	28.5	50.8	71.6	76.4	79.5

Note: a = 1985.

Sources: Byung-Nak Song, *The Korean Economy* (in Korean), second edition, Seoul, Bakyoung Sa, 1984; Economic Planning Board, *Social Indicators in Korea*, 1979, 1986, 1988, and *Major Statistics of Korean Economy*, 1987, 1988.

promoted economic development to augment the power and glory of the political leadership, rather than to improve the welfare of the people. Nor have resources been channelled to large industries without regard for the welfare of ordinary citizens. Some of the rich have become richer, but so have many of the poor.

It is interesting to note that President Roh Tae-Woo's economic platform is the 'creation of a great era for ordinary people.'[16] The essence of this platform is that, more than ever, the Korean economy is to be geared to the enhancement of the welfare of the 'ordinary people'.

Secondly, Korea lags far behind industrialized countries in per capita income and general welfare. But Koreans are better off as regards income level in terms of such consumer durables as colour televisions and automobiles.

Thirdly, housing appears to be the most important determinant of welfare for Koreans, especially given the high value Korean culture puts on family life. Most Koreans now can afford to buy most consumer durables, except housing. Housing is the most important determinant of the disparity between 'the haves and the have-nots'. Home-ownership is crucial to the formation of a strong middle class and maintenance of social stability— particularly with the Republic of Korea confronting the communist regime to the North.

Finally, access to schools, hospitals, markets, parks, police protection, and other social services are also important aspects of the quality of life for most people. At present, however, many Korean school children in large cities spend a great deal of time commuting between home and school. For the majority of Koreans who do not own a private car, a nearby public or private service may be as important as the availability of the service itself. Comprehensive and integrated development of service networks and provision of various services including, of course, basic human needs based on the concepts of 'neighbourhood' and 'community' appear to be the key to increasing the welfare of 'ordinary people'. But Korea still has far to go in successfully incorporating these concepts into regional and city development plans.

Table 10.6 Comparison of Social Indicators by Country

	Korea	Taiwan	Japan	United States	West Germany	France	United Kingdom
Income							
Per capita GNP (1988, US$)	4,040	6,053	23,358	19,760	19,857	17,002	11,830[a]
GNP (1988, billion US$)	169	120	2,859	4,863	1,212	950	503[a]
GNP share of agriculture (1987, per cent)	12	7	3	2	2	4	2
Health							
Life expectancy at birth (1986)	69	71	78	75	75	77	75
Daily calorie supply (1986, cal)	2,806	2,865	2,695	3,682	3,519	3,358	3,148
Population per physician (1981)	1,166 (86)	1,222 (86)	761 (85)	500	442	460	680
Deaths per 1,000 (1986)	6	5	7	9	12	10	12
Births per 1,000 (1986)	20	18	12	16	10	14	13
Population growth rate (1980–6, %)	1.4	1.3	0.7	1.0	−0.2	0.5	0.1
Education							
Percentage of population of age 20–24 enrolled in higher education (1985)	32	19	30	57	30	30	22
Adult literacy (1980, %)	93	82 (79)	99	99	99	99	99
Percentage of high school-aged children enrolled in school (1985, %)	94	81	96	99	74	96	89
Percentage of high school graduates advancing to higher education (1984–5)	36	—	30 (86)	46 (83)	27 (82)	27 (82)	21 (82)

Culture and leisure							
T.V. sets per 1,000 (1983)	201 (85)	—	556	790	360	375	479
Telephones per 1,000 (1983)	223 (86)	223 (86)	513	752	572	575	515
Private automobiles per 1,000 (1983)	16 (86)	49 (86)	221	527	402	376	281
Weekly hours worked, manufacturing workers (1984)	54.7 (86)	50.6 (86)	41.7	40.7	41.0	38.7	41.7
Area of urban park per person (1983, m^2)	2.0	—	3.6	23.9	37.4	12.2	30.4
Public safety							
Crimes per 100,000	1,974 (85)	—	1,328 (85)	—	2,730 (78)	1,535 (78)	2,526 (78)
Accidental death per 100,000 (1981)	14.7	—	35 (85)	57.5	61.7	76.4	35.4
Share of defence expenditure in GNP (1980, %)	6.6	—	0.8	4.9	2.7	2.8	4.6
Social and physical environment							
Unemployment rate (1986, %)	3.2	2.7	2.8	6.9	9.0	10.4	11.9
Family size (persons)	4.5 (80)	4.8 (80)	3.1 (85)	2.7 (80)	2.4 (78)	2.9 (75)	2.7 (81)
Persons per room	2.0 (80)	1.7 (80)	0.7 (85)	0.6 (70)	0.6 (78)	0.8 (78)	0.6 (71)

Table 10.6 (*continued*)

	Korea	Taiwan	Japan	United States	West Germany	France	United Kingdom
Ratio of owner's housing	58 (80)	—	62 (85)	65 (77)	34 (72)	47 (75)	50 (71)
Road pavement ratio (1983, %)	50 (85)	—	53.3 (83)	85 (81)	99	—	97
Piped-water supply ratio (%)	66 (85)	70 (80)	93.7 (84)	99.3 (78)	99.2 (72)	98.7 (78)	—
Sewage supply ratio (%)	—	—	34	72	91	65	97

Note: a = 1987. Numbers in parentheses indicate the year.

Sources: Economic Planning Board, *Social Indicators in Korea*, 1976, 1989; *Major Statistics of Korean Economy*, 1989 and *Major Statistics of Foreign Economies*, 1988. The Bank of Japan/Research and Statistics Department *Comparative Economic and Financial Statistics of Japan and Other Major Countries*, 1987, 1989. Japanese Economic Planning Agency, *New Social Indicators*, 1987. World Bank, *World Development Report*, 1988, 1989; Taiwan Executive Yuan/Council for Economic Planning and Development, *Taiwan Statistical Data Book*, 1987. World Bank, *World Development Report*, 1987, 1989.

11 Understanding the Korean Management System

Korea's Economic Life between America and Japan

Edwin O. Reischauer, in his book *My Life Between Japan and America*, describes himself as 'an American boy born and raised in Japan'.[1] Although America was the stage for most of Professor Reischauer's professional life, he comments that his whole life 'centered upon better understanding between the U.S., Japan and the rest of East Asia'. Drawing on his mixed Japanese-American cultural background, Professor Reischauer's self-perceived task was to enhance and solidify the 'strong, equal partnership of the U.S.A. and Japan', the world's two most powerful democracies.[2]

A similar book about Korea's economic position might be appropriately entitled 'Economic Growth and Survival Between Japan and America'. Both America and Japan have profoundly influenced the Korean economy, and many Korean companies live their business lives with one foot in each country. That is, they depend upon America as a market for their exports and upon Japan as a source for intermediate goods needed to manufacture those exports.

Korea relies on the United States and Japan in financial areas as well. Korea's trade surplus with America in recent years is offset by its trade deficit with Japan. In reality, a large part of the foreign exchange Korea earns from trade with America is used to pay off the deficit incurred in trade with Japan.

The Korean management style also appears to lie between the Japanese and American approaches. Most Americans appear to believe that Koreans are very much like the Japanese—and that 'Korea is a second Japan'. But when Koreans talk with Japanese they find that many Japanese consider Koreans to be more like Americans than like themselves.

Hasekawa Keitaro, a Japanese economic columnist, remarked some years ago that when President Chun Doo Hwan came to power in 1980 many Koreans over the age of 50 were dismissed from various public and private organizations. Hasekawa saw this as illustrating that the Korean management style is closer to that in America than in Japan.[3] Such generalizations are, of course, hazardous, but make a worthwhile point nevertheless.

Japanese and American Influences on the Korean System

The Korean management system can be understood through a comparison with the Japanese and American systems. Rodney Clark has done a systematic study of the Japanese management system,[4] and, based on Clark's approach, Harvey Leibenstein of Harvard recently has suggested that twelve important characteristics distinguish the Japanese and American management systems.[5] These characteristics or dimensions are used in Table 11.1 to compare the Korean management system with those of Japan and America (and the West generally).

Historically speaking, in Korea, Japanese influence on management style preceded American influence because Korea was a Japanese colony from the early years of this century until Korea's liberation in 1945. From then, until 1965, American influences dominated. After the normalization of Korea's relations with Japan in 1965, however, both the American and Japanese management styles have influenced Korea to varying degrees.

During the Japanese occupation period, Koreans were generally restricted by the Japanese authorities to the lower positions in almost all organizations, including business firms. With few exceptions, Koreans were excluded from managerial positions and consequently deprived of opportunities for managerial experience. Moreover, whatever experience Koreans did obtain solely reflected the Japanese managerial style—or more precisely, a highly discriminatory colonial version of this style. When the Japanese left in 1945, Koreans started to systematically study the American management system. Korean students who studied abroad after 1945 went mostly to the United States, where they learned the techniques they later applied to Korean enterprises.

It is worth mentioning that the military in Korea also played an important role in transferring the American management system. For example, many Korean generals studied American military and business management systems during their military-service periods. After they were discharged from the military they applied these skills to various Korean enterprises. One example is retired General Tae Joon Park, who has successfully led the

Table 11.1 The Korean, Japanese, and American (Western) Management Systems Compared

Korea	Japan	America
Company as a family-type community	Company as a community	Less emphasis on community
Sharp distinctions between owners, managers, and workers	No sharp distinction between managers and workers	Sharp distinctions
Weakly held lifetime employment ideal	Lifetime employment ideal	No lifetime employment ideal
Very strong emphasis on general hierarchical ranks	Strong emphasis on general hierarchical ranks	Management hierarchy related to function
Emphasis on loyalty and co-operation	Emphasis on co-operation, harmony, and consensus	Emphasis on individual achievement within narrow job definitions
Age and service length recognized as important criteria	Age and service length explicitly recognized as promotion criteria	Age and length of service only marginally relevant to promotion
Specific authority and diffuse responsibility	Diffuse authority and diffuse responsibility	Authority and responsibility ostensibly specific
Managerial authority limited largely by owner's policy and interests	Managerial authority limited by internal labour mobility	Managerial authority challenged by trade unions
Enterprise unions predominate	Almost exclusively enterprise unions	Trades unions
Extensive on-the-job and related training for a variety of jobs	On-the-job training for a variety of jobs	On-the-job training for specific jobs
Considerable job rotation and boundary flexibility	Job rotation and boundary flexibility	Focus on specific job with specific boundaries
Company recruits on the basis of age, experience, and education	Firm recruits on the basis of age and education	Firm recruits on the basis of skills and experience needed to fill specific jobs

Note: The characteristics for Japan and the West were suggested by Harvey Leibenstein, in a different order, in 'The Japanese Management System: An X-Efficiency-Game Theory Analysis', in Masahiko Aoki (ed.), *The Economic Analysis of the Japanese Firm*, Amsterdam, North-Holland Co., 1984.

Pohang iron and steel mill—the largest in Korea—ever since its inception.

Because of the extensive involvement of retired officers in the management of private firms in Korea, Koreans jokingly say that not a few Korean private enterprises are operated like 'military companies'. Indeed, workers in many Korean construction companies are expected to obey orders and work with the same discipline as soldiers in the army's construction and engineering commands.

The characteristics of the Korean management system described in Table 11.1 are not, of course, independent and mutually exclusive. To a large extent they are interrelated and intertwined. Nevertheless, it is useful to separately discuss the most important of these characteristics.

The Company as a Semi-familial Community

Lee Byung-Chul—founder of the Samsung business group, which is in many ways the 'grandfather' of South Korean business conglomerates—said in his autobiography that the book he valued most was the *Analects of Confucius*, and that he had studied it carefully throughout his life.[6] Chung Ju-Yung also asserts that Korea's business ethic needs to be established within the framework of Confucian ethics.[7] As noted in Chapter 3, Confucianism was the state religion or philosophy of Korea for over five hundred years—beginning with the foundation of the Yi Dynasty in 1392 and continuing until the end of the dynasty in 1910 when Korea was forcibly annexed by Japan. The profound influence of Concucianism on the values, attitudes, and behavioural norms of Koreans also has spilled over to the fundamental underpinnings of the Korean management system and human relationships within Korean companies.

Confucian ethics concerning human relationships are stated in terms of basic moral rules and principles governing the five main human relationships: father and son, kin and subject, husband and wife, elder and younger, and friend and friend. In Confucianism, society's rules and principles are largely extensions of those regulating relationships among family members.

Because of Confucianism, the values, ways of thinking, and modes of conduct of present-day Koreans still centre on family life and the family system. Koreans also value their families highly because the family has been the only social institution that, throughout Korea's long and turbulent history, including the period of harsh Japanese colonial rule, could be trusted to provide for the security and welfare of its members. For this reason, too, the influence of the family on the Korean management system—in both business and government—has been highly significant.

Traditionally, Korean élites were so-called 'Confucian gentlemen' who looked down on commercial activities and developed no body of traditional wisdom about business management. Indeed, traditional Korea gave rise to no large-scale firms to which management principles might have been usefully applied. Business activities were understood to be peculiar to the lowest social class. Moreover, while Buddhist temples and religious organizations existed during the Yi Dynasty, Buddhism was officially discouraged by the state and Buddhist organizations did not evolve into large-scale managerial enterprises. Confucian activities, for their part, took place mostly within the family unit. With the exception of government organizations, there were no areas in which Koreans could learn and apply management principles.

In the traditional Korean family the father is the respected and unquestioned head. He can wield nearly absolute power if he so desires. Haunted by poverty throughout most of their history, survival itself has been a driving force for most Koreans. The traditional Korean father had full responsibility to feed the family, to approve marriages, and to decide on the careers and future lives of his children. Daughters traditionally held the lowest status within the family, and when they were married off they were not supposed to return to their former families again. Thus, the only way for wives to survive was to fully commit themselves to their husband's family and to obey their husband and the elders of their husband's family. In all respects the traditional family was very much like 'a small state with a strong ruler'.

The relationship between the father and his eldest son is the backbone of the Korean family system. The eldest son is traditionally the successor and heir to his father's assets and role in the family and, therefore, is given priority over younger siblings in terms of educational and other opportunities. The power of the father passes to the first son. Within the family, the eldest son's responsibility goes first to his parents, then to his brothers in the order of their birth, and finally to his sisters.

Beyond the immediate family, loyalties go to near blood relatives, and finally to the clan—which consists of distant relatives descended from a common ancester. This is why many Koreans value 'blood relationships' so highly. The extended clan is called the *chiban*. The larger the *chiban* the better, because a larger *chiban* implies broader-based security for members of the clan. Korean familial values are, of course, changing with socio-economic conditions, but still maintain remarkable stability. The family remains the basic social organization and the model for values governing the behaviour of Korean managers and entrepreneurs.

When Koreans organize and manage enterprises, there is a tendency for them to organize and manage them on the basis of the principles governing the family or clan systems. Business founders in Korea are expected to feed and provide for not only their immediate family members but other relatives as well. As a result, many Korean enterprises are staffed by the relatives and fellow clan members of the owners and operate under rules which often resemble those of the clan system.

For example, it is interesting to note that Chung Ju-yung, the founder of the Hyundai conglomerate, eats breakfast together at home with his five sons, all of whom are top managers in the Hyundai business group, and after breakfast they walk together to their respective offices in the nearby Hyundai office building. Most Koreans value and envy this type of family association.

Semi-lifetime Employment Ideal

The American scholar Harvey Leibenstein contends that 'the employment ideal in the West is a short-run contractual ideal of firm association rather than a long-run belonging ideal' as in Japan.[8] He also suggests that 'employee behaviour in the West involves devotion to a particular skill or job rather than loyalty to the firm in general'. In contrast, employee behaviour in Japan involves long-term devotion to the organization that one belongs to.

The employment ideal in Korea appears to entail quasi-long-term loyalty. The loyalty of employees in Korea is chiefly to an individual, be it the owner or the chief executive. Conversely, Koreans have very little sense of loyalty to organizations as such—be they firms or government agencies—or to abstractions such as ideas and policies.[9] In politics as well, a party member's loyalty is almost solely to the leader of the party, rather than to either the party or its platform. Like business organizations, political parties are operated along the lines of the Korean family system and ruled in an authoritarian way by the heads of the parties.

These differences in the focus of commitment of loyalty are also related to the relative duration of the contractual ideal. In Japan, the belonging ideal is based on the group or the organization itself, and is potentially as enduring as the group or the organization itself. In Korea, since loyalty is mainly to the individual instead of the organization, the employee's commitment depends on the duration of a smooth human relationship between the employee and the particular individual he feels loyalty towards. Accordingly, the Korean employee's commitment to an individual gives rise to a quasi-long-term employment ideal, in contrast to the long-term ideal of Japan based on a commitment to the organization, or the short-term American ideal based on a term-specific employment contract.

The Emphasis on General Hierarchical Ranks

The well-known Japanese anthropologist Chie Nakane asserts, as mentioned in Chapter 4, that Japan is 'a homogeneous society built on a vertical organizational principle'.[10] In many ways, Korea is also a highly homogeneous society built on a vertical organizational principle.

The Korean company appears to be more hierarchical than the Japanese company, because of the great influence of the strongly-hierarchical traditional family system. The Korean sociologist Kim Kyung-Tong argues, moreover, that the Korean military has also had a profound influence on the structure of Korean business organizations. Above all, many of Korea's recent national leaders have been retired generals, including Presidents Park Chung Hee, Chun Doo Hwan, and Roh Tae Woo. In addition, many employees of Korean companies have been in the military, and many executives are retired officers. Employees of almost all Korean companies are expected to undergo regular military training of various sorts, such as the monthly civil-defence drills and reserve army training for young male employees. In fact, every big company is expected to establish and maintain a reserve army training unit as part of the company's organization. This organization structure can be particularly effective in performing tasks that require military-style co-ordination.

The Korean managerial system is more top-down than the combined top-down and bottom-up style that is characteristic of Japan. In the case of Japan, the mutual sense of obligation between *oyabun* (boss) and *kobun* (subordinate) is very strong, as is the sense of reciprocal obligation between the individual and the organization.

In the West, with the emphasis placed on individualistic behaviour within the bounds of a narrow job commitment, hierarchical considerations are not as strong as in either Korea or Japan. The American style employer-employee relationship, with the primacy it gives to contractually defined rights and responsibilities, strikes many Koreans as impersonal and mechanical. In fact many Koreans working for American companies in the United States complain that the life inside the company is very rigid and socially cold and isolating. In terms of management style, values, personal loyalty, and non-specific co-operation, the Korean system is closer to the Japanese model than to the American one. Nevertheless, Korean-style management appears to place more importance on loyalty, paternalism, and co-operation than on Japanese-style consensus and harmony.

A more organic and humanistic approach to organizational behaviour may be one of the most important characteristics of the Korean management style. This has even proved sucessful in America, and one of the reasons the Huntsville, Tennessee, factory of the Lucky-Goldstar Electronics Company has been so successful in managing employee-employer relations is because it relies on this type of organizational style.

The Evolution of the Korean Management System

How will the Korean management system change in the future? What changes would be desirable? Answering this question is extremely difficult. One approach is to examine the apparent advantages of the Japanese management system over the American management system. According to the framework suggested by Harvey Leibenstein, the Japanese management system is successful because it is well suited to the attitudes, values, and norms of behaviour which characterize Japanese society.

Leibenstein identifies the following four major characteristics as significant contributing factors in the success of the Japanese management style:

(a) The Japanese style of consensus formation achieved in small groups leads to the mobilization of greater efforts by the broader membership of the organization.

(b) The spirit of harmony facilitates the smooth and efficient operation of the organization, and, thus, raises productivity.

(c) The Japanese consensus-achieving system links together the welfare of the firm and the welfare of the employee. Employees and management both share the sense of 'being in the same boat'.

(d) The lifetime-employment ideal, in particular, and the emphasis on co-operation and harmony, in general, work to eliminate employee resistance to technical changes and innovation. In contrast, in the West it is quite common for factory workers to resist the introduction of new machinery or production equipment because they fear losing their jobs.

An employment system based on the contract ideal encourages employees to improve their specific skills or job qualifications. The lifetime employment ideal, however, encourages employees to become familiar with the variety of skills they are likely to need during their lengthy employment with the firm. This is also made possible because the lifetime employment system involves job rotation and job variety, making it more conducive to technological innovation than a short-term contract employment system.

As to the broader reasons why Japanese managers have achieved better results than their American counterparts, Leibenstein further suggests that:[11]

(a) The Japanese management system offers a better mix of non-monetary rewards to the employee. Examples of such non-monetary rewards are various titles, citations, and honorary treatment.

(b) The Japanese system also motivates employees better and ensures greater efforts by employees. Due to the lifetime-employment system, job rotation, commitment to the company as a community, and steady movement up in the company hierarchy, the employees in a Japanese company are motivated to work harder and better than the employees in American companies that lack these features.

(c) Japanese cultural and psychological characteristics are such
    that Japanese employees are more responsive than American
    employees to non-monetary incentives.

Leibenstein's points suggest some future directions for the improvement of Korean management systems. Because Koreans,
like the Japanese, appear to be very responsive to non-monetary
rewards, especially rewards from a close community relationship,
it is important to develop and offer an appropriate mix of monetary and non-monetary rewards to the employees in the Korean
company. Following the damaging labour strike at the Hyundai
automobile company in August 1987, I gave a lecture on the
Korean economy to a group of labour-union leaders there, which
led to a discussion session. They told me that they were particularly dissatisfied with the existing system of non-monetary rewards and the mechanical management of human relationships.
The managers of the automotive company also told me that the
poor non-monetary reward system coupled with low wages were
the two major reasons for the violent labour action the company
had experienced. Managers in other Korean companies have
frequently told me the same thing.

Wages were, of course, clearly the centre of the recent labour
disputes and are likely to remain so in the future. But non-wage
factors were also an important cause for recent disputes. According to a Ministry of Labour analysis, the number of labour disputes over wages was 57.3 per cent. The rest were due to factors
such as working conditions, unfair treatment, lay-offs, unsatisfac-
tory employer-employee relationships, and excessive working
hours.[12].

For countries like Korea, which have been profoundly influenced by Confucianism with its emphasis on human relations
and the non-material aspects of life, an appropriate mix of non-
monetary rewards may prove to be even more important motivators than monetary rewards. This may be increasingly the case as
Korea's per capita income increases. To date, Korean business
firms and other organizations have tried to raise the overall level
of employee effort chiefly by invoking such national goals as the
need to escape the vicious circle of poverty, the achievement of
superiority over North Korea in economic 'warfare', the repay-
ment of foreign debts, and the elevation of Korea's international
image and honour. This outdated and crude approach to motivat-

ing workers loses its effectiveness once workers' incomes and sophistication surpass a certain level, however.

To be successful in the future, Korean firms will have to develop a mixture of monetary and non-monetary rewards that effectively promote efficiency and productivity. In general, the ideal of a long-term commitment to the firm based on lifetime employment appears more appropriate to Korea's circumstances than a short-term commitment based on a fixed-term contract. Accordingly, Korean firms still need to improve the existing semi-lifetime employment system and to promote a genuine communal tie between employers and employees.

To achieve its maximum potential, the Korean management system also will have to better suit the psychological and cultural characteristics of the Korean people. The differences in the psychological and cultural characteristics between Korea and Japan appear to be significant. These differences, as well as important similarities, can be described in terms of several key concepts relating to Korean and Japanese values and behaviour— a sense of belonging, obligation, loyalty, integrity, and consensus.

One of the most striking differences between Japanese and Koreans is the much weaker sense among Koreans of what the Japanese psychologists call *amae*—a need for a sense of belonging that fosters attitudes of subordinate dependence and mutual dependence between the employee and the firm, and between an individual employee and his peer group in the firm. Indeed, even the term *amae* has no equivalent in Korean. While Koreans also are relatively group-oriented, they also have a strong individualistic streak like most Westerners. Koreans frequently joke that an individual Korean can beat an individual Japanese, but that a group of Koreans are certain to be beaten by a group of Japanese. The cultural origins of the tendency for Koreans to be highly individualistic are unclear, but may be related to the need to survive by one's own resources in periods of extreme uncertainty. Many Koreans feel they still have to learn how to structure organizations that can function harmoniously and to behave as members of such organizations.

Koreans also seem to have a much weaker sense of indebtedness (*un* in Korean, *on* in Japanese) to an organization and one's fellow members. Once the organizational bonds are strained or broken by internal frictions, Koreans are less likely than the Japanese to feel guilty and more likely to feel anger and a sense of betrayal.

On the other hand, the concept of loyalty (*chung* in Korean, *chu* in Japanese) is similarly important to Koreans and Japanese. But the loyalty ideal in Korea is typically from subordinate to superior—from employee to the employer in a firm—rather than a two-way reciprocal obligation. As to the general concept of integrity (Korean *uiri*, Japanese *giri*) to others in everyday life, there appears to be almost no difference between Korean and Japanese attitudes.

The process of informal consensus formation (Korean *sajeon-hyupui*, Japanese *nemawashi*), prior to the making of a final decision, is also similar in Korea and Japan. Koreans adhere to this process less firmly than the Japanese, however. For example, foreigners in Japan observe that it is often impossible to reverse or change decisions in a formal meeting because the de facto final decision has already been made through *nemawashi*. The formal meeting in Japan frequently is no more than a ritualistic endorsement of the informal consensus.

These cultural differences account, in part, for differences between the Korean and Japanese management systems. In many ways, Koreans are closer to the Japanese than to Westerners in terms of race, culture, values, and social institutions. It is very important for Korean firms to properly combine the advantages of each of the three approaches to management. If Korean firms can do this, they will be well on the way to achieving optimum levels of organizational efficiency.

Part III
Korea's External Relations

12 Korea's External Economic Relations

Survival among the Giants

The sense of national insecurity, especially geopolitical insecurity, affects immensely the economic behaviour of Koreans, who have to survive facing an unpredictable and antagonistic North Korea, and are surrounded by world giants—China, Japan, the United States, and the Soviet Union. Many economic decisions in Korea have been made on the basis of security rather than economic considerations. The phrases *anbo ch'eil* ('security first') and *anbojok ch'awon* ('the security dimension') have been popular catchwords among the policymakers and national leaders. They have often used these words to justify unpopular decisions and to compel Korean firms to comply with government policies.

Many Westerners new to Asia often assume that the peoples of Korea and Japan are virtually identical. But Koreans and Japanese recognize very significant differences between themselves. What are these differences? And are there also similarities? The following remarks by Sony Corporation co-founder and chairman Akio Morita in his best-selling book, *Made in Japan*, are illuminating:

We Japanese are obsessed with survival. Every day, literally, the earth beneath our feet trembles. We live our daily lives on these volcanic islands with the constant threat not only of a major earthquake, but also of typhoons, tidal waves, savage snowstorms, spring deluges. Our islands provide us with almost no raw materials except water, and less than a quarter of our land is livable or arable. Therefore, what we have is precious to us.[1]

Koreans also, like Japanese, are obsessed with survival. In the case of Japan, what trembles is the earth beneath the feet; but in Korea what trembles is the conflict-ridden and turbulent geopolitical atmosphere that surrounds Korea and fuels anxieties. As Alvin Toffler points out in his book, *Korea and The Third Wave*, the Korean peninsula is one of those places in the world where conflicting ideologies, powers, and interests of the great powers confront each other most keenly and dangerously.[2]

Koreans live their daily lives confronting the keenly conflicting interests of the most powerful countries on earth, as well as the not necessarily imaginary threat of one of the world's most unpredictable communist regimes, namely North Korea. We are constantly reminded of the turbulent economic and political currents swirling between neighbouring China, the USSR, and Japan, as well as the United States. Japan, at least, has the advantage of being a world giant itself, but in Korea we face the same survival issues from a much weaker position. In the case of Japan, the threat to survival comes mainly from nature; in Korea nature is less threatening than the danger of conflict between Great Power interests or from North Korea.

Learning to survive among giants has been the historic destiny of the Korean people. In modern times Koreans have been under the influence of all four big powers. And Korea had long been under the influence of China before the peninsula was forcibly annexed by Japan in 1910. Liberation from 35 years of Japanese domination came in 1945, at the end of World War II. Soon thereafter, the cold war between the United States and the Soviet Union resulted in the division of the country and the tragedy of the Korean War. In the 'good old days' before the great powers were in conflict, Korea was known as 'the Land of Morning Calm'. Korea is no longer calm: ideological, political, and economic dust swirls continuously about the Korean peninsula.

Only a few countries in the world have been totally free of foreign domination throughout their history. Thailand is one of the most famous examples, and the Thais are famous for their so-called 'bamboo diplomacy'. Thais point out that the bamboo bows when the wind blows, and the seasoned bamboo bows even before the wind blows. In Korea, however, high school history books teach that Korea has been attacked by stronger neighbours more than nine hundred times during her history. We Koreans regret that we do not have the Thais' wisdom to handle our powerful neighbours as skilfully—like the seasoned bamboo bending before the strong wind.

All of Korea's neighbours are world giants, incomparably stronger than Korea in both population and territory (see Table 12.1). For instance, China's population is larger than Korea's by about 25 to one, while even Japan holds a three-fold advantage. In terms of land area the differences are even greater.

As a result of Korea's national and geopolitical characteristics, Koreans have had to deal with a number of clear-cut constraints

Table 12.1 Korea and the Major Powers Compared

	Area		Population		GNP (billion US$)	Per Capita GNP (US$) 1986
	1,000 Km²	South Korea = 100	Millions, 1986	South Korea = 100		
Korea						
South	99	100ᵃ	42.1	100ᵇ	113.2	2,690
North	121	122	20.7	49	19.4	936
Total	219	221	62.8	149	132.6	2,111
China	9,561	9,658	1,068.5	2,538	309.9	290
Japan	378	382	122.1	290	1,924.3	15,760
USA	9,373	9,468	243.8	582	4,517.6	18,530
USSR	22,402	22,628	283.1	579	2,570.3	9,079

Note: a: 99 = 100; b: 42.1 = 100

Sources: Computed from the World Bank, *World Development Report*, 1987, 1988, and 1989. North Korean figures are from Ha-Chung Yeon, 1986, 1987. Soviet GNP and per capita GNP figures are computed on the basis of the Samuelson-Nordhaus method. See Samuelson and Nordhaus, 1989, p. 841.

and necessities for survival. Korea has to live with—not in isolation from—these giants, and its outward-looking growth strategy
appears to have been the proper strategy for Korea to follow.
However, of the four global giants, Korea so far has had close
economic relations with only two—Japan and the United States.
If Korea can normalize her economic relations with the others,
namely China and the Soviet Union, her economic growth will be
greatly strengthened, as happened when Korea normalized economic relations with Japan in 1965.

Economic normalization would bring great benefits to the global giants as well. If Korea is wise and lucky enough, it may be in
a position to promote economic co-operation among the four
giants and become a pivotal point in the East Asian region. In
fact, Seoul is centrally located with respect to such major international cities as Tokyo, Osaka, Beijing, Shanghai, and Vladivostok. If Koreans act wisely, they can turn these geopolitical and
locational characteristics to their advantage, rather than face
them as handicaps as in the past.

Economic Rivalry between North and South Korea

The North-South split led each side to follow very different
strategies as they continued their rivalry. One strategy, that of
the North, seemed to work well for a time, but by the 1970s that
strategy had led to the widening gap observed in statistics.

Per capita gross national product (GNP) in North Korea
appears to have been higher than in the South during the 1950s
and until the mid-1960s, as Table 12.2 indicates. Indeed, even in
terms of trade the North was ahead of the South until the early
1960s. Table 12.3 shows that exports from the North were much
larger than from the South, and that the North was less dependent on imports.

Hakan Hedberg, a Swedish journalist famous for his accurate
forecasts about Japan, notes that North Korea was ahead in the
North-South rivalry until 1968. In 1969, however, the South
overtook the North in per capita GNP, as well as in many other
areas. Hedberg indicates that the North was superior to the
South in 17 areas in 1960, including the production of electricity,
cement, coal, fertilizer, and tractors. However, according to
Hedberg, the South started to lead the North in almost all of
these sectors after 1969.[3]

Table 12.2 Total and Per Capita GNP of North and South Korea
(In current prices)

	GNP (billion US$)			Per Capita GNP (US$)		
	South Korea (A)	North Korea (B)	Ratio A/B	South Korea (A)	North Korea (B)	Ratio A/B
1965	3.0	1.3	2.3	105	108	0.97
1970	7.8	2.8	2.8	243	198	1.23
1975	20.2	7.4	2.7	573	464	1.24
1980	61.2	14.7	4.2	1,605	822	1.95
1985	83.7	15.4	5.4	2,150	755	2.85
1987	118.6	19.4	6.1	3,098	936	3.31

Note: Computed from the data compiled by Ha-Cheong Yeon. His data were adjusted to fit the actual and per capita GNP of South Korea. See Ha-cheong Yeon, *North Korean Economic Policy and Management*, Korea Development Institute Research Report No. 57 (in Korean), December 1986. Figures for 1987 are from The National Unification Board, *An Overall Appraisal of the North Korean Economy (87 Nyun Bukhankyung-jae Jonghabpyungka)*, Seoul, 1988, and *An Overview of the the North Korean Economy*, 1989. North Korean population figures in 1987 were, according to the NUB, 20.7 million, smaller than the Economic Planning Board figure of 21.3 million.

In Beijing I met a Chinese scholar, an expert on the North Korean economy, who confided to me that per capita income in the North is presently no more than one-third the level in the South. The personal possessions of most North Koreans consist of little more than utilitarian clothing, grain coupons, and low-quality daily necessities provided by the state. The scholar's estimate of the status of the North Korean economy is consistent with the GNP statistics shown in Table 12.2. Other foreign visitors also have commented on the generally very low quality of life in North Korea. Because the North Korean economy is military-oriented and inward-looking, the trade volume of the North is also very small compared with that of the South, as indicated in Table 12.3. South Korean and Japanese experts on the North Korean economy give the following reasons for the North Korean economy's structural problems.[4]

Firstly, because of its almost entirely self-dependent develop-

Table 12.3 The Foreign Trade of North and South Korea Compared (in million US dollars)

	Total			Exports		Imports		Trade Deficit	
	South Korea A	North Korea B	Ratio A/B	South Korea	North Korea	South Korea	North Korea	South Korea	North Korea
1960	350	320	1.1	32	154	316	166	−284	−12
1970	2,820	680	4.1	835	341	1,984	378	−1,149	−37
1975	12,360	1,840	6.7	5,081	806	7,274	1,155	−2,193	−349
1980	39,800	3,350	11.9	17,505	1,642	22,292	1,710	−4,787	−68
1985	61,419	3,185	19.3	30,283	1,285	31,136	1,900	−853	−615
1987	88,301	4,060	21.7	47,281	1,670	41,020	2,390	6,261	−720

Sources: Ha-Cheong Yeon, 'The North Korean External Economic Relations in Recent Years: Structure and Development' (in Korean), in *Korea Development Review*, Vol. 9, No. 3, Fall 1987. Ha-Cheong Yeon, *North Korean Economic Policy and Management* (in Korean), Seoul: Korea Development Institute Research Report No. 57, December 1986. Ministry of Finance, *Fiscal and Financial Statistics*, June 1988, and The National Unification Board, *An Overall Appraisal of the North Korean Economy, 1977* (*87 Nyun Bukhankyungjae Jonghabpyungka*), Seoul 1988.

ment strategy, the North has rejected large-scale use of foreign capital and technology. As a result of this closed-economy approach, North Korea lags far behind the South in tapping outside sources of technological improvement and capital formation. Because of this, North Korea recently introduced its own 'Joint Management Law' which has some similarities to free-world laws governing joint ventures. So far, however, there is little evidence that the North has had significant success in attracting foreign investors.

Secondly, North Korea's economic management style is still very similar to that adopted by the USSR during the Stalin era. The North still places excessive emphasis on machinery and steel and autarchical development. The resulting losses in efficiency due to this highly centralized and autarchical economic system are enormous.

Thirdly, the overall industrial structure is highly imbalanced. The top national priority is given to heavy industries and the military, with the result that the growth of light manufacturing industries and infrastructure industries has been seriously restricted. Consequently, consumer goods—a principal tool in motivating workers—are in chronic short supply.

The North Korean economy appears, in fact, to be permanently on a war footing. Pyongyang allocates about 22 per cent of its GNP to the military (see Table 12.4), much more than the 5 per cent of GNP spent on defence in South Korea. The driving force behind the allocation of economic resources in North Korea is the maintenance and strengthening of its military power. The distortions caused by excessive military expenditures have resulted in serious economic problems, including default on some foreign debts.

Lastly, because North Korea relies on the 'Stakhanovite' approach that puts overwhelming emphasis on the role of increased labour mobilization to expand production, the North Koreans have given technical innovation comparatively low priority.

Economic Relations between Korea and the United States

Economic relations between Korea and the United States have undergone drastic changes as Korea has developed. Until the

Table 12.4 Major Economic Indicators for North and South Korea, 1987

	South Korea	North Korea
Total land (Km)	99,091	122,370
Arable land (Km)	21,670	20,690
Rice paddies	13,520	6,300
Dry fields	8,510	14,390
Per farm household (ha)	1.15	1.60
Population ('000)	42,082	20,690
GNP (billion US$)	118.6	19.4
Per capita GNP (US$)	3,098	936
Economic growth rate (per cent)	12.0	3.3
Defense Expenditure/GNP (per cent)	5.0	21.8
Foreign debts (billion US$)	35.6	5.2
Electricity generation capacity (million kW)	19.0	6.4
Oil refinery capacity (million M/T)	35.6	3.5
Iron production (million M/T)	18.5	4.8
Number of automobiles (1'000)	1,611	189
Television sets ('000, 1983)	8,850	200

Sources: Ha-Cheong Yeon. *North Korean Economic Policy and Management* (in Korean), Korea Development Institute Research Report No. 57, December 1986, Economic Planning Board, *Major Statistics of Korean Economy*, Seoul, Korea, 1988. The National Unification Board, 1987.

mid-1960s, when Korea was still very poor and at the stage of a 'less developed country', its economic relations with the United States were mainly that of the recipient/donor type. According to Edward Mason, 'during the period 1953 through 1962, foreign aid (to Korea), 95 percent of which came from the United States, amounted to some 8 percent of Korean GNP, 77 percent of fixed capital formation, and financed about 70 percent of imports. Until 1965 almost all U.S. economic assistance was in the form of grants.'[5] Korea was then the third largest recipient of foreign aid in the world, after Vietnam and Israel.

As Korea graduated from underdeveloped country status in the early 1960s and approached NIC (newly industrializing country) status around 1970, United States economic assistance gradually declined and increasingly took the form of loans. The relationship between Korea and the United States from the mid-1960s to the mid-1980s shifted to one of borrower and lender or debtor and creditor. Korea's heavy foreign borrowing after the mid-1960s eventually made it the fourth largest debtor nation in the world. The United States was, of course, the largest lender to Korea. Foreign debt peaked at US$46.7 billion in 1985, but declined rapidly thereafter.

Economic relations between Korea and the United States entered into a new phase from 1986 as Korea's trade balance with the United States turned positive for the first time. By 1988 Korea had become one of the top five trade surplus countries in the world—the others being Japan, West Germany, Taiwan, and Canada. Korea's trade surplus with the United States grew from $4.3 billion in 1985 to $9.6 billion in 1987 and $8.7 billion in 1988 respectively (see Table 12.5). The United States is Korea's largest trade partner and accounts for most of Korea's positive trade balance. Economic relations between Korea and the United States since 1986 have increasingly turned on the trade-balance issue, and if the present trend continues, the previous debtor/creditor relationship between the two countries will be reversed.

Many Americans believe that Korea's *embarras de richesse* is due chiefly to the maintenance of unfair trade barriers and an undervalued currency. Conversely, many Koreans see the large United States trade deficit as being mainly of America's own making, and feel that the United States is blaming Korea for its own shortcomings. Many Koreans also believe the United States fails to recognize that Korea is still a developing country with a large foreign debt, and still undergoing rapid and difficult socio-economic transformation and political democratization. As a result, economic relations between Korea and the United States have become increasingly contentious, especially towards the American use of section 301 of the Trade Act of 1974 and the so-called 'super 301' provisions of the omnibus trade act to pressure Korea to open its markets and revalue its currency. Koreans suspect, however, that even if they take steps to revalue the Korean won and liberalize trade, it will be mainly Japan, not America, that will benefit. Koreans doubt that such measures would significantly reduce Korea's trade surplus with the United States. Korean businessmen argue that they import more from Japan than from the United States despite the rising Japanese yen because Japanese goods are still more competitive than

Table 12.5 Korea's Trade with Neighbouring Countries and the United States (in million US dollars)

To and From	1965 Amount	%	1975 Amount	%	1985 Amount	%	1988 Amount	%
U.S.A.								
Exports	62	35.4	1,536	30.2	10,754	35.5	21,404	35.3
Imports	182	39.3	1,881	25.9	6,489	20.8	12,747	24.6
Balance	−120	—	−345	—	4,265	—	8,657	—
Japan								
Exports	45	25.7	1,293	25.4	4,543	15.0	12,004	19.8
Imports	175	37.8	2,434	33.5	7,560	24.3	15,929	30.7
Balance	−130	—	−1,141	—	−3,017	—	−3,925	—
Taiwan								
Exports	2	1.1	63	1.2	196	0.6	954	1.6
Imports	10	2.2	162	2.2	333	1.1	1,071	2.1
Balance	−8	—	−99	—	−137	—	−117	—
China								
Exports	—	—	—	—	40	0.1	372	0.6
Imports	—	—	—	—	478	1.5	1,387	2.7
Balance	—	—	—	—	−438	—	−1,015	—
Total Trade								
Exports	175	100.0	5,081	100.0	30,283	100.0	60,696	100.0
Imports	463	100.0	7,274	100.0	31,136	100.0	51,810	100.0
Balance	−288	—	−2,193	—	−853	—	8,886	—

Sources: Economic Planning Board, *Major Statistics of Korean Economy 1985, 1989.* Ministry of Finance, *Fiscal and Financial Statistics,* Seoul, MoF, March 1989.

American goods. Moreover, in many cases appropriate United States substitutes do not exist.

Key Reasons for Korea's Trade Surplus

There appear to be two basic reasons for Korea's large trade surplus and strong economic performance since 1986. One is favourable external conditions, known, as we have seen, as the 'three lows,' namely, low oil and natural resource prices, a low dollar, and low international interest rates. Since 1986, these three factors have given a great boost to the Korean economy, especially exports. The other reason is the sweeping economic reforms that were carried out by the Korean government in the early 1980s to achieve price stability and improved efficiency through competition.

At the time, the government employed tight monetary and fiscal policies to bring inflation, measured in wholesale prices, down from 39 per cent in 1980 to −1.5 per cent in 1986. At the same time, the fiscal deficit was reduced from 4.7 per cent of GNP to 0.1 per cent between 1981 and 1986. Controlling inflation involved such unpopular measures as freezing the salaries of civil servants and not raising the grain purchase price. These unpopular measures cost the government party votes in the presidential and parliamentary elections of 1987–8.

The measures taken by the government to increase economic efficiency have included privatization of government-owned banks and public enterprises, reduction or removal of various administrative controls, and enactment of the fair trade and anti-monopoly law in 1981. Imports and foreign investment were also liberalized to introduce foreign competition in order to promote efficiency at home that would translate into greater external competitiveness. Korea's import liberalization ratio was 68.6 per cent in 1980, but increased to 94.8 per cent by the time of the 1988 Seoul Summer Olympics. The government also liberalized foreign investments through a 'negative list' system under which the industries not on the negative list were opened to foreign investment. At present, 97.5 per cent of all manufacturing industries are open to foreign investment.

Korea's industrial policy has also been restructured. As the international competitiveness of Korean firms expanded, the government switched from a policy of supporting specific industries with preferential loans and interest rates to a more general policy of providing technical guidance, information, and manpower training. The government also shifted from favouring the larger firms to a more balanced policy designed to promote small and medium-sized firms as well as large ones.

The former Minister of Finance Il Sakong argues that:

these structural reforms have been very successful. During the last few years, prices have stabilized, industrial productivity has increased, the overall efficiency of the economy has improved significantly, and as a result, so too has Korea's external competitiveness. Because of these reforms, [Koreans] were fully able to exploit favourable developments in the external economic environment, and Korea has made great progress since the beginning of 1986.[6]

Korea's large trade surplus arises directly from the improved international competitiveness of the Korean economy since the early 1980s, rather than from the maintenance of unfair trade barriers or an undervalued currency. Undervaluation, of course, as pointed out by MIT's Rudiger Dornbusch, helped to raise Korea's international competitiveness and growth in productivity.[7] But currency undervaluation alone cannot account for Korea's large trade surplus.

Important Reasons for America's Large Trade Deficits

Rudiger Dornbusch also points to the budget deficit as the underlying cause for America's widening trade deficit.[8] Martin Feldstein, former chief economic advisor to President Reagan, shares this opinion, asserting that 'the primary reason for our deteriorating trade imbalance was the 70 per cent rise of the dollar that occurred between 1980 and the spring of 1985.' The main reason for the sharp rise in the dollar was, according to Feldstein, high interest rates on dollar securities due to the sharp rise in current and expected future budget deficits.[9]

Recently both American and Korean experts on United States-Korea trade issues convened at the Institute for International Economics in Washington, D.C. Thomas O. Bayard of IIE summarized the views presented in the conference as follows:

It was generally accepted that many US-Korean conflicts stem largely, if not exclusively, from global macroeconomic imbalances ... The solution to these global imbalances lies in cooperation among all the major trading nations. For its part, the United States must cut its budget deficit substantially in the next three to four years. Many Koreans ... accept that Korea, too, should contribute to the reduction of the global trade imbalance.[10]

Policies towards United States-Korea Economic Relations

United States policymakers have called for Korea to liberalize trade and appreciate the won to help reduce America's trade deficit. Koreans believe these measures will also help the healthy growth of the Korean economy, but believe that changes must be introduced of a speed and scope appropriate to the current stage and phase of Korea's economic growth. The escalation of United States pressure on Korea to liberalize trade and revalue its currency has caused ordinary Koreans to feel that the United States wants them to sacrifice themselves for Americans. Such thinking has stirred up anti-American feelings.

There are deep differences of perception surrounding United States-Korea trade issues. The average Korean's perception is that the United States is incomparably stronger than Korea, and that opening Korean markets to the United States will lead to the collapse of many Korean industries and badly hurt domestic agriculture. Such Koreans fail to realize the increased importance of Korea's economy in the global economy or the seriousness of America's widening trade deficit. They also retain a 'developing country mentality', which leads them to expect special treatment from the United States and other advanced countries. Americans, however, also have a misperception that 'Korea may be a second Japan' and that United States-Korea trade relations are basically the same as United States-Japanese relations.

These perceptions on the part of Koreans are obstacles to Korea's trade liberalization and currency appreciation. Rapid political democratization since June 1987 also has invigorated various interest groups such as farmers, consumers, labour unions, students, and dissident unions. Large scale protests by farmers against the government agricultural policy have reflected this trend, and Korean policymakers are under heavy pressure to go slowly on import liberalization.

None the less, Korea needs to steadily liberalize trade by removing various market-distorting elements such as non-tariff barriers and administrative practices that deter foreign investment. Although trade liberalization needs to be co-ordinated with other policies, liberalization is preferable to currency re-valuation and should take priority.

Factors such as labour disputes are already exerting adverse effects on trade performance, and the lag effects of previous revaluations and liberalizations, and uncertainty with respect to inflationary pressure and domestic savings behaviour could re-duce the Korean trade surplus rather significantly in the near future. Foreign observers such as Rudiger Dornbusch of MIT and Ann Krueger, former vice president of the World Bank, also have noted that Korea must find its proper speed and scale of trade liberalization and currency appreciation.[11] Indeed, Krueger believes that Korea still needs to reduce its large amount of foreign debt, and probably needs to maintain a current account surplus for a few more years.[12] One way to lessen the United States-Korea trade imbalance in the interim is to use Korea's large trade surplus to purchase American goods, especially high-tech items.

Korea also needs to avoid creating American suspicions of its intentions of taking steps to co-operate with America in reducing trade frictions. As Soo-Gil Young advocates, the Korean govern-ment decision-making and policy process must be clear-cut in order to avoid misunderstandings.[13] It is very important to reduce unnecessary suspicions that may arise because of the differences between the two countries in decision-making processes, culture, and way of thinking. It goes without saying that Korea and the United States need to co-operate closely to resolve conflicts over trade and macroeconomic policies. They also need to devise more basic and long-term solutions, possibly to include a free-trade agreement as proposed by Dornbusch.[14]

Economic Relations with Neighbouring Countries

Korea's largest neighbouring country, in terms of trade, is Japan. For two full decades from the end of the Japanese colonial period in 1945 until 1965, when relations were normalized, there were no formal economic relations between the two countries. Since then, economic relations have expanded rapidly (Table 12.5).

Korea has consistently had a trade deficit with Japan since 1965. This is in part because Korea's trade pattern is similar to that of Japan, but Korean goods and services have not yet become competitive with Japanese goods and services. Moreover, Korea has been dependent upon Japan for machinery, equipment, and other parts needed in manufacturing export goods, and shifting to American substitutes has been slow and difficult.

In terms of exports and total trade, America has been Korea's largest trade partner. But in terms of imports and foreign direct investment, Japan has been Korea's major partner. Korean businessmen usually list the following reasons for Korea's dependence on the United States for export markets and on Japan for import goods and foreign investment. They form the similarity between Korea and Japan in the pattern of industrial growth, proximity, ease of communication between Koreans and Japanese, and timely after-sales service provided by Japanese firms.

Korea's other major neighbouring countries are China and Taiwan. Korea's economic relations with Taiwan go back to the 1940s, when the two countries were liberated from Japan, but trade with Taiwan has not been large. Because of Korea's substantial food imports from Taiwan, Korea has had a trade deficit with Taiwan for most of this period.

Korea's economic relationship with China during the post-war period started in 1978 with the beginning of China's open-door policy, but it was not until 1985 that trade between the two countries started to expand rapidly (see Table 12.5.) Since then, trade between Korea and China has, if indirect trade through Hong Kong is included, exceeded that between Korea and Taiwan. President Roh Tae Woo's 'Bukbang (northward) policy', aiming at opening up relations with socialist countries like China and the USSR, has accelerated non-traditional economic ties. China is presently Korea's largest trade partner among the socialist countries, accounting for three-fourths of Korea's total trade with the socialist bloc. Korea's second largest trade partner in the bloc is the USSR, although the actual trade volume remains quite small.

South Korea's trade with North Korea had been officially prohibited by both sides until recently, but from 1988 North-South trade began on a very small scale, and is still mainly conducted through third-party brokers. The South imports mainly primary goods such as coal and fish, and exports industrial goods. However, future prospects for North-South trade depend greatly upon the unpredictable behavior of Kim Il Sung and the ups and downs in the political dialogue between the two sides.

The Emerging East Asian Era

Japan is now the second-ranking economy in the world. Many experts, both Japanese and non-Japanese, speculate that the size of Japan's economy may catch up with or even exceed that of the United States economy towards the year 2000. By the end of 1987, Japan's per capita GNP exceeded that of the United States (See Table 12.6) and there is no doubt that the relative size of the Japanese economy will continue to increase.

According to projections made by the Economic Planning Agency of Japan,[15] the aggregate size of the economies of all the other East and South-east Asian countries, namely, Korea, China, Taiwan, Hong Kong, and the ASEAN nations (Singapore, Indonesia, Malyasia, the Philippines, and Thailand) is presently about half the size of the Japanese economy—actually 44.2 per cent in 1987 according to Table 12.7. Because of the high growth rates of these economies, however, their aggregate size probably will be about the same as the Japanese economy towards the year 2000. This implies that the total economic size of the East and South-east Asian region will equal about twice the Japanese economy towards the year 2000—making the area the de facto centre of the world economy at the turn of the 21st century. As the region's economies grow, their stages of development will change accordingly. I have projected the stages of development of these countries using the Chenery-Syrquin framework[16] and the growth projections made by the Japanese Economic Planning Agency. The projections for Chinese growth between 1985 and 2000 employ the estimates of Dwight H. Perkins of Harvard University, who places income figures for China at $500 in 1985 rising to $1,200–1,500 by the year 2000.[17] Making GNP comparisons by using official exchange rates is highly treacherous, especially when comparisons include countries with different economic systems. Nevertheless, the results indicate that all the presently developing countries in the region will 'graduate' to newly industrializing country (NIC) status by the year 2000, while almost all the current Asian NICs will have achieved more developed country or advanced country status (see Table 12.8).

From the point of view of Korea, this means that Korea will have on its eastern side the huge Japanese economy and on its western and southern sides the burgeoning economies of China and South-east Asia, whose combined size will be comparable to

Table 12.6 Economic Indicators for South Korea and its Major Trading Partners

	1984	1985	1986	1987	1988
Korea					
1. GNP per capita, US$	2,044	2,060	2,503	3,098	4,040
2. GNP growth rate (%)	8.4	5.4	12.3	12.0	12.1
3. Unemployment (%)	3.8	4.0	3.8	3.1	2.5
4. Inflation (%)	2.3	2.5	2.8	3.0	7.1
5. Exports (billion $)	29.2	30.3	34.7	47.3	60.7
Imports (billion $)	30.6	31.1	31.6	41.0	51.8
6. Increase in labour productivity (%)	9.2	4.9	14.5	9.6	13.9
Taiwan					
1. GNP per capita, US$	3,091	3,191	3,841	5,043	6,053
2. GNP growth rate (%)	10.5	5.1	11.7	11.9	7.3
3. Unemployment (%)	2.4	2.9	2.7	2.0	1.7
4. Inflation (%)	0.0	−0.2	0.7	0.5	1.3
5. Exports (billion $)	30.4	30.7	39.8	53.5	60.6
Imports (billion $)	22.0	20.1	24.2	35.0	49.7
6. Increase in labour productivity (%)	3.0	2.7	12.0	11.8	7.5
Japan					
1. GNP per capita, US$	10,463	11,176	16,173	19,553	23,358
2. GNP growth rate (%)	5.1	4.9	2.5	4.5	5.7
3. Unemployment (%)	2.7	2.6	2.8	2.8	2.5
4. Inflation (%)	2.3	2.0	0.6	0.1	0.7
5. Exports (billion $)	170.1	175.6	209.2	229.2	246.9
Imports (billion $)	136.5	129.5	126.4	149.5	187.5
6. Increase in labour productivity (%)	6.1	1.5	3.0	4.0	7.9
United States					
1. GNP per capita, US$	15,882	16,706	17,419	18,570	19,760
2. GNP growth rate (%)	6.8	3.4	2.8	3.4	3.8
3. Unemployment (%)	7.5	7.2	7.0	6.2	5.5
4. Inflation (%)	4.3	3.6	1.9	3.7	4.1
5. Exports (billion $)	224.0	218.8	227.2	254.1	321.8
Imports (billion $)	346.4	352.5	382.3	424.4	441.6
6. Increase in labour productivity (%)	3.9	4.3	3.7	2.7	3.8

Note: Inflation is based on consumer price index.
Sources: The Bank of Korea, *Economic Indicators of Major Countries*, 20 March 1989, and *Monthly Bulletin*, February 1989. Korea Labour Institute, *Wages and Related Statistics, 1989*. The Bank of Japan Research and Statistics Department, *Comparative Economic and Financial Statistics — Japan and Other Major Countries*, Tokyo, BOJ, 1989.

Table 12.7 Major Economic Indicators for East and South-east Asian Countries

	Population (millions) 1987	GNP per Capita		Area ('000 km^2)
		Dollars 1987	Growth Rate (%) (1965–87)	
ASEAN				
Indonesia	171.4	450	4.5	1,905
Malaysia	16.5	1,810	4.1	330
Philippines	58.4	590	1.7	300
Thailand	53.6	850	3.9	514
Total	299.9	624		3,049
Asian NICs				
Hong Kong	5.6	8,070	6.2	1
Korea	42.1	2,690	6.4	98
Singapore	2.6	7,940	7.2	1
Taiwan	19.5	5,043	6.6	36
Total	69.8	3,975		136
China	1,068.5	585	5.2	9,561
Japan	122.1	15,760	4.2	378
ESA total (A)	1,560.3	1,932	—	13,124
World total (B)[a]	4,638.6 (5,010.1)[b]	3,264[c]	—	106,890 (133,535)[b]
Ratio (A/B, %)	33.6% (31.1%)[b]	59.2%	—	12.3% (9.8%)[b]

Notes: China's per capita GNP figure for 1985 was US$500 according to Dwight H. Perkins. It was updated by the author for 1987. See Dwight H. Perkins, 1988. ESA = East and South-east Asian countries.
a. Excludes USSR and Eastern Europe.
b. Includes USSR and Eastern Europe.
c. Excludes USSR, Eastern Europe, and countries for which national income data are not available.

Sources: World Bank, *World Development Report*, 1989. Taiwan, *Taiwan Statistical Data Book*, 1988, 1989, and Economic Planning Board/National Bureau of Statistics, *Major Statistics of the Korean Economy*, 1989.

GDP (US$ billion)		Average Annual GDP Growth Rate		Merchandise Trade (US$ billion)	
1965	1987	1965–80	1980–7	Exports	Imports
3.8	70.0	8.0	3.6	17.2	14.5
3.1	31.2	7.4	4.5	17.9	12.5
6.0	34.6	5.9	−0.5	5.6	7.1
4.4	48.2	7.2	5.6	11.7	13.0
17.3	184.0			52.4	47.1
2.2	36.5	8.6	5.8	48.5	48.5
3.0	121.3	9.5	8.6	47.2	40.9
1.0	19.9	10.1	5.4	28.6	32.5
2.8	97.2	9.3	7.3	53.5	35.0
9.0	274.9			177.8	156.9
65.6	591.9	6.4	10.4	39.5	43.4
91.1	2,376.4	6.3	3.8	229.1	146.0
183.0	3,427.2	—	—	498.8	393.4
1,749.6	15,139.8	4.1	2.9	2,390.2	2,477.7
10.5%	22.6%	—	—	20.9%	15.9%

Table 12.8 The Stages in the Development of the Economies of East and South-east Asia

Number of Stages	Type of Stage	Per Capita GNP (in 1982 US$)	Per Capita GNP, 1985 (in 1985 US$)	Per Capita GNP, 2000 (in 1982 US$)
1.	LDC Stage I	Below 364		
2.	LDC Stage II	364	China (500), Indonesia (530), Philippines (580)	
		728		
3.	NIC Stage I	1,456	Thailand (800)	China (1,250), (1,500)
4.	NIC Stage II	2,912	Malaysia (2,000), Korea (2,150)	Philippines (1,600), Indonesia (1,670), Thailand (2,310)
5.	NIC Stage III	5,456	Taiwan (3,145)	Korea (4,950)
6.	MDC Stage I	8,736	Hong Kong (6,230), Singapore (7,420)	Malaysia (5,550), Taiwan (6,538)
7.	MDC Stage II	13,104	Japan (11,300)	Hong Kong (13,010)
8.	MDC Stage III	Over 13,104		Singapore (15,280), Japan (19,220)

Note: China's per capita GNP figures in this table are from Pwight H. Perkins, 1988, pp. 632. Hollis Chenery's stage classification corresponds to stages 2-7 in our classification scheme as presented in this table. Our classification scheme, thus, is more comprehensive than that of Chenery and Syrquin, 1986b, in that it also includes LDC stage I and MDC stage III.

Sources: Per capita GNP figures for the year 1985 are from the World Bank, *World Development Report*, 1987, and for the year 2000 are from Japanese Economic Planning Agency, *Prospects for the Pacific Age-Economic Development and Policy Issues of the Pacific Region to the Year 2000*, July 1985. Figures for Taiwan are those projected by Lawrence Klein, 1986.

that of Japan. This opens the possibility that in the future Korea may become a key centre of the East Asian regional economy.

As a central country in the region (see Fig. 12.1), Korea needs to cope appropriately with changes that are expected to take place in the western Pacific in connection with the change in the patterns and stages of national and industrial development and interdependence in the region towards the year 2000.

In terms of industrial development, countries presently at the early (foods and textiles) or middle (wood products and chemicals) industrial stage will advance to the middle or late (electronics and machinery) stage. Countries already at the middle or late industry stage will advance to the late or high-tech industry (computer, robotics, bio-technology) stages. This development process can be explained in terms of the 'multi-layer' or 'multi-tier' catching-up process. This process will lead, on the one hand, to an increasing interdependence among the major blocs of the region by means of international inter-industry linkages, and, on the other hand, increased competition among them.

This multi-tier catching-up process will lead to a multi-tier interdepedence among the region's economies as countries move up the technology ladder and patterns of comparative advantage change. For instance, some ASEAN countries at the early-to-middle stage of development are dependent upon Asian NICs for late industries. Asian NICs which are at the late-industries stage are in turn dependent upon Japan for high-tech industries.

Development strategies of most least developed countries in the region are expected to be re-oriented away from an inward-looking or neutral strategy towards an outward-, industry-oriented growth strategy. The resource-rich countries, which are at present mostly ASEAN nations, are expected to switch their future development strategies from an emphasis on primary products to manufacturing. This shift in strategy will be due largely to the following factors: shifts in final demand away from agricultural products with rising income, shifts in comparative advantage away from primary products, and overall excess production capacity of many primary product sellers.

Malaysia, as represented by its Look East policy and its Industrial Master Plan, and Thailand, aiming to be the forerunners of the ASEAN nations, have already taken extensive action to re-orient their strategies away from primary products and towards industrialization. Indonesia and the Philippines are expected to

Fig. 12.1 Korea as a Regional Centre of East Asia

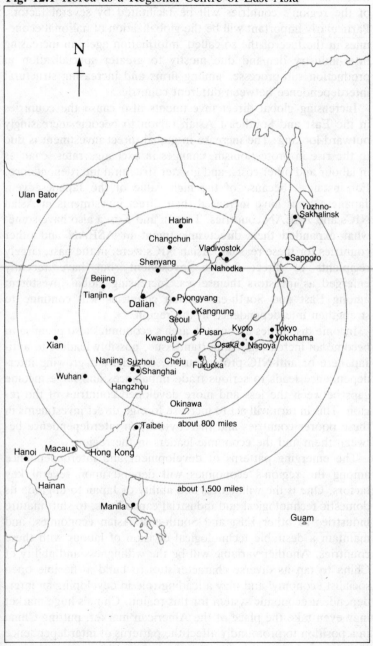

follow suit. The adoption of outward-looking strategies by most of the region's countries will be facilitated by several factors. Particularly important will be the globalization of national economies in the face of the so-called 'information age', an increasing inter-industry demand due mostly to greater specialization in production sub-processes among firms and increasing structural interdependence between different countries.

Increasing global direct investments also cause the countries in the East and Southeast Asian region to become increasingly outward-looking. The increase in global direct investment is due to the rise in protectionism, changes in exchange rates, changes in labour and other costs, and greater structural interdependence. For instance, because of the high value of the Japanese yen, Japanese firms have increased their direct investments in Asian NICs and ASEAN countries. Taiwan and Korea also have somewhat expanded their direct investment in ASEAN and other countries for these reasons. Asian NICs were, in the past, largely recipients of direct foreign investment, but have recently emerged as investors themselves. Increasing global investment among East and South-east Asian countries will continue to strengthen interdependence in the region.

Income disparities among the area's economies also promise to become an increasingly important issue, possibly leading to anti-Japanese or anti-NIC protectionism, especially if growing interdependence leads to serious trade imbalances and large income gaps between the less and more developed countries of the region. This in turn will act to increase foreign direct investments in these poorer countries and thereby deepen interdependence between them and the economic leaders in the region.

The emerging patterns of development and interdependence among the region's economies will depend upon several key factors. One is the willingness and ability of Japan to upgrade its domestic technological and industrial capabilities, to shift mature industries to other East and South-east Asian economies, and maintain a desirable technological division of labour with these countries. Another variable will be the willingness and ability of China to tap its diverse characteristics to build a 'flexible open socialist economy' and play a leading role in developing an interdependent economic system for this region. China's huge market may even take the place of the American market, putting China in a position to profoundly affect the patterns of interdependence in the region. China's industrialization may provide the other area economies with new frontiers and act as a driving force for the region's economy as a whole. A third factor is the willingness of the region's less developed countries to adopt an outward- and industry-oriented development strategy, and to upgrade their technological and industrial capabilities.

Because all the region's countries will be inseparable parts of an increasingly interdependent economic system, each will have to accept its 'global responsibility' regarding the division of labour and structural integration among the region's economies.

13 Prospects for the Future

Korean and Japanese Stereotypes

Domestic and foreign experts have offered many explanations for the rapid economic growth in Korea in comparison with that in Japan. Hugh Patrick and Henry Rosovsky have succinctly presented the most typical explanations of Japanese growth in the concluding chapter of their work, *Asia's New Giant—How the Japanese Economy Works*. Their conclusions reflect an analysis of the results of collaborative research on various aspects of the Japanese economy by 23 American and Japanese economists.[1] The framework used by Patrick and Rosovsky is also a useful way to put the Korean case in a comparative perspective.

In one widely accepted view, Japanese growth policy has been rooted in a drive to catch up. That is, Japan pursued rapid growth in order to catch up with the advanced western countries. Koreans have speculated that Japan, as the loser in the military contest of World War II, has driven itself to win the economic battle with the advanced countries, especially the United States. According to Japanese scholars Yamamura and Yasuba, however, Japan had already caught up in terms of industrialization in the 1970s, and is now in a post catch-up growth stage.[2]

In contrast to Japan's unchanging 'catch-up' growth philosophy, Korea's growth philosophy has changed several times since the beginning of rapid growth in the early 1960s. In the early years it was 'to escape dire poverty and exceed North Korea'. This was repeatedly emphasized by President Park Chung Hee and reflected in planning documents prepared in the 1960s[3]. However, as South Korea's per capita income moved ahead of North Korea's in 1969, and the country achieved newly-industrializing-country status, the goal of economic growth changed. In the 1970s it became to expand the country's economic power as much as possible. Accordingly, Korea's trade promotion was carried out in a highly mercantilist way. Specifically, in the *Long-Term Perspective Plan (1972–1981)* prepared by the Economic Planning Board, a key target was to greatly expand the heavy and chemical industries and to increase Korea's total exports to US$10 billion and per capita income to US$1,000 by 1981.[4]

With the advent of the Chun Doo Hwan government in 1981, however, Korea's growth philosophy became *Sunjin chokuk Changjo* (creation of an advanced fatherland). This was stressed repeatedly by President Chun and accepted as the keystone of various growth policies and planning documents in the early 1980s. The most systematic and representative projection of Korea's growth potential is summarized in *Korea Year 2000: Prospects and Issues for Long-Term Development* prepared by the Korea Development Institute[5]. The focus in Korea on becoming an advanced country contrasts with Japan's goal of catching up with and perhaps surpassing Western advanced countries. Because Korea's population is much smaller than that of Japan or the United States, Korea cannot realistically expect to catch up in aggregate economic power, but aims at reaching advanced-country status in terms of per capita income. Japan, however, appears to aim at matching or passing the advanced countries in terms of both per capita income and aggregate economic power.

A second point is that demand management in Korea was, as in Japan, basically aimed at maximizing growth, rather than towards achieving stable growth. Nevertheless, in Japan the government intentionally slowed growth at times to control inflation and balance-of-payments problems—while Korea always pushed almost expansionary policies in spite of rising inflation and balance-of-payment deficits. Especially in the 1960s and 1970s, this 'growth-at-any-cost policy' was accompanied by various economic problems, including high inflation, and growing disparities between large and small firms. As a result, Korea's growth policy shifted to 'growth with stability' in the early 1980s.

Thirdly, the expansion of manufacturing production capacity in Korea was undertaken primarily to expand exports. In the case of Japan, Patrick and Rosovsky indicate that, except in the 1960s and early 1970s, Japanese growth was led by domestic demand rather than foreign demand. Lawrence Krause and Sueo Sekiguchi also indicate the same thing. They reject the notion that Japanese growth was led primarily by exports.

Another feature is that the Korean economy is a large-firm economy. Economic expansion has been achieved mainly through the expansion of large business conglomerates (*jaebol*), and Korea's industrial organization is highly concentrated. Contrary to the widespread belief that Japanese growth was also achieved through the expansion of large financial-industrial groups, Caves argues that the concentration of manufacturing industries in Japan is about the same as in the United States.[6] This is because Japan has a relatively well-developed medium and small enterprise sector. The need for Korea to promote small and medium enterprises in the future is stressed in the new constitution enacted in 1987.

Japan's technology strategy is often called the 'strategy of number two'. The Japanese have not invested much money in experimental technology such as space exploration, in which they are behind the United States and the USSR. The main interest of the Japanese has been in importing and commercializing existing technologies through adroit product development and management. Japan has always been ahead in maintaining its position as runner up in the area of technology. Japan benefited greatly from the technology gap with advanced countries. But after it caught up in the 1970s, the possibility of benefiting from this gap shrank. Korea continues to benefit greatly from a large technology gap with Japan and other advanced countries. As this gap narrows, however, the cost of obtaining technology from advanced countries will increase.

Patrick and Rosovsky indicate that the Japanese financial system was very inefficient because of tight control of interest rates, discrimination against small firms, the absence of a bond market, and overborrowing. The same can be said for Korea. The Korean system was, as indicated by Cole and Park, characterized not only by internal disequilibrium, but also by a large and active informal financial sector.[7]

Japan's small expenditures on defence and general social welfare was the major cause for the low tax burden, which acted as a stimulant to economic growth. In the case of Korea the burden of the tax system has been rather high because of large expenditures on defense and large subsidies given to agriculture.

All specialists agree that the rapid growth of Korea and Japan cannot be principally ascribed to any single factor such as education, cheap labour, or capital formation. Rather, it was the result of a combination of many factors, none of which predominates.

Patrick and Rosovsky indicate too that while Japanese labour relations were harmonious, harmony was achieved at the expense of the worker. The same thing can be said in the case of Korea, although since mid-1987 labour relations have become increasingly antagonistic and confrontational, and the wages of workers have risen rapidly.

Also, the concept of 'Japan, Inc.' or 'Korea, Inc.' is misleading. The private sector in both countries is highly competitive and has influenced the process of economic growth at least as much as government policy directives.

Finally, the notion that Japan and Korea alone are suffering from various urban problems such as severe congestion, poor housing, environmental pollution, and high urban density is wrong. Large metropolitan areas all over the world tend to have similar urban ills.

The Rise of the Korean Economy towards the Year 2000

The 1960s and the 1970s marked Korea's 'great leap toward a semideveloped state', and the 1970s and 1980s saw the 'transition from semidevelopment to economic maturity' in Korea. Can Korea continue to grow rapidly and follow Japan into the ranks of non-Western advanced countries? Both Korean and foreign experts have tried to answer this question. Generally, foreigners tend to be more optimistic than Koreans about the future of the Korean economy.

Lawrence R. Klein, Nobel laureate economist and world authority on economic forecasting, has projected that if Korea's per capita income continues to grow at 6 per cent a year, Korea will become an advanced country by the year 2000. Klein argues that Korea's 'highly favorable supply of high-quality human capital makes me confident that the numerical projections to the year 2000 are sensible.'[8] Other important reasons for optimism, according to Klein, are that Korea's successful industrial policies and Korean's work ethic have given rise to high productivity matched by a high propensity to save and a strong entrepreneurial spirit. The projection made by Walt W. Rostow, former economic advisor to Presidents Kennedy and Johnson, is also optimistic about the future of the Korean economy. He says that Korea's past trend of growth will continue in the future and her per capita income will become US$5,917 (in 1981 dollars) by the year 2000. Korea then will be at the level of the presently advanced industrial market economies and will enjoy what he calls 'the advantages and costs of high mass consumption'. He stressed that Korea's single most precious asset is 'a talented, competent, energetic new generation of workers, technicians, public servants, and private entrepreneurs'.[9] Correct policies, government commitment to economic development, technical competence and the passionate determination of Koreans to develop the nation are also important factors that led him to be optimistic about Korea's future.

Somewhat less optimistic projections are given by Miyohei Shinohara, former Chairman of the Japanese Institute of Developing Economies. He projects that the rate of growth of Korea's per capita income will be only 4 per cent per annum to the year 2000[10]. However, the Japanese Economic Planning Agency projects that the rate of growth of Korea's GDP will increase at 7 per cent per annum towards the year 2000—in terms of per capita income this implies an annual growth rate of a little over 5 per cent.[11] The projections made by the Korea Development Institute show a growth rate of 7.9 per cent between 1984 and 1990 and 7.2 per cent bewteen 1991 and 2000.[12] The projected slowing in the 1990s is attributed to a gradual decline in the contribution of labour input. Long-term projections, however, are subject to a wide margin of error because of possible changes in values, institutions, domestic politics, and global economic and political trends. Accordingly, the precise projection itself is without great meaning—what is important is that Korean experts stress the continuation of a relatively rapid growth of the economy, albeit with the expectation of some slowdown towards the year 2000.

Hugh Patrick and Henry Rosovsky state that their optimism about the Japanese economy rests on their confidence that the basic institutions of Japan and its economy are fundamentally sound. Moreover, they assert, 'Japan's people possess organizational ability, education, and skills, combined with a tradition of hard work, none of which is apt soon to evaporate.'[13]

To a large extent, the same thing may be said about the future of the Korean economy. Koreans' overall ability to manage their economy may fall somewhat behind that of the Japanese, but Korea has some other advantages over Japan. For instance, Japan now faces such developed-country problems as an ageing population and a severe shortage of manpower, while Korea's population is still very young, with the average age of Koreans being only 27.7 as of 1985.

The steady rise of the Korean economy to advanced country status will depend on how well Korea manages to deal with changing domestic and international circumstances. The expectation among Korean experts of somewhat slower economic growth in the 1990s reflects uncertainty about changes in these factors.

Domestic Factors

Labour-related problems is the factor most likely to cause a slowdown in future economic growth. Wages in Korea rose rapidly after President Roh's Democratization Declaration on 29 June 1987 liberalized labour relations. As a result, the wages of manufacturing workers rose to about the same level as those of Korea's major competitors—Taiwan, Hong Kong, and Singapore. Moreover, Korea's low unemployment rate, 2.5 per cent in 1988, is even lower than in Japan. Cheap labour is a thing of the past and labour supplies in Korea, especially of well-educated workers, have tightened substantially.

As pointed out by T. Scitovsky, insufficient domestic savings and the need to borrow investment capital from abroad have been an important constraint on Korean growth until very recently.[14] This changed only in the late 1980s. The gross savings ratio in Korea rose from 21.9 per cent of GNP in 1980 to 35.3 per cent in 1988. This increase, together with the trade surplus, turned Korea into a net creditor nation in 1989. If these conditions persist, capital should not be a constraining factor in the 1990s. However, the rate of return on capital may decrease due to the increased research and development costs associated with the promotion of what Walt W. Rostow calls the 'fourth industrial revolution' based on micro-electronics, genetics, robots, new synthetic materials, communications, and lasers.[15] Korea has benefited from having wide-open oportunities to borrow and utilize a backlog of existing declining-cost technologies, but in the 1990s these opportunities are likely to shrink greatly. The KDI projections suggest that half of Korea's economic growth after 1991 will be due to technological improvement. Already, the ratio of R&D expenditure to GNP has risen from one per cent in 1983 to 2.6 per cent in 1989.[16] At the same time World Bank experts have cautioned that 'Korea has a limited domestic market for some of the high-tech products, and care must be taken not to put too many eggs in the higher-tech basket.'[17]

The restructuring of policy priorities may also contribute to slower growth in the next decade. 'Growth at any cost' in the 1960s gave way to 'growth first' in the 1970s and 'growth with equity' in the 1980s. Since the beginning of all-out social democratization in 1987, and, as per capita income moves toward US$5,000, Koreans have voiced demands for improved equity. Demands for better housing, improved health care, better education, better public and social services, and better environmental quality have also increased, creating pressure for a shift in priorities to 'growth with higher quality of life'. All these represent pressing needs. Addressing such social needs is clearly an urgent problem. This will divert resources from directly productive investments to meet public and social needs and may lead to slower growth.

There are, of course, growth-promoting factors present as well. For instance, sizeable pockets of unused or underused labour still exist. There is also much room to increase labour productivity by moving workers from less productive or declining sectors to more productive or growing sectors, rationalizing the backward service sector, and transforming less productive agricultural land into more productive industrial uses.

International Circumstances

The international circumstances facing Korea and Japan are similar in some ways. Both are dependent on foreign countries for both raw materials and markets—although the degree of dependency is much higher in Korea. For instance, in 1986, exports and imports comprised less than a quarter of GNP in the case of Japan, but more than three quarters of GNP in Korea. Korean businesses also find themselves in competition with more experienced Japanese firms for foreign markets and raw materials. As Korea's growth pattern and export structure become increasingly similar to Japan's, such competition will become increasingly acute. Competition between Korean and Japanese consumer electronics in American markets is already very severe.

Because of its higher dependency on global markets, Korea suffered more than Japan from the oil crises in the 1970s. Korea is likely to remain one of the most trade-oriented countries in the world, and its future growth will depend in part on raw material prices.

The first oil crisis in 1973 delivered an almost deadly blow to the Korean economy. It caught inexperienced Korean policy makers totally unprepared, and at one point foreign bankers stationed in Korea feared the Korean economy was on the verge of bankruptcy. Fortunately, Korea was able to recycle earnings from Middle East construction projects to buy oil. The Middle East construction boom that began around 1976 enabled the Korean economy not only to recover from the depression caused by the first oil crisis, but also to finance a spurt of industrial investment. Unfortunately, the influx of oil dollars from construction exports to the Middle East made Korean policy makers overly optimistic and resulted in premature investments in heavy and chemical industries, including shipbuilding, right on the eve of the second oil crisis. Morris Adelman of MIT, a world expert on energy and resources, once told me that he had suggested to Korean policymakers in the late 1970s that they not make massive investment in the maritime transportation industry because a second oil crisis was on the horizon. They did not listen, and the second oil crisis dealt a damaging blow to Korea's infant heavy and chemical industries. The marine transportation sector still suffers from this setback, but other sectors have almost fully recovered as a result of the 'three lows'—low oil prices, low dollar prices, and low interest rates—that began around 1985.

Another constraint may be the strong pressure on Korea from abroad to liberalize trade and open domestic markets, including those for agricultural goods, to foreign competition. Pressure from the United States is already very acute. The situation has been aptly described by Rudiger Dornbusch of MIT. 'The Washington answer to Korea's *embarras de richesse* is plain: liberalize imports and the capital account, spend, invest, import, don't export, appreciate, raise wages, cut taxes, have a ball!'[18] Korea needs further liberalization, including of agricultural markets, albeit as part of its overall restructuring and adjustment *pari passu* of other policies.

The rapid growth of the Korean economy in the future has the potential to become a source of contention, especially with Korea's major trade partners. Korea needs to consider possible repercussions from major trade partners. Korea is, as already mentioned, at present under heavy pressure from the United States to open markets for goods such as agricultural products in which Korea has severe comparative disadvantages. Korea may face increasing pressure from America and other countries. The opening-up of domestic markets will have to move apace with the restructuring of Korean industry in a way that is compatible not only with changing factor proportions in Korea but also with future changes in Korean-American trade patterns. Increasingly, maintaining good trade relations with the rest of the world will be crucial for the continued growth of the Korean economy, requiring an effective and flexible adaptation to a changing global economic system.

Possible Adverse Factors

The factors Patrick and Rosovsky listed in the 1970s as possibly adversely affecting the future growth of the Japanese economy also apply to Korea.[19] These include the possibility of serious confrontations between labour and management, an increasing desire for leisure, internal political instability, and possible political or economic retaliation from foreign countries. Many people tend to be optimistic about the future of the Korean economy in spite of these adverse factors. The reasons are similar to those given by Patrick and Rosovsky for their optimism on the future of the Japanese economy. In all likelihood, Korea will continue to have a highly motivated, industrious, and disciplined labour force, experienced and venturesome entrepreneurs, effective co-operation between government and business, and competent and flexible policymakers attuned to changing domestic and international circumstances. Indeed, though Korea will need to grow strongly in order to cope with the internal and external difficulties that are likely to arise in the future, and even under an optimistic scenario, Korea's growth will not be as smooth and stable as Japan's growth was in the past.

Korea's most serious problem is the labour-management confrontation that began in 1987. Korean labour relations are still in their infancy and are reminiscent of those of the United States in the 1920s. Korean policy makers are particularly worried about the possibility of serious labour disputes that may impede growth. Rudiger Dornbusch of MIT believes 'labour relations in Korea are already exerting adverse effects on trade performance',[20] but

many businessmen remain optimistic about Korean labour relations in the future. The reasons may be stated as follows. Some
large Korean firms have been able to maintain smooth labour
relations without labour unions, and the proportion of Korean
workers belonging to labour unions is still relatively low. It was
22.0 per cent in 1988 [21]. Labour conflict may continue for some-
time in the future, but hopefully will be limited to certain firms
and industries. Related to the labour-union issue is the emergence of the working class as a new power group, as Korea moves
towards a more pluralistic political system. This will require
changes in Korea's highly centralized decision-making process
and increase the cost of reconciling conflicting interests.

Secondly, an increasing desire for leisure among Koreans may
adversely affect the growth of productivity. Sunday store closings
and the reduction of daily working hours from over 10 to 8 hours
recently have been gaining acceptance in Korea, but Korea is not
likely to soon depart from the pattern of hard work and a long
work day—the longest in the world according to the International
Labour Organization.

Korean consumers, like their Japanese counterparts, are highly
materialistic and have a strong desire to achieve a high and
continually rising standard of living. Because the social welfare
system is poorly developed, Korean workers are expected to
provide for their own retirement, guaranteeing a continued commitment to hard work and a high rate of savings.

Korea is currently in the transitional stage between authoritarian rule and a fully realized democratic system. Transitional
political instability may cause some social turmoil and affect
economic growth adversely in the coming years. Korea's political
development is far behind its economic development and domestic politics may constrain economic development for some time.
The dilemma may be that, although the economy becomes increasingly similar to the economy of industrial countries, politics
is still at the stage of a developing country. Korea's problem is to
reduce this 'economy-politics gap'. Fortunately, most opposition
party leaders support the free market economic system and realize the importance of economic growth. Korea's entrepreneurs
and managers also appear to be in a position to influence politicians rather than vice versa. Overall, one can optimistically
speculate that the Korean economy will be able to weather the
growing pains of domestic politics.

Finally, Parvez Hasan and D. C. Rao of the World Bank indicate that a favourable world economic environment is one of the three fundamental conditions for sustaining Korea's continuous growth into the future—the other two being greater efforts toward product and market diversification and enhancement of social equity.[22] Korea's heavy reliance on the American market makes a favourable economic environment in the United States and sustained access to its markets particularly vital. Uncertainties about the world economy and pressures from industrial countries to prematurely open domestic markets may hinder the future growth of the Korean economy.

Korea has always been influenced greatly by Great Power interests. The United States, Japan, China, and the USSR have been grouped into two systems—one capitalist and the other socialist. But both systems and the relations between them are now in transition as the rigid bipolarity of the world economy based on these two systems gradually loses force. Korea has been especially influenced by the ideological confrontation between the two systems and sees this systemic transition as an opportunity to open up relations with China, the USSR, and other socialist countries. If well managed, this trend may greatly stimulate Korean economic growth, as did the normalization of relations with Japan in 1965.

One negative change in the world economic order is the apparent tendency towards the breakdown of the world trading system into competing blocs. There is a danger this could lead to increased protectionism at both the national and trading bloc levels in reaction to a recession or balance-of-payments deficits. The emerging intrabloc and interbloc economic and political dynamics and the dispersal of world economic powers among blocs will create new international circumstances for Korea to navigate.

General Lessons from the Korean Experience

One of the important lessons from the Korean experience is that the success of the Korean economy is not the result of any single growth factor or some unique cultural characteristic. It is the result of a combination of many favourable domestic and international factors and supportive government policies. Rapid growth is not only the result of hard-working workers or government policy. As Edward Mason notes, 'too many other factors were involved in the Korean case.'[23]

Another lesson is that the OIG-oriented, that is, outward-, industry- and growth-oriented strategy appears to be the only right development strategy, not only for Korea, but perhaps also for *any* developing country that wants to sustain economic development for a long period of time.

Economic success hides many blemishes and tends to justify even transitional failures in other aspects. The Korean successes were accompanied by rising pollution, environmental deterioration, urban congestion, and shortages in housing and urban amenities, but over the longer term they may also generate the resources necessary to redress these problems.

Successful growth appears to be the best remedy for the numerous socio-economic diseases of underdevelopment. Politically, successful growth has been a powerful factor in enlisting the support of the people and in weakening the appeal of competing ideologies, thereby promoting a social atmosphere favourable to further growth. Korea's experience has indicated, however, that there is a limit to how long the public will accept political impotence as the price of economic development.

Korea, like Japan, succeeded by aggressively attacking adversity rather than retreating from it. Lawrence Krause explains that:

because of Japan's isolation and its ignorance of the outside world, the general trading company was developed, which proved to be tremendously efficient in conducting international commerce. Because of the lack of domestic raw materials and the consequent need to import, Japan pioneered the development of bulk carriers, which reduced the cost of water transportation, and created the most advanced shipbuilding industry in the world. Japan also developed tidewater sites for processing plants to make the best use of these carriers. Because these sites required large investments, they could be justified only by large plants, which in turn permitted the capturing of economies of scale in manufacturing.[24]

Korea has used many of the same techniques to make the best of adversity.

Three aspects of the Korean government-business relationship are worth emphasizing.[25] One is that close co-operation between government and business has been generally growth-promoting and efficiency-enhancing. A second is that this close co-operation between government and business makes it possible to maintain a consistent set of goals and implement them in a systematic way. The third is that the private-enterprise system, if promoted effectively by the government, can be a highly effective mechanism for generating economic growth and elevating the living standards of the general population. Left alone, the private enterprise system may not in most real-world circumstances realize its potential for improving material welfare. Although it may sail well in a calm lake, it needs government support to cross a stormy ocean.

In Korea, the government has intervened in the economy to strengthen the functioning of the market system, and relied mainly upon the private enterprise system in expanding foreign trade. The relationship between the highly centralized government and the business community has not been always smooth, and Korea now needs to substantially decentralize its public decision-making and further vitalize its private sector. While the Japanese government acted as a countervailing power, in the case of Korea the government exercised more of a controlling or regulating role, sometimes with the result of discouraging private initiative. The increasing complexity of the economy and interrelationships with foreign countries necessitate less government intervention and more freedom for private decision-making.

On the negative side, the Korean government has allowed an 'LDC agrarian mentality' to become entrenched through the protracted overprotection and underdevelopment of agriculture. This has resulted in prices for agricultural products which are much higher than international prices. Moreover, land-use policies overprotecting agricultural land has led to a severe shortage of urban land and dramatic increases in prices of land and housing in urban areas.

Finally, the willingness and eagerness of Koreans to study, emulate, and adapt the experiences of other countries has facilitated the rise and transformation of their economy.

Some Implications for Developing Countries

Assuring Leadership Commitment

An important psychological barrier to the development of Korea, especially in the years following Japanese colonial rule and the

Korean War, was the people's mistrust of one another and of their national leaders. The most serious legacy of colonial rule may be the loss of trust and hope among people, and between the government and the governed. This sense of mistrust was greatly strengthened during the Korean War. The major reason why Koreans did not deposit their money in the government-owned banks in the past was this lack of trust in government policies and government-owned banks.

The Korean government appears to have been relatively successful in maintaining people's faith in their leaders, instilling hope for the future, and mobilizing the people's support for and active participation in the pursuit of national economic development. Throughout his tenure, President Park Chung Hee repeatedly proclaimed that 'our ultimate task is the achievement of economic and industrial modernization.'[26]

Concrete measures taken by the government assured Koreans of their leaders' full commitment to development. Such measures included establishing the Economic Planning Board to take charge of overall economic planning and policy, the Korea Trade Promotion Agency to oversee trade promotion, the Korea Advanced Institute of Science and Technology, and the monthly Trade Expansion Conferences attended personally by President Park from 1971 onwards. President Park's continuous emphasis on the utmost importance of economic development, along with the creation of implementing appropriate institutions, was more than enough to assure people's support of, and faith and hope in, the future of the economy. But people's faith in his commitment to economic development gradually faded as the president took an increasing number of measures to hold on to personal political power.

Building a Leadership Class

The leadership required for economic development may be divided into two types. The first is the political leadership needed to guide socio-political development. The role of the political leadership is to assure the socio-political stability of the country and to engineer political, demographic, institutional, and educational changes in a way that is conducive to economic development and thereby to build up faith and confidence between the government and the governed. The second type is the economic leadership or entrepreneurship needed to direct productive activities. The emergence and development of entrepreneurs is also crucial in modernizing countries. The quality of political leadership determines the quality of infrastructure or, in Hirschman's words, 'social overhead capital' in a broad sense. At the same time, the quality of economic leadership determines the quality of 'directly productive activities'.

The continuous and rapid development of the Korean economy has depended on having talented and fully committed Korean leaders of both types. Many countries apparently fail to engineer economic development because they lack capable national leaders. Indeed, one of the most serious legacies of colonial rule is the destruction of the leadership corps. According to Korean economic historian Byung-Jik Ahn, the total number of Korean graduates of colleges or universities during the 35 years of Japanese colonial rule was less than one thousand. Following the liberation of the country in 1945, however, the number grew to about 70,000 by 1959—only fourteen years later.

It can take developing countries several decades or more to build up fully a capable leadership class. As pointed out by Nobel laureate economist Arthur Lewis, 'what cannot be predicted or prescribed is the quality of leadership that will see a country through its crisis.'[27] There is no easy way to improve the quality of national leaders, especially socio-political leaders. Because socio-political activities are almost totally country-specific, there is no way for these skills to be learned or honed through international competition, and the quality of political leaders may remain at relatively low domestic levels. However, the quality of economic leaders—or entrepreneurs—may rise to international standards through competition. The gap between the two can increase with a rise in income and act as a hurdle to further growth.

Fortunately, even in the early stages of development, Korea's political leaders appeared to be rather capable and their commitment to economic development very firm. Because businessmen became confident about the leadership's commitment to economic modernization, they devoted their money and efforts almost totally to industrial development.

Good political leadership is most important in the early stages of development, when political decisions dominate economic factors and economic leaderships. In the case of Japan, which is known as an entrepreneurial society, entrepreneurs now influence politicians rather than the other way around—although the reverse was true when Japan first began to develop. In the case of Korea, politicians still have the upper hand over entrepreneurs.

Given the importance of creating an environment favourable to entrepreneurs, it is my belief that the national or socio-political leaders in developing countries must be well attuned to economic factors and entrepreneurs' concerns. I also believe that developing countries need a deliberate policy for creating an 'incubator' to produce or train nascent entrepreneurs. For example, certain areas in the capital city or other large cities may be designated as entrepreneurial zones in which people can start businesses or learn business skills with minimum restrictions and maximum government support. Those who start or learn a business in the designated incubator areas should be especially protected from government red tape. In the case of Korea, Chonggaechon in downtown Seoul and Youngdungpo, an industrial area in the southwestern part of Seoul, appear to have served as quasi-incubators. The difficult problem, however, is to wean the neophytes from the incubator before they become completely dependent on it. Developing countries need to consider maintaining several active incubator zones until they reach NIC status.

Government-directed Growth

The Korean economy has been mostly government-directed, government-led, or government-propelled. In effect, Korea has pursued a 'government-led market economy', in contrast to Hong Kong's 'market-led market economy'. Although the Korean government has interfered in the economy extensively and continuously, it has not created permanently sick industries which need huge subsidies. In general, the Korean government has used its 'strong visible hand' to reinforce and facilitate the function of the market economy.

Government intervention in the economy was crucial in developing the market system itself and also rectifying market failures of various types. Up until the early 1970s, the market system still functioned very poorly and the government virtually ignored the allocative function of the market mechanism. Instead, the government itself took over the allocative function of the market system, with the justification that this would speed up economic growth. Foreign exchange, bank credit, the appointment of senior managers, sites for industrial location, infrastructure facilities, and even housing sites and units were directly allocated or controlled by the government. The heads of various private economic organizations such as the Chamber of Commerce, and the Korea Traders Association were also appointed by the government. During this period, the Korean economy resembled a 'command economy' or 'directed market economy'. Korea was then, in Myrdal's term, truly a 'hard state' capable of implementing its policy measures firmly and effectively.

The chairman of 'Korea, Inc.' has been the President himself, while business groups such as Samsung, Hyundai, Lucky-Goldstar, and Daewoo have been its production units. The relationship between the government and business groups in Japan has been nearly bilateral or horizontal, whereas in the case of Korea it has been vertical or hierarchical. So also has been the relationship between the government and political parties in the two countries. In Korea, until recently, economics has driven politics more often than the reverse. Because of this, Mason and others contend that 'Korea, Inc.' is a more apt term than 'Japan, Inc.'[28] According to Murakami the nexus of party-government-industry relations is the major characteristic of the Japanese model of political economy,[29] while the vertical government-industry relations may be the major characteristic of the 'Korean model of government-directed, export-led industralization'.

In Korea, what is needed is the improvement and modernization not only of the market and the government, but also of the relationship between the government and industry.

Educating Society on Economic Principles

As a consultant on economic education at the Economic Planning Board, I found it extremely difficult to get the tradition-bound, change-resistant and command-oriented bureaucrats and national leaders to understand the basic principles of a free market economy, including the true meaning of supply and demand. President Park Chung Hee said that 'the economy is truly hard to handle'.[30] There is a strong tendency for national leaders of poor countries to choose the command economic system rather than the market economic system, out of simple ignorance about how the 'invisible hand' of the free market works and its advantages. At an early stage of development there are typically very few individuals who fully comprehend the basic principles of a market economy and can explain them in plain language to ordinary people.

Because of the threat from the communist North, South Korean economists as well as the government have tried to keep Marxist economics and ideologies out of Korean society. For instance, until the early 1980s, customs inspectors were ordered by the government to search for any one who tried to bring in any book on Marxism or Marxist economics. Those who tried to popularize Marxist ideologies in Korea were subject to legal punishment. In this respect, economics as taught and applied in Korea has been almost purely economics for a free enterprise, market economy.

Any developing country attempting to get economic development off the ground, or sustain it, needs a critical minimum number of economists who understand the basic principles of the market economy and can form a social force to counteract anti-growth forces and persuade the people and their leaders of the advantages of the free enterprise, market-economy system. In developing countries which lack effective, innovative entrepreneurs, economists are needed to promote entrepreneurship among the tradition-bound people. In such countries economists have to be the innovators themselves, or promoters of innovators.

Educating the public on economics appears to be crucial in the early stages of development to mobilize national leaders as well as the general public behind economic development. Poor countries hoping to promote economic development need to give high priority to societal education in economics.

Notes

Notes to Chapter 2

1. Economic Planning Board, National Bureau of Statistics, *Korea Statistical Yearbook 1987*, p. 61.
2. Akio Morita, 1987, p. 226.
3. Soo-il Kwack, 1988b.
4. Kenichi Omae, 1986. Especially Chapter 3.
5. Urban population here also includes population of urban areas with population of less than 20,000. Thus, it is larger than the same figure in Table 2.4.
6. Government of the Republic of Korea, *National Land Development Plan (1972–1981)*, Seoul, 1971.
7. On this point see Byung-Nak Song and Sang-Chuel Choe, 1981, and Sang-Chuel Choe and Byung-Nak Song, 1985.
8. Edwin S. Mills and Byung-Nak Song, 1979, pp. 36–43.
9. The average level of urbanization for 58 middle-income countries was 48 per cent in 1986. See World Bank, *World Development Report, 1988*, pp. 248–85.
10. See Arthur Lewis, 1984.
11. Hollis B. Chenery and Moshe Syrquin, 1986b.
12. Tae Hwan Kwon, a sociologist and expert on Korean population, told me that the period of the Korean 'baby-boom' was 1955–60.
13. Economic Planning Board, *The First Five-Year Economic Development Plan (1962–1966)*, 1961, p. 20.
14. Economic Planning Board, National Bureau of Statistics, *Population and Housing Census*, 1966, 1975, 1985. Refer also to Table 10.5.
15. See World Bank, *World Development Report, 1988*, pp. 280–1.

Notes to Chapter 3

1. The discussion of Korean history in this chapter is based on Ki-baik Lee, 1984; Korea Overseas Information Service, 1987; Jon Carter Covell, 1985; Hochin Choi, 1984; and Edward Mason and others, 1980.
2. Edwin Reischauer, 1986, p. 67.
3. Ki-baik Lee, 1984, pp. 94–7 and Jon Carter Covell, 1985, pp. 62–4.
4. Edward E. Adams, 1983, pp. 294–5.
5. See Dwight Perkins in Edward S. Mason, 1980, chapter 3.
6. Edward E. Adams, 1983, pp. 290–1.
7. See note 5 above.

8. Jon Carter Covell, 1985.

9. See note 5 above.

10. Hochin Choi, 1984, p. 169.

11. Isabella S. Bishop, 1970, p. 66, as quoted by Edward S. Mason and others, 1980, p. 69.

12. Tu Wei-Ming, 1984, p. 87.

13. See Sung Hwan Ban, 1974, Sang-Chul Suh, 1978, and Edward S. Mason 1980, pp. 74–82 (written by Dwight H. Perkins). Sang-Chul Suh's estimate of the average annual growth rate of material product during this period was 3.8 per cent. Dwight H. Perkins estimated the average annual growth rate of Korean GNP during the colonial period to be about 4 per cent. See Edward S. Mason and others, Chapter 2, pp. 74–82. Kazushi Ohkawa and Henry Rosovsky's (1973) estimate of the growth rate of Japanese GNP between 1910–40 was 3.6 per cent a year.

14. See Edward S. Mason and others, 1980, p. 75.

15. Edward S. Mason and others also made the same point, saying that 'the conclusion seems almost inescapable that little of importance was left over from the Japanese period'. Mason and others (1980), p. 77.

16. Hochin Choi, 1984, pp. 273–87 and Korea Overseas Information Service, 1987, pp. 102–6.

17. Edward S. Mason and others 1980, p. 448.

18. Korea Overseas Information Service, 1987, pp. 103–5.

19. Kazushi Ohkawa and Henry Rosovsky, 1973, p. 22.

20. Kazushi Ohkawa and Henry Rosovsky, 1973, p. 198.

Notes to Chapter 4

1. Edwin O. Reischauer, 1985, p. 196.

2. Edward S. Mason and others, 1980, p. 70.

3. Alvin Toffler, 1985, p. 117.

4. Akio Morita, 1987, pp. 226–7.

5. Edwin O. Reischauer, 1985, p. 224.

6. Economic Planning Board, National Bureau of Statistics, *Population and Housing Census*, 1985.

7. Spencer J. Palmer, 1986, p. *vii*.

8. As quoted by Chang-Keun Choo, 1988. See also Yi Kwang-su, 'The Impact of the Christianity on Choson', *Chong-chun*, July 1917.

9. Roderick Macfarquhar, 1980.

10. This argument is based on Tu Wei-Ming, 1984, p. 21.

11. Tu Wei-Ming, 1984, pp. 110–11.

12. Nathan Glazer, 1976, p. 816.

13. Ruth Benedict, 1946 and Chie Nakane, 1984. See also Nathan Glazer, 1976, pp. 816–17.

14. Tu Wei-Ming, 1984, p. 110.

15. Lee Iacocca, 1984, p. 349.
16. Myung Sook Kim, 1986.
17. Chie Nakane, 1964, pp. 434–8. See also Nathan Glazer, 1976, p. 817.
18. Yong-un Kim, 1985, p. 167.

Notes to Chapter 5

1. Hollis B. Chenery and Moshe Syrquin, 1977 and 1986b.
2. The 'normal', 'average', 'typical', or 'expected' level here implies that estimated by Hollis Chenery and Moshe Syrquin using data for 101 countries for the period 1955–75. See H. Chenery and M. Syrquin, 1977.
3. See Myung Sook Kim, 1986.
4. See World Bank, *World Development Report, 1988*, and Chapter 10 of this book.
5. See Byung-Nak Song, 1982. The Chenery-Shishido-Watanabe method is used. See H. Chenery, S. Shishido, and T. Watanabe, 1962.
6. See Byung-Nak Song, 1982, and H. Chenery, S. Shishido, and T. Watanabe, 1962.
7. See Kwang Suk Kim and Joon Kyung Park, 1985.
8. Simon Kuznets, 1973.
9. Economic Planning Board, National Bureau of Statistics, *Establishment Census*, 1981 and 1986.
10. Edwin S. Mills and Byung-Nak Song, 1979, pp. 36–42.
11. Walt W. Rostow, 1983.
12. Ryoshin Minami, 1986, pp. 298–307.
13. John C.H. Fei and Gustav Ranis, 1975.
14. Edward S. Mason and others, 1980, p. 466.
15. Lawrence Klein, 1986.
16. Walt W. Rostow, 1983.
17. Yutaka Kosai and Yoshitaro Ogino, 1984.
18. World Bank, *World Development Report, 1989*, pp. 164–5.

Notes to Chapter 6

1. Gustav Ranis, 1971, 1989.
2. H. Chenery and M. Syrquin, 1986b, p. 64.
3. H. Chenery and M. Syrquin, 1986a, pp. 91–4.
4. H. Chenery, S. Shishido and T. Watanabe, 1962.
5. Hugh Patrick and Henry Rosovsky, 1976, p. 11.
6. Lawrence Klein, 1986, p. *xii*.
7. Lawrence Krause, 1981.
8. As quoted by Nicholas Georgescu-Roegan, 1988.
9. See Georgescu-Roegan, note 8 above, p. 303.

10. Kazushi Ohkawa and Henry Rosovsky, 1973, p. 173.

11. Peter Drucker, 1986.

12. Park Chung Hee, *The Country, The Revolution, and I* (in Korean), Seoul, Hollym Corporation, 1963, pp. 82, 259–60.

13. Shin, Bong-shik, 1988.

14. The World Bank, 1987a, p. 37.

15. Hong, Wontack, 1988.

16. See David C. Cole and Yung Chul Park, 1983, p. 284. Tae-won Kwack also stressed this point, stating that 'credit allocation seems to have played the most critical role.' See Taw-won Kwack (1986), p. 125.

17. See Yung Whee Rhee and others (1984), p. 72.

18. Dong-Sung Cho, 1987, pp. 50–8.

19. Lawrence Krause and Sueo Sekiguchi, 1976.

Notes to Chapter 7

1. See Korea Traders Association, 1988.

2. Lawrence Krause and Sueo Sekiguchi, 1976.

3. Hollis Chenery and Lance Taylor, 1968.

4. See World Bank, *World Development Report, 1988*, pp. 226–7.

5. World Bank, *World Development Report, 1988*, pp. 282–3.

6. See Government of the Republic of Korea, 1973, and also Korea Development Institute, 1978. I participated in the formulation of these plans as head of The Industrial Policy Division, Korea Development Institute, the principal research institute for the Economic Planning Board.

7. See Bong-Shik Shin, 1988.

8. The World Bank, 1987b, p. 28.

9. The World Bank, 1987b, p. 31.

10. Leroy Jones, 1980, p. 149.

11. Economic Planning Board, Fair Trade Commission, 1989. I served as Fair Trade Commissioner at EPB.

12. Economic Planning Board, Fair Trade Commission, 1987.

13. Masu Uekusa, 1987, p. 203.

14. Robert L. Heilbroner and Lester C. Thurow, 1984, pp. 561–5.

15. Miyohei Shinohara, 1982, pp. 21–35.

16. Masu Uekusa, 1987, p. 212.

17. Miyohei Shinohara, 1982, pp. 21–53.

18. The Bank of Korea, *The Input-Output Table for the Korean Economy, 1985*, and *Statistics of Japan, 1986*, Prime Minister's Office, Japan. For computational procedures, see Byung-Nak Song, 1977.

19. Miyohei Shinohara, 1982, pp. 24–6.

20. Lawrence B. Krause, 1985. p. 35.

21. Discussion in this section is based on Samsung Conglomerate, 1988.

Notes to Chapter 8

1. According to Paul A. Samuelson and William D. Nordhaus (1985, pp. 759–62), the government's proper economic functions are creating an appropriate economic or legal framework, ensuring stability, and promoting efficiency and equity.

2. Economic Planning Board, *The Second Five-Year Economic Development Plan (1966–71)*, p. 129.

3. Yutaka Kosai and Yoshitaro Ogino, 1984, pp. 123–4. See also Yutaka Kosai, 1987, pp. 555–64, and Kozo Yamamura and Yasukichi Yasuba, 1987, pp. 33–90.

4. Kakuei Tanaka, 1972.

5. Arthur Lewis, 1968.

6. Discussion in this section is based on the Economic Planning Board, *Guidelines for the Preparation of the Sixth Five-Year Plan (1987–91)*, Seoul EPB, August 1985.

7. For more dètailed discussion of the Korea's incentive and disincentive systems, see Chapter 6.

8. The average debt ratio of Korean manufacturing firms reached its peak at 487.9 per cent in 1980. It decreased to 340.1 per cent in 1987. See Bank of Korea, *Economic Statistics Yearbook*, 1989, pp. 192–3.

9. Yutaka Kosai and Yoshitaro Ogino, see note 3 above, 1984, pp. 124–6.

10. For further discussion of this point see Chapters 5, 7, and 11.

Notes to Chapter 9

1. See, for instance, Byung-Nak Song, 1981, and Sung Y. Kwack, 1986.

2. Arthur Lewis, 1984.

3. Yong-un Kim, 1985, pp. 166–7.

4. Arthur Lewis, 1954, 1984.

5. See, for instance, Byung-Nak Song, 1981, and Jeffrey G. Williamson, 1977, 1979.

6. The World Bank, *World Development Report, 1989*, p. 225.

7. In formal terms, the equation is as follows:

$$C = 5.66 + 0.85YR + 0.91YUW + 0.64YUK$$
$$(4.47)^a \quad (0.25)(0.07) \qquad (0.07)$$

where: $R^2 = 0.99$; a = standard error; Durbin Watson = 2.43; Standard

error of regression = 1.20, C : consumption, YR : rural income, YUW :
urban workers' income, and YUK : urban capitalists' income.

8. Tibor Scitovsky, 1986, pp. 168–78.

9. Tibor Scitovsky, 1986, pp. 170–80.

10. Miyohei Shinohara, 1982, especially Chapter 10: 'Japan's High
Savings Ratio: Its Determinants and Behavior Patterns — With Some
Comparisons with Asian NICs', pp. 153–81.

11. For explanation of this hypothesis, see Byung-Nak Song, 1981,
and Miyohei Shinohara, 1982.

12. Jeffrey Williamson, 1976, p. 67.

13. Paul A. Samuelson and William D. Nordhaus, *Economics*, twelfth
edition, 1985, p. 131.

14. The Federation of Korean Industries, 1987b.

15. Tibor Scitovsky, 1986, pp. 170–1.

16. Lawrence J. Lau, 1986, p. 4.

17. Yung Chul Park and David C. Cole, 1983, p. 128.

18. Yung Chul Park and David C. Cole, 1983, p. 114.

19. Yung Chul Park and David C. Cole, 1983, p. 114.

20. Jeffrey Williamson, 1977, p. 3.

Notes to Chapter 10

1. See The Bank of Korea, *Economic Statistics Yearbook*, 1989, p.
81, and *Economic Indicators of Major Foreign Countries*, March 1989.

2. For more detailed aspects of this movement see In-Joung Whang,
1986b.

3. See Richard J. Sza, 1980. See also Soon Cho, 1988, and Sung Y.
Kwack, 1988.

4. Lawrence J. Lau, 1986, p. 8.

5. Kuo, Shirley W.Y., Gustav Ranis, and John C.H. Fei, 1981, p.
143.

6. Economic Planning Board, *The 1968 National Wealth Survey*, 1970,
and *The 1977 National Wealth Survey*, 1979. The Third National Wealth
Survey was conducted in 1989. But the results will be published in 1990.

7. See Parvez Hasan and D.C. Rao, 1979, p. 36.

8. Hakchung Choo, 1987.

9. Dwight H. Perkins, 'Income Distribution', in Edward S. Mason
and others, 1980.

10. Adelman, Irma and Mahn Je Kim, 1969.

11. Prud'homme, Remy, 1983, p. 178.

12. Edward S. Mason, 1980, p. 482.

13. Economic Planning Board, *Social Statistics Survey*, 1980, 1986.

14. *Joong-ang Daily News*. 'Survey of Opinions on National Life,
1985, 1986 and 1987'.

15. Economic Planning Board, *Social Indicators in Korea, 1979–1988.* I participated in the development of the current system of social indicators as recommended by the UN Statistical Commission on Social Indicators and the application of it to Korea while I was research economist at the Korea Development Institute.

16. Roh Tae-Woo, 1987.

Notes to Chapter 11

1. Edwin O. Reischauer, 1986.
2. Edwin O. Reischauer, 1986, pp. 353–4.
3. Hasekawa Keitaro, 1984, pp. 14–38, 247–8.
4. Rodney Clark, 1979.
5. Harvey Leibenstein, 1984.
6. Byung-Chul Lee, 1986, p. 269.
7. Chung Ju-Yung, 1986, p. 187.
8. Harvey Leibenstein, 1984.
9. Paul S. Crane, 1978, p. 98.
10. Chie Nakana, 1984.
11. Harvey Leibenstein, 1984.
12. Korea Labour Institute, 1988, p. 53.

Notes to Chapter 12

1. Akio Morita, 1987, p. 226.
2. Alvin Toffler, 1985., p. 94.
3. Hakan Hedberg, 1978, pp. 149–53.
4. See, for instance, Ha-Cheong Yeon, 1986 and 1987.
5. Edward S. Mason, 1980, p. 455.
6. Il Sakong, 1989, p. 10.
7. Rudiger Dornbusch, 1989, pp. 66–71.
8. See 'A Survey of the World Economy', *Economist*, 24–30 September 1988.
9. Martin Feldstein, 1986, p. 7.
10. Thomas O. Bayard and Soo-Gil Young, 1989, p. 5.
11. Rudiger Dornbusch, 1989, p. 68, and Ann Krueger, 1989, pp. 159–65.
12. Ann Krueger, 1989, p. 162.
13. Soo-Gil Young, 1989.
14. Rudiger Dornbusch, 1989, p. 71.
15. Japan: Economic Planning Agency, 1985.
16. Hollis Chenery and Moshe Syrquin, 1986b.
17. Dwight H. Perkins, 1988.

Notes to Chapter 13

1. See Hugh Patrick and Henry Rosovsky, 1976, Chapter 13.
2. See Kozo Yamamura and Yasukichi Yasuba, 1987.
3. See Park Chung Hee, 1963 and 1970.
4. See Government of the Republic of Korea, 1973.
5. See Korea Development Institute, 1986.
6. See Richard E. Caves, 1976.
7. See David C. Cole and Yung Chul Park, 1983.
8. See Lawrence R. Klein, 1986.
9. See Walt W. Rostow, 1986.
10. See Miyohei Shinohara, 1986, pp. 59–61.
11. See Japanese Economic Planning Agency, 1985.
12. See Korea Development Institute, 1986, p. 33.
13. See Hugh Patrick and Henry Rosovsky, 1976, pp. 908–9.
14. See Tibor Scitovsky, 1986.
15. See Walt W. Rostow, 1983.
16. See Economic Planning Board, 1989.
17. See World Bank, 1987a.
18. Rudiger Dornbusch, 1989.
19. See Hugh Patrick and Henry Rosovsky, 1976.
20. Rudiger Dornbusch, 1989.
21. See Korea Labour Institute, 1989, p. 40.
22. Parvez Hasan and D.C. Rao, 1979, p. 8.
23. Edward S. Mason and others, 1980, chapter 13.
24. Lawrence B. Krause and Sueo Sekiguchi, 1976, p. 450.
25. A similar point was made in the case of Japan by Patrick and Rosovsky. See Hugh Patrick and Henry Rosovsky, 1976, pp. 921–2.
26. Park Chung Hee, 1963, pp. 82, 259–60.
27. Arthur Lewis, 1984, p. 9.
28. Edward S. Mason, and others, 1980, pp. 485.
29. Yasusuke, Murakami, 1987, p. 70.
30. Park Chung Hee, 1963, p. 260.

Appendices

Appendix A Input-Output Table for the Korean Economy, 1985 (in billion won)

		Intermediate Demand			
	Output / Input	1. Primary Industry	2. Secondary Industry	3. Tertiary Industry	4. Sub-total
Producing Sector	1. Primary industry	1,363	7,600	187	9,150
	2. Secondary industry	2,596	42,916	10,545	56,057
	3. Tertiary industry	656	11,263	10,097	22,016
	4. Sub-total	4,615	61,779	20,829	87,223
Payment Sector	5. Households (wages)	1,325	13,856	17,168	32,349
	6. Government (tax subsidy)	37	5,369	2,104	7,510
	7. Foreign sector (imports)	262	21,547	2,784	24,593
	8. Capital sector (depreciation)	457	4,140	3,233	7,830
	9. Others (profit, rent, etc.)	7,947	9,884	13,327	31,159
	10. Sub-total	10,028	54,796	38,616	103,441
	11. Input total	14,643	116,576	59,445	190,664

Notes: Exchange rate: 1 US dollar = 890.2 Korean won in 1985. Secondary industry implies mining and manufacturing industries.

Source: Compiled from the 65-sector *Input Output Table for the Korean Economy*, prepared by the Bank of Korea, 1985.

Final Demand						
5. Households (consumption)	6. Government (consumption)	7. Foreign sector (exports)	8. Capital Formation	9. Inventory	10. Subtotal	11. Output total
4,371		563	157	403	5,494	14,643
19,659		21,715	18,812	333	60,518	116,576
22,475	8,075	5,439	1,324	115	37,429	59,445
46,505	8,075	27,717	20,293	851	103,441	190,664
						32,349
						7,510
1,121			3,452	−79	4,494	29,087
						7,830
						31,159
						103,441
47,626	8,075	27,717	23,745	772	132,528	

Appendix B Korea's Input-Output Relations Showing Direct and Indirect Input Requirements

Year	Direct Input Coefficients			Leontief Inverse of Direct plus Indirect Coefficients		
1985a	0.0931	0.0652	0.0031	1.1278	0.1210	0.0301
	0.1773	0.3681	0.1774	0.3448	1.6730	0.3588
	0.0448	0.0966	0.1698	0.1010	0.2012	1.2479
1985b	0.0941	0.0856	0.0031	1.1538	0.2232	0.0605
	0.1892	0.5307	0.2034	0.5235	2.3507	0.5927
	0.0498	0.0985	0.1906	0.1347	0.2998	1.3113
1980	0.0897	0.0948	0.0003	1.1288	0.1683	0.0435
	0.1538	0.3361	0.2091	0.2905	1.6158	0.4133
	0.0385	0.1093	0.1823	0.0920	0.2239	1.2802
1970	0.1105	0.0729	0.0069	1.1395	0.1160	0.0283
	0.1060	0.2515	0.1522	0.1782	1.3952	0.2370
	0.0450	0.1320	0.0989	0.0830	0.2102	1.1459

Note: 1985a: Domestic input coefficients.
1985b: Both domestic and imported input coefficients. Thus, the difference between the two shows imported input coefficients.

Sources: Computed from The Bank of Korea, *Input-Output Table for the Korean Economy, 1970, 1980 and 1985.*

Bibliography

Principal Statistical Sources

Bank of Korea (*Han'guk Unhaeng*), *Economic Statistics Yearbook*, 1960–1989, Seoul (in both Korean and English).

_____ *National Income Accounts*, Seoul, 1984 (text in Korean, statistics in both Korean and English).

_____ *New National Accounts*, Seoul, 1986 (text in Korean, statistics in both Korean and English).

_____ *Annual Report*, Seoul, 1950–1988 (in Korean).

_____ *Monthly Bulletin*, Seoul, April 1969–July 1989 (text in Korean, statistics in both Korean and English).

_____ *The Input-Output Table for the Korean Economy*, 1963, 1966, 1968, 1970, 1973, 1976, 1978, 1980, 1983, and 1985 (text in Korean, statistics in both Korean and English).

_____ *Economic Indicators of Major Countries*, March, 1989.

Economic Planning Board, National Bureau of Statistics *Korea Statistical Yearbook*, Seoul, 1952–1988 (in both Korean and English).

_____ *Report on Mining and Manufacturing Census*, Seoul, 1963, 1966, 1976, and 1984 (in both Korean and English).

_____ *Mining and Manufacturing Survey*, 1987.

_____ *Annual Report on the Economically Active Population*, 1963–1988. (text in Korean, statistics in both Korean and English).

_____ *Social Statistics Survey*, Seoul, 1980, 1986 (in Korean).

_____ *Migration Statistics*, Seoul, 1988 (in both Korean and English).

_____ *Major Statistics of Foreign Economy*, Seoul, 1981–1988 (in both Korean and English).

_____ *Major Statistics of the Korean Economy*, Seoul, 1989 (Korean and English).

_____ *Social Indicators in Korea*, Seoul, 1979–1988 (in both Korean and English).

_____ *Population and Housing Census*, Seoul, 1960–1985 (in both Korean and English).

_____ *The 1968 National Wealth Survey, Seoul, 1970* (in Korean).

_____ *The 1977 National Wealth Survey*, Seoul, 1979 (in Korean).

_____ *Establishment Census*, Seoul, 1981, 1986 (in both Korean and English).

_____ *Annual Report on the Family Income and Expenditure Survey*, Seoul, 1971–1988 (in both Korean and English).

International Monetary Fund, *International Financial Statistics*, 1966–1988.

Japan, Bank of, Research and Statistics Department, *Comparative Economic and Financial Statistics: Japan and Other Major Countries*, 1987.

―― *Economic Statistics Annual*, Tokyo, 1983, 1987, 1988.

―― *Annual Report of Foreign Economic Statistics*, Tokyo, 1979, 1987 (in both Japanese and English).

Japan, Economic Planning Agency, *Handbook of the Japanese Economy*, Tokyo, 1989.

Japan: General Affairs Agency, *Nipponno Tokei* (Statistics of Japan), 1987.

Japan: Prime Minister's Office, Statistics Bureau (Sorifu, Tokeikyoku), *Statistics of Japan*, Tokyo, 1989 (in Japanese).

―― *International Statistics*, 1983, 1989 (in both Japanese and English).

Japan: The Tokyo Chamber of Commerce & Industry, *Japan and the World in Statistics,* 1989.

Korea Traders Association, *Statistical Yearbook of Foreign Trade*, 1987, 1989 (in both Korean and English).

―― *Major Indicators of the Trend of Foreign Trade*, Seoul, 1985, 1988 (in Korean).

Ministry of Agriculture and Fisheries, *Report on the Results of Farm Household Economic Survey*, 1965–1988 (text in Korean, statistics in Korean and English).

―― *Major Statistics of Agriculture and Fisheries*, Seoul, 1989 (in both Korean and English).

Ministry of Finance, *Fiscal and Financial Statistics (Jaejung Gumyung Tonggae)*, Seoul, July 1989 (in Korean).

Ministry of Home Affairs, *Municipal Yearbook of Korea*, 1972–1989 (in both Korean and English).

Taiwan: Council for Economic Planning and Development, *Taiwan Statistical Data Book*, 1983, 1986, 1988 (in English).

General

Adams, Edward B., *Korea Guide—A Glimpse of Korea's Cultural Legacy*, Seoul, International Tourist Publishing Co., seventh edition, 1988.

Adelman, Irma (ed)., *Practical Approaches to Development Planning: Korea's Second Five-Year Plan*, Baltimore, Johns Hopkins University Press, 1969.

―― and Mahn Je Kim. 'An Econometric Model of the Korean Economy', in Irma Adelman (ed)., *Practical Approaches to Development Planning: Korea's Second Five-Year Plan (1967–1971)*, Baltimore, Johns Hopkins University Press, 1969.

Ahn, Choong Yong, 'Structure and Prospect of Korea-China Trade',

Paper Presented at the Conference on Economic Development of Korea and China, Seoul, Sejong Institute, 1988.

Allgeier, Peter F., 'Korean Trade Policy in the Next Decade: Dealing with Reciprocity', *World Development*, Vol. 16, No. 1, January 1988.

Amsden, Alice H., *Republic of Korea—Country Study*, World Institute for Development Economics Research of the United Nations University, Helsinki, Finland, 1987.

Aoki, Masahiko, *The Economic Analysis of the Japanese Firm*, Amsterdam, North-Holland Co., 1984.

Bai, Moo-ki, 'The Turning Point in the Korean Economy', *Developing Economies*, Vol. 20, No. 2, June 1982.

—— 'Export-led Industrialization and Wages and Labor Conditions in Korea', paper presented at the Workshop on Wages and Labour Conditions in the NICs of Asia, held at the Thamasat University, Bangkok, Thailand, 9–11 June 1986.

Balassa, Bela, 'Korea's Development Strategy for the Fourth Five-Year Plan Period (1977–81)', in Economic Planning Board (ed.), *Discussion Papers on The Draft of the Fourth Plan (1977–81)*, Seoul, EPB, 1976.

—— 'The Role of Foreign Trade in the Economic Development of Korea', in Walter Galenson (ed.), *Foreign Trade and Investment: Economic Development in the Newly Industrializing Asian Countries*, The University of Wisconsin Press, 1985.

—— 'Korea During the Fifth Five-Year Plan Period (1982–86)' in Il Sakong (ed.), *Macroeconomic Policy and Industrial Development Issues*, Seoul, Korea Development Institute Press, 1987.

—— 'The Lessons of East Asian Development: An Overview', *Economic Development and Cultural Change*, Vol. 36, No. 3, April 1988 (Supplement).

—— and Associates, *Development Strategies in Semi-industrial Countries*, Baltimore, Johns Hopkins University Press, 1982.

Ban, Sung Hwan, *The Growth of Korean Agriculture, 1968–1971*, Seoul, Korea Development Institute, 1974.

Bank of Korea, *Jeochook Chonglam* (An Overview of Savings), Seoul, BOK, 1988 (in Korean).

Bayard, Thomas O., and Soo-Gil Young, *Economic Relations Between the United States and Korea: Conflict or Cooperation?*, Washington, D.C., Institute for International Economics, Special Report 8, IIE, January 1989.

Benedict, Ruth, *The Chrysanthemum and the Sword: Patterns of Japanese Culture*, Houghton Mifflin Co., 1946.

Bergsten, C. Fred, 'US International Macroeconomic Policy', in Thomas O. Bayard and Soo-Gil Young (eds.), *Economic Relations Be-*

tween the US and Korea: Conflict or Cooperation?, Washington, D.C., Institute for International Economics, Special Report 8, 1989.

Bishop, Isabella B., *Korea and Her Neighbors*, Seoul, Yonsei University Press (Reprint), 1970.

Brown, Gilbert T., *Korean Policies and Economic Development in the 1960s*, Baltimore, Johns Hopkins Press, 1973.

Byun, Hyung Yoon, 'Growth and Transformation of The Korean Economy', in Won Taek Lim and others (eds.), *Understanding The Korean Economy*, Seoul, Beebong Co., 1987 (in Korean).

Calverley, John, *Korea: Exporting to Survive*, A Euromoney Special Study, London, Euromoney Publications Ltd., 1982.

Caves, Richard E., 'Industrial Organization', in H. Patrick and H. Rosovsky (eds.), *Asia's New Giant: How the Japanese Economy Works*, Washington D.C., The Brookings Institution, 1976.

Chen, Edward K.Y., *Hyper-growth in Asian Economies: A Comparative Study of Hong Kong, Japan, Korea, Singapore and Taiwan*, London, The Macmillan Press, 1979.

Chenery, Hollis B., and Lance Taylor, 'Development Patterns Among Countries and Over Time', *Review of Economics and Statistics*, November 1968.

Chenery, Hollis B., and Moshe Syrquin, *Patterns of Development, 1955–1975*, London, Oxford University Press, 1977.

——— 'The Semi-industrial Countries', in H. Chenery, S. Robinson, and M. Syrquin, *Industrialization and Growth: A Comparative Study*, London, Oxford University Press, 1986a.

——— 'Typical Patterns of Transformation', in Hollis Chenery and others, *Industrialization and Growth: A Comparative Study*, London, Oxford University Press, 1986b.

Chenery, Hollis B., S. Robinson, and M. Syrquin, *Industrialization and Growth: A Comparative Study*, London, Oxford University Press, 1986.

Chenery, Hollis B., S. Shishido, and T. Watanabe, 'The Patterns of Japanese Growth, 1914–1954', *Econometrica*, January 1962.

Cho, Dong-Sung, *The General Trading Company—Concept and Strategy*, New York, Lexington Books, 1987, pp. 50–58.

Cho, Soon, 'Equity Issues in Korea', Paper Presented at the Korean Economic Association Meeting, Seoul, 2–3 August 1988 (in Korean).

Cho, Soon and others (eds.), *The Theory and Reality of the Korean Economy*, Seoul, Seoul National University Press, 1987 (in Korean).

Choe, Sang-Chuel, and Byung-Nak Song, 'Spatial Distribution of Industries and Important Location Factors in the Seoul Region', World Bank Report No. UDD-89, November 1985.

Choi, Hochin, *The Economic History of Korea (Hankuk Kyongjaesa)*, revised edition, Seoul, Bakyongsa Co., 1984 (in Korean).

Choo, Chang-Keun, 'A Note on The Troubles of the Korean Church', in *Seongseo Hankook* (The Korean Bible), January 1988.

Choo, Hakchung, 'Income Distribution', in Soon Cho and others (eds.), *The Theory and Reality of the Korean Economy*, Seoul, Seoul National University Press, 1987 (in Korean).

Chung, Ju-Yung, *In Excitement This Morning As Well (Onul Achimedo Sulleimeul Ango)*, Seoul, Samsung Publishing Co., 1986.

Clark, Rodney, *The Japanese Company*, New Haven, Yale University Press, 1979.

Cole, David C., and Princeton N. Lyman, *Korean Development: The Interplay of Politics and Economics*, Cambridge, Mass., Harvard University Press, 1971.

Cole, David C., and Yung Chul Park, *Financial Development in Korea, 1945–1978*, Cambridge, Mass., Harvard University Press, 1983.

Corbo, Vittorio, and Sang Woo Nam, 'Korea's Macroeconomic Prospects and Policy Issues for the Next Decade', *World Development*, Vol. 16, No. 1, January 1988.

Council for the Centennial Anniversary of The Korean Church, *An Outline of the Memorial Works for the Centennial Anniversary of the Korean Church*, Seoul, 1984.

Covell, Jon Carter, *Korea's Colorful Heritage*, Seoul, Si-sa-young-o-sa, Inc. 1985.

Crane, Paul S., *Korean Patterns*, published for the Korea Branch of the Royal Asiatic Society, fourth edition, Seoul, 1978.

Dahl, Robert, *A Preface to Economic Democracy*, Berkeley, University of California Press, 1985.

Daniels, Michael J., *Korea's Thirty Years of Growth and Change (1957–1987)*, Seoul, Myung Hwa Press, 1987.

Denison, Edward F., 'Trends in American Economic Growth, 1929–1982', Washington D. C., Brookings Institution, 1985.

—— 'On Estimation of The Sources of Economic Growth in Korea', Seoul, Korea Development Institute, mimeo, December 1977.

—— and William K. Chung, *How Japan's Economy Grew So Fast: The Sources of Post-War Expansion*, Washington, D.C., The Brookings Institution, 1976.

Dornbusch, Rudiger, 'Discussion', in 'Korean International Macroeconomic Policy', by Mahn-Je Kim and Sung-Tae Roh in T.O. Bayard and Soo-Gil Young, (eds.), *Economic Relations Between the US and Korea: Conflict or Cooperation*, Washington, D.C., Institute for International Economics, 1989.

_____ and Yung Chul Park, 'Korean Growth Policy', paper prepared for the Brookings Panel on Economic Activity, Washington, D.C., 10–11 September 1987.

Drucker, Peter, 'The Changed World Economy', *Economic Impact*, No. 56, April 1986.

Economic Planning Board, *The First Five-Year Economic Development Plan, 1962–1966*, Seoul, EPB, 1961.

_____ *The Second Five-Year Economic Development Plan, 1967–1971*, Seoul, EPB, 1966.

_____ *The Third Five-Year Economic Development Plan, 1972–1976*, Seoul, EPB, 1971.

_____ *The Fourth Five-Year Socio-Economic Development Plan, 1977–1981*, Seoul, EPB, 1976.

_____ *The Fifth Five-Year Socio-Economic Development Plan, 1982–1986*, Seoul, EPB, 1981.

_____ *Reports of Foreign Consultants for the Revision of the Fifth Five-Year Plan, 1982–1986*, and *Revised Fifth Plan (1984–86)*, Seoul, EPB, 1981, 1983.

_____ *The Sixth Five-Year Socio-Economic Development Plan, 1987–1991* and *Revised Sixth Plan (1988-91)*, Seoul, EPB, 1986, 1988.

_____ *Guidelines for the Preparation of the Sixth Five-Year Plan, 1987–91*. Seoul, EPB, August 1985.

_____ *White Paper on Public Enterprise*, Seoul, EPB, 1988.

_____ *Future Population of Korea by Region*, Seoul, EPB, 1989.

_____ *White Paper on the Korean Economy*, Seoul, 1988 (in Korean).

Economic Planning Board, Fair Trade Commission, *Monopoly Regulation and Fair Trade Law*, Seoul, EPB, 1987 (in English).

_____ 'Report on the Designation of Business Conglomerates for the Year 1989,' Seoul, EPB, March 1989 (in Korean).

_____ *Monopoly Regulation and Fair Trade in Korea*, Seoul, EPB, May 1989 (in English).

Economist, 'A Survey of the World Economy', *Economist*, 24–30 September 1988.

Edwards, Sebastian, 'Financial Deregulation and Segmented Capital Markets: The Case of Korea', *World Development*, Vol. 16, No. 1, January 1988.

Federation of Korean Industries, *A Forty-Year History of The Korean Economy*, Seoul, FKI Press, 1985.

_____ *A Survey of Korean Economic Development*, Seoul, FKI Press, 1987a.

_____ *A Study on Informal Transaction*, Seoul, FKI Press, 1987b.

_____ *Korea's Economic Policies, 1945–1985*, Seoul, FKI Press, 1987c.

Fei, John C.H., and Gustav Ranis, 'A Model of Growth and Employment in the Open Dualistic Economy: The Case of Korea and Taiwan', *Journal of Development Studies,* Vol II, No. 2, January 1975.

Feldstein, Martin, 'The Changing Environment for World Trade', Remarks to the Korean Traders Association, Seoul, 27 October 1986.

Frank, Charles R., Jr., Kwang Suk Kim, and Larry Westphal, *Foreign Trade Regimes and Economic Development: South Korea,* New York, National Bureau of Economic Research, 1975.

Friedman, Milton, *Capitalism and Freedom,* Chicago, The University of Chicago Press, 1982.

_____ and Rose Friedman, *Free To Choose,* New York, Penguin Books, 1980.

Galenson, Walter (ed.), *Economic Growth and Structural Change in Taiwan,* Ithaca, Cornell University Press, 1979.

_____ *Foreign Trade and Investment: Economic Development in the Newly Industrializing Countries,* The University of Wisconsin Press, 1985.

Georgescu-Roegan, Nicholas, 'Closing Remarks: About Economic Growth—a Variation on a Theme by David Hilbert', *Economic Development and Cultural Change* (Supplement) Vol. 36, No. 3, April 1988.

Gillis, Malcolm, and others, *Economics of Development,* New York, W.W. Norton & Co., 1983.

Glazer, Nathan, 'Social and Cultural Factors in Japanese Economic Growth', in Hugh Patrick and Henry Rosovsky, (eds.), *Asia's New Giant—How the Japanese Economy Works,* Washington, D.C., The Brookings Institution, 1976.

Government of the Republic of Korea, *National Land Development Plan, 1972–1981,* Seoul, 1971.

_____ *The Second Comprehensive National Physical Development Plan, 1982–1991,* Seoul, 1981.

_____ *Long-Term Perspective Plan, 1972–1981,* Seoul, 1973.

Hankel, Wilhelm, 'Some Comments and Recommendations to Macro-Issues, Sectoral Priorities and Selective Incentives with Regard to the Fifth Five-Year Development Plan of Korea', In Il Sakong (ed.), *Macroeconomic Policy and Industrial Development Issues,* Seoul, Korea Development Institute Press, 1987.

Hasan, Parvez, and D.C. Rao, *Korea: Policy Issues for Long-Term Development,* Baltimore, Johns Hopkins University Press, 1979.

Hedberg Haken, *The New Challenge: South Korea!,* Seoul, Chongno Book Center Co., 1978.

Heilbroner, Robert L., and Lester C. Thurow, *The Economic Problem,* seventh edition, New York, Prentice-Hall Inc., 1984.

Hirschman, Albert O., *The Strategy of Economic Development,* New Haven, Yale University Press, 1958.

Hong, Wontack, 'Market Distortions and Trade Patterns of Korea: 1960–85', Seoul, Korea Development Institute Working Paper No. 8807, September 1988.

_____ and L.B. Krause (eds.), *Trade and Growth of the Advanced Developing Countries in the Pacific Basin,* Seoul, Korea Development Institute Press, 1981.

_____ and Yung Chul Park, 'The Financing of Export-Oriented Growth in Korea', in A. Tan and B. Kapur (eds.), *Pacific Growth and Financial Interdependence,* New York, Allen & Unwin, 1986.

Iacocca, Lee, *Iacocca: An Autobiography,* New York, Bantam Books, 1984.

Inoguchi, Takashi, and Daniel I. Okimoto, *The Political Economy of Japan,* Vol. 2, *The Changing International Context,* Stanford, Ca., Stanford University Press, 1988.

Japan: Economic Planning Agency, *Prospects for the Pacific Age: Economic Development and Policy Issues of the Pacific Region to the Year 2000,* Tokyo, EPA, July 1985.

_____ *New Social Indicators,* Tokyo, EPA, 1987, 1989.

Japan: Institute for Social and Economic Affairs, *Japan 1987—An International Comparison,* Tokyo, Keizai Koho Center, 1987.

Japan: Research Institute of International Affairs, *Republic of Korea and Democratic People's Republic of Korea,* Tokyo, 1987.

Jeong, Chang Young, 'Rates of Return on Investment in Education: The Case of Korea', Seoul, Korea Development Institute, Working Paper 7408, 1974.

Jones, Leroy P., 'Jaebul and the Concentration of Economic Power in Korean Development: Issues, Evidence and Alternatives', Seoul, Korea Development Institute Consultant Paper Series, No. 12, Seoul, KDI, July 1980.

_____ and Il Sakong, *Government, Business and Entrepreneurship in Economic Development: The Korean Case,* Cambridge, Mass., Harvard University Press, 1980.

Joong-ang Daily News, *Survey of Opinions on National Life,* 1985, 1986, 1987.

Kang, Shin-il, *A Study on Privatization of Public Enterprises (Kongkiupui Minyonghwae Kwanhan Yeonku),* Korea Development Institute, April 1988 (in Korean).

Keitaro, Hasekawa, *Challenging Korea,* Tokyo, Komoonsa Co., 1984 (in Japanese).

Kim, Jung-Soo, and Funkoo Park, 'Industrial Structural Changes and Manpower Policy', *Korea Development Review (Hankook Gaebal Yeonku),* Vol. 8, No. 1, Spring 1986.

Kim, Myung Sook, 'Study on Public Expenditures on Education', *Korea Development Review*, December 1986.

Kim, Kwang Suk, and Joon Kyung Park, *Sources of Economic Growth in Korea, 1963–1982*, Seoul, Korea Development Institute, 1985.

Kim, Kwang Suk, and Larry Westphal, 'Industrial Policy and Development in Korea', World Bank Staff Working Paper, No. 263, Washingtong, D.C., World Bank, 1977.

Kim, Kihwan, 'Korea in the 1990s: Making the Transition to a Developed Economy', *World Development*, Vol. 16, No. 1, January 1988.

Kim, Wan-Soon, and K.Y. Yun, 'Fiscal Policy and Development in Korea', *World Development*, Vol. 16, No. 1, January 1988.

Kim, Yong-un, *Values of Japanese and Koreans (Ilboningwa Hankooki-nui Euisik Kuzo)*, Seoul, Hangillsa Co., 1985.

Kim Young Chin, and Jene K. Kwon, *Capital Utilization in Korean Manufacturing, 1962–1971*, Seoul, Korea Development Institute, 1973.

Klein, Lawrence R., 'Foreword', in Lawrence J. Lau (ed.), *Models of Development: A Comparative Study of Economic Growth in South Korea and Taiwan*, San Francisco, Institute for Contemporary Studies, 1986.

Korea Development Bank, *Industry in Korea, 1988*, Seoul, KDB, 1989.

Korea Development Institute, *Long-Term Prospect for Economic and Social Development, 1977–91*, Seoul, KDI 1978.

―― *Korea Year 2000: Prospects and Issues for Long-Term Development*, Seoul, KDI, 1986.

―― *Industrialization and Development Strategies*, Seoul, KDI, 1986.

Korea Institute for Economics and Technology, *Comparison of Korea's Overall National Power (Wooreeui Jonghap Kukryuk Beegyo)*, Seoul, KIET, August 1988 (in Korean).

―― *Korea's Industrial Policy*, Policy Research Series (F) 88–12, Seoul, KIET, 1988.

Korea Labor Institute, *Quarterly Labor Review*, Vol. I, No. 1, and Vol. II, No. 1, Seoul, KLI, 1988, 1989.

Korea Overseas Information Service, *A Handbook of Korea*, sixth edition, Seoul, International Publishing House, 1987.

―― *Facts About Korea*, 18th edition, Seoul, Hollym Co., 1986.

Kosai, Yutaka, 'The Politics of Economic Management', in Kozo Yamamura and Yasukichi Yasuba (eds.), *The Political Economy of Japan*, Stanford, Ca., Stanford University Press, 1987.

―― and Yoshitaro Ogino, *The Contemporary Japanese Economy*, (translated by Ralph Thompson), New York, M.E. Sharpe, Inc., 1984.

Krause, Lawrence B., 'Summary of the Eleventh Pacific Trade and

Development Conference on Trade and Growth of the Advanced Developing Countries', in Wontack Hong and L.B. Krause (eds.), *Trade and Growth of the Advanced Developing Countries in the Pacific Basin*, Seoul, Korea Development Institute Press, 1981.

____ 'Introduction', in Walter Galenson (ed.), *Foreign Trade and Investments: Economic Development in the Newly Industrializing Asian Countries*, Madison, The University of Wisconsin Press, 1985.

____ and Sueo Sekiguchi, 'Japan and the World', in Hugh Patrick and Henry Rosovsky, (eds.), *Asia's New Giant—How the Japanese Economy Works*, Washington, D.C., The Brookings Institution, 1976.

Krueger, Anne O., *The Development Role of the Foreign Sector and Aid*, Cambridge, Mass., Council on East Asian Studies, Cambridge, Mass., Harvard University Press, 1979 (in Korean).

____ and others (eds.), *Export-Oriented Development Strategies: The Success of Five Newly Industrializing Countries*, Boulder, Colorado, Westview Press, 1985.

____ 'Discussion' in 'Korean Trade Policy: Implications for Korean-US Cooperation', in T.O. Bayard and Soo-Gil Young (eds.), *Economic Relations Between the US and Korea: Conflict or Cooperation?* Washington, D.C., IIE, 1989.

Kuo, Shirley W.Y., Gustav Ranis, and John C.H. Fei, *The Taiwan Success Story—Rapid Growth with Improved Distribution in the Republic of China, 1952–1979*, Boulder, Colorado, Westview Press, 1981.

Kuznets, Paul W., *Economic Growth and Structure in the Republic of Korea*, New Haven, Yale University Press, 1977.

____ 'An East Asian Model of Economic Development', *Economic Development and Cultural Change*, Vol. 36, No. 3, April 1988 (Supplement).

Kuznets, Simon, 'Modern Economic Growth: Findings and Reflections', *American Economic Review*, Vol. 63, No. 3, 1973.

Kwack, Soo-il, 'A Study on the Privatization of Public Enterprise', in Korea Economic Research Institute (ed.), *Conceptualization of Economic Democratization (Kyungjae Minjuhwaui Gibongusang)*, Seoul, KERI, April 1988 (1988a).

____ 'Regrettable Status of Real Estate Price', *Chosonilbo* (daily newspaper), 13 August 1988 (1988b).

Kwack, Sung Y, 'The Economic Development of the Republic of Korea, 1965–1981', in Lawrence J. Lau (ed.), *Models of Development: A Comparative Study of Economic Growth in South Korea and Taiwan*, San Francisco, Institute for Contemporary Studies Press, 1986.

—— 'The Growth and Equity Issues for the Korean Economy', paper prepared for the Third International Conference of the Korean Economic Association, 2–3 August 1988.

Kwack, Tae-Won, 'Industrial Restructuring Experience and Policies in Korea in the 1970s', in Kyu-uck Lee (ed.), *Industrial Development Policies and Issues,* Seoul, Korea Development Institute, 1986.

Kwon, Tai Hwan, Hae Young Lee, Yunshik Chang, and Eui-Yong Yu, *The Population of Korea,* Seoul, The Population and Development Studies Centre, Seoul National University, 1975.

Kwon, Tai Hwan, and Yong-Ha Shin, 'An Attempt to Estimate Population of the Choson Dynasty', *Tong-a Munwha,* Seoul, December 1977.

Lau, Lawrence J., *Models of Development—A Comparative Study of Economic Growth in South Korea and Taiwan,* San Francisco, Ca., ICS Press, 1986.

Lee, Byung-Chul, *Hoamjajeon (My Autobiography),* Seoul, The Joongang Daily News Co., 1986 (in Korean).

Lee, Kyu-uck, 'The Concentration of Economic Power in Korea: Causes, Consequences and Policy', in Kyu-uck Lee (ed.), *Industrial Development Policies and Issues,* Seoul, Korea Development Institute, 1986.

—— and Sung Soon Lee, *Business Integration and Concentration of Economic Power,* Seoul, Korea Development Institute Research Report 85–02, September 1985.

Lee, Ki-baik, *A New History of Korea* (translated by Edward W. Wagner), Seoul, Ilchokak Publishers and Cambridge, Mass., Harvard University Press, 1984.

Leibenstein, Harvey, 'The Japanese Management System: An X-Efficiency-Game Theory Analysis', in Masahiko Aoki (ed.), *The Economic Analysis of the Japanese Firm,* Amsterdam, North-Holland Co., 1984.

Leipziger, Danny M., 'Korea: Transition to Maturity', *World Development* (Special Issue), Vol. 16, No. 1, January 1988.

—— 'Industrial Restructuring in Korea', *World Development,* Vol. 16, No. 1, January 1988.

Lewis, W. Arthur, 'Economic Development with Unlimited Supplies of Labour', The Manchester Business School, Vol. 22, No. 2, May 1954.

—— 'Economic Planning: Development Planning', in D. L. Sills (ed.), *International Encyclopedia of Social Sciences,* 1968.

—— 'The State of Development Theory', *The American Economic Review,* Vol. 74, No. 1, March 1984.

Liang, Kuo-shu, and Ching-ing Hou Liang, 'Development Policy Formation and Future Policy Priorities in the Republic of China', *Economic Development and Cultural Change,* Vol. 36, No. 3, April 1988 (Supplement).

Lindauer, David, 'Labor Market Behavior in Developing Countries', Unpublished Ph.D. dissertation, Harvard University, 1980.

Lluch, C., and R. Williams, 'Dualism in Demand and Savings Patterns: The Case of Korea', *Economic Record,* No. 51, March 1975.

Lo, Fu-chen, (ed.), *Asian and Pacific Economy Towards the Year 2000,* Kuala Lumpur, Asian and Pacific Development Centre Press, 1987.

Lundberg, Erik, 'Fiscal and Monetary Policies', in Walter Galenson (ed.), *Economic Growth and Structural Change in Taiwan,* Ithaca, Cornell University Press, 1979.

Ma, Hong, *New Strategy for China's Economy,* Beijing, New World Press, 1983.

Macfarquhar, Roderick, 'The Post-Confucian Threat to the West', *Economist,* 8 February 1980.

Mason, Edward S. and others, *The Economic and Social Modernization of the Republic of Korea,* Cambridge, Mass., Harvard University Press, 1980.

McGinn, Noel F., Donald R. Snodgrass, Yung Bong Kim, Shin-Bok Kim, and Quee-Young Kim, *Education and Development in Korea,* Cambridge, Mass., Harvard University Press, 1980.

Mills, Edwin S., 'Procedures for Allocating Land in Korea', in Il Sakong (ed.), *Human Resources and Social Development Issues,* Seoul, Korea Development Institute Press, 1987.

_____ and Byung-Nak Song, *Urbanization and Urban Problems,* Cambridge, Mass., Harvard University Press, 1979.

Minami, Ryoshin, *The Economic Development of Japan—A Quantitative Study,* London, Macmillan Press, 1986.

Ministry of Home Affairs, *Municipal Yearbook of Korea,* 1972, 1974, 1982, 1987, and 1988.

Morita, Akio, *Made in Japan,* London, Fontana/Collins, 1987.

Murakami, Yasusuke, 'The Japanese Model of Political Development', in Kozo Yamamura and Yasukichi Yasuba (eds.), *The Political Economy of Japan,* Stanford, Stanford University Press, 1987.

Nakane, Chie, 'Logic and Simile: When Japanese Meet Indians', *Japanese Quarterly,* Vol. 11, October-December 1964, pp. 434–8.

_____ *Japanese Society,* Tokyo, C.E. Tuttle Co., 1984.

National Unification Board, *An Overall Appraisal of the North Korean Economy,* Seoul, NUB, 1980.

Nugent, Jeffrey B., and Mustapha K. Nabli, *The New Institutional Economics and Development: Theory and Applications to Tunisia,* Amsterdam, North-Holland Co., 1989.

Ohkawa, Kazushi, and Henry Rosovsky, *Japanese Economic Growth,* London, Oxford University Press, 1973.

Omae, Kenichi, *The New Wealth of Nations,* Tokyo, Kodansa, 1986 (in Japanese).

Palmer, Spencer J., *Korea and Christianity,* Seoul, Seoul Computer Press, 1986.

Park, Chong Kee, 'Taxation and Economic Development', Korea Development Institute Working Paper 7807, July 1978.

Park, Chung Hee, *The Country, the Revolution and I,* Seoul, Hollym Corporation, 1963.

—— *Our Nation's Path,* Seoul, Hollym Co., 1970.

Park, Se-Il, 'Labor Issues in Korea's Future', *World Development,* Vol. 16, No. 1, January 1988.

Park, Yung Chul, *Financial Development Issues and Policies in Korea,* Seoul, Korea University Press, 1988 (in Korean).

—— and David C. Cole, *Financial Development in Korea, 1945–1978,* Cambridge, Mass., Harvard University Press, 1983.

Patrick, Hugh, and H. Rosovsky, *Asia's New Giant—How the Japanese Economy Works,* Washington, D.C., The Brookings Institution, 1976.

Perkins, Dwight H., 'Reforming China's Economic System', *Journal of Economic Literature,* Vol. 26, No. 2, June 1988.

—— *China: Asia's Next Economic Giant?,* Seattle, University of Washington Press, 1986.

—— 'The Historical Foundations of Modern Economic Growth', in Edward S. Mason and others (eds.), *The Economic and Social Modernization of the Republic of Korea,* Cambridge, Mass., Harvard University Press, 1980 (Chapter 2).

—— 'Government as an Obstacle to Industrialization: The Case of Nineteenth-Century China', *The Journal of Economic History,* December 1967.

Phisit Pakkasem, *Leading Issues in Thailand's Development Transformation, 1960–1990,* Bangkok, Thailand, National Economic and Social Development Board, March 1988.

Prud'homme, Remy, 'A Study on Regional Policies', in Economic Planning Board (ed.), *Reports of Foreign Consultants for the Revision of the Fifth Five-Year Economic and Social Development Plan,* Seoul, December 1983.

Pu, Shan, 'China and the Asian-Pacific Economy Towards the Year 2000', in Fu-chen Lo (ed.), *Asian and Pacific Economy Towards the Year 2000,* Kuala Lumpur, Malaysia, Asian and Pacific Development Centre Press, 1987.

Ranis, Gustav, 'The Role of the Industrial Sector in Korea's Transition to Economic Maturity', paper presented at ILCORK Conference, 22–29, August 1971, Seoul, Korea

—— 'The Political Economy of Development Policy Change: A Comparative Study of Taiwan and Korea', Korea Development Institute Working Paper No. 8916, Seoul, KDI, June 1989.

Reischauer, Edwin O., *My Life Between Japan and America,* New York, Harper & Row Inc., 1986.

—— *The Japanese,* Tokyo, Charles E. Tuttle Co., 1985.

Renaud, Bertrand, 'Economic Growth and Income Inequality in Korea', World Bank Staff Working Paper No. 209, Washington, D.C., 1976.

Reynolds, Lloyd G., 'Gunnar Myrdal's Contribution to Economics, 1940–1970', *Swedish Journal of Economics*, 1984.

Rhee, Yung Whee, Bruce Ross-Larson, and Pursell, *Korea's Competitive Edge: Managing Entry into World Markets,* Baltimore, The Johns Hopkins Press, 1984.

Roh Tae-Woo, *Great Era for the Ordinary People (Wedaehan Botongsaramdului Seedae),* Seoul, Eulyoumoonwhasa, 1987.

Rostow, W.W., 'Korea and the Fourth Industrial Revolution, 1960–2000', paper presented at the Federation of Korean Industries, September 1983.

Sakong, Il (ed.), *Macroeconomic Policy and Industrial Development Issues,* Seoul, Korea Development Institute, 1987.

—— 'The International Economic Position of Korea', in T.O. Bayard and Soo-Gil Young (ed.), *Economic Relations Between the US and Korea: Conflict or Cooperation?*, Washington, D.C., IIE, January 1989.

Samuelson, Paul A., and William D. Nordhaus, *Economics,* twelfth edition, New York, McGraw-Hill Co., 1989.

Samsung Conglomerate, *Samsung Osipnyunsa* (A Fifty-year History of Samsung), Seoul, Samsung Group, March 1988.

Scitovsky, Tibor, 'Economic Development in Taiwan and South Korea, 1965–1981', in Lawrence J. Lau (ed.), *Models of Development: A Comparative Study of Economic Growth in South Korea and Taiwan,* San Francisco, Institute of Contemporary Studies Press, 1986.

Shin, Bong-Shik, 'Measures to Simplify Government Permission, Inspections and Approaches', paper presented at the Conference on the Rationalization of Economic Regulation by the Government held at the Korea Chamber of Commerce, August 17 1988.

Shinohara, Miyohei, *Industrial Growth, Trade and Dynamic Patterns in the Japanese Economy,* Tokyo, University of Tokyo Press, 1982.

—— 'The Dynamics of Development in East Asia', in Keizai Koho

Center (ed.), *Economic Views from Japan*, Tokyo, Keizai Koho Center, 1986.

_____ 'Trends of the Asian-Pacific Economies, 1960–2000', The Institute of Economics, Academia Sinica, Chung-Hua Series of Lectures No. 10, June 1985, Taipei, Taiwan.

_____ and Fu-chen Lo, *Global Adjustment and the Future of the Asian-Pacific Economy*, Institute of Developing Economies, Tokyo, Japan, 1989.

Sloboda, John E., 'Housing, Land, and Socio-Economic Integration—Viewed Through the Housing Problem in Seoul, Korea', Cambridge, Mass., Harvard University, unpublished paper, 1972.

_____ 'Migration', in Edwin S. Mills and Byung-Nak Song, *Urbanization and Urban Problems*, Cambridge, Mass., Harvard University Press, 1979, Chapter 5.

Song, Byung-Nak, 'The Production Structure of the Korean Economy: International and Historical Comparisons', *Econometrica*, Vol. 45, No. 1, January 1977.

_____ 'Empirical Research on Consumption Behavior: Evidence from Rich and Poor LDCs', *Economic Development and Cultural Change*, Vol. 29, No. 3, April 1981.

_____ 'The Pattern of Korean Growth, 1963–1973: An International Perspective With Special Consideration of the Japanese Pattern', *Korean Economic Journal*, January 1982.

_____ 'Comparative Growth Strategy of Korea, China and Japan', paper presented at the Joint Korea-China Seminar on Economic Development, Sejong Institute, Seoul, November 1988.

_____ *The Korean Economy*, second edition, Seoul, Bakyoungsa Publishing Co., 1984.

_____ 'Economic Issues and Policies on Korean Jaebol (Conglomerates)', in Federation of Korean Industries (ed.), *Issues and Policies on Korean Jaebol*, Seoul, FKI, 1989.

_____ and Irma Adelman, 'A Note on Rates of Change in Productivity in Korea', Seoul, Korea Development Institute Working Paper No. 7215, September 1972.

_____ and Choe, Sang-Chuel, 'Review of Urban Trends and Policies in Korea', World Bank Urban and Regional Report No. 81–2, May 1981.

_____ and Fu-chen Lo, 'Industrial Restructuring of the East and Southeast Asian Economies', paper presented at the Beijing Conference on the Asian-Pacific Economy Towards the Year 2000, Beijing, November 1986.

_____ Fu-chen Lo, and Shunichi Furukawa, 'Patterns of Development and Interdependence Among the ESA (East and Southeast Asian)

Economies', paper presented at the Tokyo Conference on Global Adjustment and the Future of the Asian-Pacific Economy, Tokyo 11–13 May 1988.

Song, Dae-hee, 'The Role of the Public Enterpirse in the Korean Economy', in Kyu-uck Lee (ed.), *Industrial Development Policies and Issues*, Seoul, Korea Development Institute, 1986.

―― 'Issues and Policy Directions for the Public Enterprise Sector in Korea', paper presented at the EPB-KDI Conference on Industrial Restructuring, Seoul, Korea Development Institute, 1988 (in Korean).

Steinberg, David I., 'Sociopolitical Factors and Korea's Future Economic Policies', *World Development*, Vol. 16, No. 1, January 1988.

Suh, Sang-Chul, *Growth and Structural Change in the Korean Economy, 1910–1940*, Cambridge, Mass., Harvard University Press, 1978.

Suh, Sang-mok, 'Economic Growth and Change in Income Distribution: The Korean Case', Korea Development Institute Working Paper 8508, Seoul, 1985.

―― 'Development Strategies: The Korea Experiences', in Korea Development Institute, (ed.), *Industrialization and Development Strategies*, Seoul, KDI, 1986.

Szal, Richard J., 'Emerging Trends in Income Distribution in Korea and Their Implications for Future Planning', Korea Development Institute Consultant Paper Series No. 2, Seoul, May 1980.

Tanaka, Kakuei, *Building a New Japan*, Tokyo, The Simul Press, Inc., 1972.

Toffler, Alvin, *Hankookinkwa Jaesamui Moolkyul* (Korea and the Third Wave), Seoul, Hankook Economic Newspaper Co., 1985 (in Korean).

Tu, Wei-Ming, *Confucian Ethics Today—The Singapore Challenge*, Singapore, Federal Publications, 1984.

Uekusa, Masu, 'Monopoly Regulation and Fair Trade Policy in Korea', in Il Sakong (ed.), *Macroeconomic Policy and Industrial Development Issues*, Seoul, Korea Development Institute Press, 1987.

Westphal, Larry E., 'The Republic of Korea's Experience with Export-led Industrial Development', *World Development*, Vol. 6, No. 3, 1978.

―― and Kwang Suk Kim, 'Korea', in B. Balassa and others (eds.), *Development Strategies in Semi-Industrial Countries*, Baltimore, Johns Hopkins University Press, 1982.

Whang, In-joung, *Social Development in Action: The Korean Experience*, Seoul, Korea Development Institute, 1986.

―― 'The Saemaul Undong: A Participatory Approach to Rural Development in Korea', in Korea Development Institute (ed.), *Industrialization and Development Strategies*, Seoul, KDI, 1986.

Williamson, Jeffrey G., 'Private Domestic Savings in Korea: Can A
    Pessimistic Past be Reconciled with An Optimistic Plan?', in Eco-
    nomic Planning Board (ed.), *Discussion Papers on the Draft of the
    Fourth Five-Year Plan*, Seoul, March 1976.
_____ 'Have Koreans Saved Too Little in the Past and Will They Do So
    In The Future?', Seoul, Korea Development Institute Consultant
    Report, Seoul, July 1977.
_____ 'Why Do Koreans Save "So Little"?', *Journal of Development
    Economics*, 5: 343–362, 1979.
World Bank, *Korea: Development in a Global Context*, A World Bank
    Country Study, Washington, D.C., 1984.
_____ *Korea—Managing the Industrial Transition*, Vol. I *The Conduct of
    Industrial Policy*, Washington, D.C., 1987a.
_____ *Korea—Managing the Industrial Transition*, Vol. II *Selected Topics
    and Case Studies*, Washington, D.C., 1987b.
_____ *World Development Report*, 1981, 1987, and 1988.
Woronoff, Jon, *Korea's Economy: Man-Made Miracle*. Seoul, Si-sa-
    yong-o-sa Publishers, 1983.
Yamamura, Kozo, and Yasukichi Yasuba, *The Political Economy of
    Japan*, Stanford, Stanford University Press, 1987.
Yeon, Ha-Cheong, 'North Korean Economic Policy and Management',
    Seoul, Korea Development Institute Research Report No. 57,
    December 1986 (in Korean).
_____ 'North Korean External Economic Relations in Recent Years:
    Structure and Development', *Korea Development Review*, Vol. 9,
    No. 3, Fall 1987 (in Korean).
Young, Soo-Gil, 'Korean Trade Policy: Implications for Korean-US
    Cooperation', in Thomas O. Bayard and Soo-Gil Young (eds.),
    *Economic Relations Between the US and Korea: Conflict or Co-
    operation?* Washington, D.C., IIE, 1989.
Yusuf, Shahid, and Kyle Peters, 'Savings Behavior and Its Implications
    for Domestic Resource Mobilization: The Case of the Republic of
    Korea', World Bank Staff Working Paper, No. 628, 1984.
Zymelman, Manuel, 'Some Thoughts on Human Resources Develop-
    ment in Korea', in Il Sakong (ed.), *Human Resources and Social
    Development Issues*, Seoul, Korea Development Institute Press,
    1987.

Index